Field Guide

Insects

of Britain & Northern Europe

Bob Gibbons

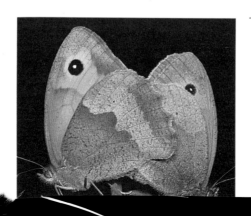

First published in 1995 by
The Crowood Press Ltd
Ramsbury, Marlborough
Wiltshire SN8 2HR

British Library Cataloguing in Publication Data
A catalogue record for this book is available from the British Library.

ISBN 1 85223 895 X HB
    1 85223 937 9 PB

Artwork by Christine Hart-Davies

Front cover photographs: Green Shieldbug, *Palomena prasina* (upper); 6-spot Burnet moth, *Zygaena filipendulae* (lower).
Back cover photographs: Male Banded Agrion, *Calopteryx splendens* (upper); a solitary bee, *Anthidium manicatum* (lower).
Title page photograph: Meadow Brown butterflies mating, *Maniola jurtina*.

Photographic Acknowledgements

Photographs supplied by Natural Image. All taken by Bob Gibbons and Peter Wilson except for those below. Each photograph is referenced by a page number followed by a number indicating its position on the page working from left to right and top to bottom.
David Element 55.6, 89.4, 93.4, 95.2, 123.1, 135.2, 157.1, 159.3, 161.2, 163.3, 169.4, 181.1, 185.1, 189.3, 191.1, 191.2, 191.4, 193.4, 195.4, 199.3, 207.3, 215.1, 219.2, 219.5, 223.6, 225.3, 229.3, 229.4, 231.4, 233.1, 243.4, 245.3, 255.1, 255.2, 255.3, 257.1, 257.4, 261.1, 263.1, 277.4, 295.4, 299.5, 301.2; Robin Fletcher 159.6, 259.2; Alec S Harmer 123.3, 125.1, 125.2, 125.5, 127.1, 129.5, 131.4, 131.5, 131.6, 135.1, 135.5, 135.6, 139.5, 141.7, 141.8, 145.3, 149.4, 155.6, 157.2, 169.2, 171.2, 171.3, 173.3, 283.3; Tom Leach 57.4; RJ Orr 159.4, 271.2; PR Perfect 39.2, 105.1, 159.2, 167.2, 169.3, 171.5, 177.1, 179.4, 185.4, 195.1, 277.2; Michael Woods 153.3, 261.4.

Edited and designed by
D & N Publishing
DTP & Editorial Services
Crowood Lane, Ramsbury
Marlborough, Wiltshire SN8 2HR

Contents

A common ichneumon wasp, the Yellow Ophion.

How to Use this Book

This book is intended as an introduction to the marvellous range of insects to be found in Britain and adjacent parts of north Europe (see map for area of coverage). No single portable volume can possibly cover the full range of insects that occur within this area, and this book is highly selective in the insects that it includes. Although the whole range of insect orders is covered, within this framework I have selected examples that have one or more of the following features:

• They are readily noticed by the average naturalist, either singly or *en masse*. This includes species that may be noticeable by some aspect other than simply their visible adult stage. For example, some larvae are especially noticeable (even though their adult phase may be drab or inconspicuous); some insect products are especially noticeable, such as the froth, known as 'cuckoo spit' produced by froghopper nymphs; and occasionally insects may be more noticeable by their sound than by their appearance, such as house crickets. As far as possible, it is the conspicuous feature that has been illustrated, since this is what people notice most.

• They are reasonably frequent and widespread. There are a few exceptions to this, where particularly distinctive insects are involved; or within the key groups of Odonata (dragonflies and damselflies), butterflies, and Orthoptera (grasshoppers and crickets), where we have aimed to include all UK species, and most NW European species, whether they are common or rare.

• They are identifiable in the field. In practice, this is not as simple as it sounds, since many apparently distinctive species have a number of close relatives that differ only in minor characteristics. In these cases, it is the group of species that is distinctive and identifiable, and this is usually made clear in the text. Apart from the main groups of larger insects, most groups of insects require specialized texts and detailed study for their certain identification. Some of the more appropriate specialized guides are listed in the Bibliography.

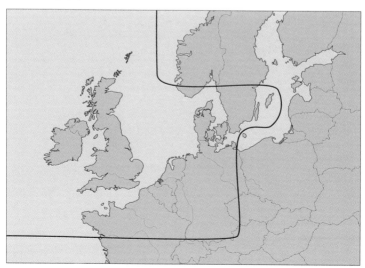

The black line delineates the main area covered by this book.

IDENTIFYING INSECTS

When using the book to try to identify an insect, ideally you should have the book there at the time; it is designed to be portable, and used in the field. It is surprisingly easy to see an insect that appears to be highly distinctive at the time and to find, on later examination of illustrations, that there are several similar-looking species. It can then be very difficult to recall which key features 'your' insect possessed!

If you already know which order the insect belongs to, it is a quick process to flick through the pictures to see if there is anything like it. If so, check the timing and distribution to see if its occurrence is likely, then read the 'similar species' to see if anything fits better. If you are uncertain where the insect fits into the scheme of things, you can use the illustrated key to the main groups of adult insects. For this, you need to be able to see the details clearly; it can be helpful to catch the insect and examine it in a clear container, releasing it afterwards. Alternatively, you can scan through the photographs in the whole book, leaving aside groups to which the insect obviously *does not* belong. For example, if you had a stonefly, it would be readily obvious that it was not a butterfly, dragonfly, grasshopper or cricket, even though you had no idea what it actually was. Once narrowed down, the procedure is the same as above.

LAYOUT OF SPECIES DESCRIPTIONS

The layout of each species description follows a roughly constant pattern, though this is necessarily altered at times, according to the type of insect.

• If the whole description is preceded by the symbol ★ , this denotes that the insect does not normally occur in the UK. This speeds up the process of checking through possibilities if you are working within the UK.

• This is followed by the English name, where there is one. Many insects are not well enough known to have an English name, and in such cases the description starts with the scientific name, in italics. In a few instances, where the name has been changed recently and the old one was familiar, alternative scientific names have been given.

• Next comes a description of the insect, beginning with a general indication of size, shape, colour and key anatomical features, particularly mentioning any variations from the illustrated type and highlighting features which need close examination.

• The section beginning **Habitat** describes the habitats in which the insect commonly occurs, indicating any differences between countries, and especially differences between the UK and mainland Europe, if appropriate. (It is surprising how often such differences exist.) This section can only be a guide, as many insects occur in too wide a spectrum of habitats to mention them all, and others – such as larger dragonflies and butterflies – can range widely through almost any habitat, if only in passing.

• The part of the description beginning **Status and distribution** indicates the rough distribution of the insect, and its relative abundance. Where appropriate, the UK distribution is described separately. The terms used, in order of decreasing abundance, are: abundant, common, frequent, local and rare, qualified as necessary, though they should only be taken as a guide, and there can be enormous annual variations with some insects. There are also many species for which this information is simply not fully available.

• The abbreviation **Season** indicates the period when the insect is most likely to be seen. Unless otherwise qualified, it refers to active adults. There is a good deal of potential variation within this, according to geographical location, the weather in a particular year, and the habits of individual species. Generally species appear earlier and survive later in warmer places: in the UK, coastal south-western areas are especially mild, and on the Continent, the W coast of France, and southern areas in general, are the warmest. A mild frost-free autumn may extend the flight period of many summer insects well into November. Some insects, especially aquatic ones, may remain adult all year, but they become less active, or totally inactive, in cold weather; in these cases, only the period during which they are most likely to be seen are given.

• A subsection headed 'Similar species' may follow the general description. This describes closely related or very similar species that are not usually illustrated. In many cases there are large numbers of similar species, and it is not possible to describe them all. Occasionally, where one insect may be confused with another that is described elsewhere in the book, this section may draw attention to this possible source of confusion.

ORDER OF SPECIES

The order of species follows the generally accepted order of families, progressing from the most primitive to the most advanced. Species are all grouped taxonomically, with related species placed together. There is one exception to this: all the galls have been collected together at the end of the book in a special section. Galls are a fascinating study in themselves, and the larger ones readily attract attention. However, it is not possible to classify the insect that caused the gall simply by looking at the gall, and the insects themselves are rarely seen, so it is more useful to group all these insects together. Most such insects come from the orders Hymenoptera or Diptera, though a few other groups are involved, and there are also a number of non-insect gall-formers. Common examples of non-insect galls, such as those caused by mites, are included. Where the gall-forming insect is also likely to be noticed in its adult stage, it appears under the normal taxonomic grouping as well.

What is an Insect?

The term 'insect' refers to a vast group of animals, belonging to over 30 different orders, with a wide variation in structure and behaviour, so it is difficult to describe common characteristics which apply to all of them. The insects are one group of the huge biological tribe (phylum) known as the arthropods, which also includes spiders, crustaceans, millipedes and many other groups, whose primary characteristics include a hard external shell or skeleton, and soft flexible joints at appropriate places which allow the animals to move. These are collectively known generally as 'invertebrates' (i.e. animals that have no backbone). Insects are most likely to be confused with other arthropods such as woodlice, spiders or centipedes. Their main distinguishing characteristics are:

• Insects have six legs, in three pairs. Many insects have one or more pairs of legs missing, modified or reduced, but virtually all insects have six legs at some point in their life-cycle.

• Most insects have wings at some point in their life-cycle. If an invertebrate has wings, it *must* be an insect. However, a small group of insects (the Apterygota, see pp.38–41) never have wings, and there are species scattered through the insect orders that have lost their wings through specialization; e.g. the fleas.

• Insect bodies are divided into three sections: head, thorax and abdomen. The head usually bears one pair of antennae (though these may be very small); the thorax bears the legs and wings, if present; the abdomen never bears legs, though it may have outgrowths associated with mating or other processes.

Immature stages of insects, such as caterpillars, are often much more difficult to categorize, and smaller examples could easily be mistaken for some non-insect invertebrates. There is no guaranteed way of identifying an immature stage as an insect, though many larvae and most nymphs retain the characteristic three pairs of legs.

The Structure of Insects

Nowadays, with good reason, most of the interest in insects centres on their ecology, behaviour and economic or conservation significance. However, in order to identify them, it may be necessary to understand their general anatomy, and their role in nature can be better understood if some aspects of their structure and biology are known.

As already described, the insect body is divided into three main parts: **head**, **thorax** and **abdomen**. There are basically 20 segments in an insect body, with six in the head, three in the thorax, and 11 in the abdomen. By no means all of these are usually distinguishable, as they have become fused together without visible joins. The segments are protected by hard plates, known as sclerites, composed mainly of chitin, which protect the internal contents. Between these plates, there are flexible joints, which may or may not correspond to the divisions between segments.

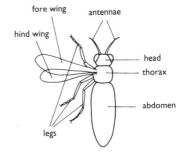

THE HEAD

The head varies enormously in shape from one insect to another. The six structural segments that form it are welded together to form a tough capsule, and usually the segmental divisions are not visible. The head bears the antennae or 'feelers', the mouthparts (which vary widely in structure), and the eyes. Parts of the head are given specific names, as shown in the accompanying diagram of a grasshopper head.

The **antennae** are organs of smell and touch, and virtually all insects possess them, even in their younger stages. There is one pair only, and they vary enormously in structure from being virtually absent to being much longer than the body. Their size and structure relates to their function, and a number of different types can be recognized. For example, male moths use their antennae to detect the presence of female moths, and they are receptive to just a few molecules of scent produced by a female that could be a considerable distance away. This ultrasensitive detection of scent is made

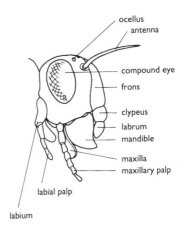

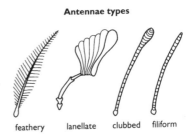

Antennae types

feathery   lanellate   clubbed   filiform

possible by the finely divided nature of the antennae, producing a much greater surface area for molecules to land on. By contrast dragonflies, which have highly developed eyes which they use for finding prey, have very reduced antennae. Some common types of antennae are shown in the diagram. The number of segments varies enormously, from just one or two (for example in some beetles) to over 100 (for example in bush-crickets).

Insects can possess **eyes** of two types: simple eyes known as ocelli, and compound eyes. The compound eyes are the structures usually referred to as the eyes of an insect, as prominent paired struc-

Antennae of a male Convolvulus Hawk-moth.

tures on the top or side of the head. Each compound eye is composed of a number of separate units known as ommatidia, each of which has its own lens at the surface of the eye. An insect's eye may be composed of just a few ommatidia, or up to tens of thousands (for example in dragonflies), and generally speaking, the more ommatidia there are, the better the insect's vision will be. The ommatidia are visible on close examination (including in good magnified photographs of insects) as facets on the surface of the eye. Each ommatidium transmits the signal for an image to the brain of the insect, which is then turned into a composite picture. Obviously, more ommatidia allow greater detail to be resolved, and it also follows that insects are particularly good at detecting movement as an object moves from one ommatidium to another.

Virtually all adult insects have compound eyes, with very few exceptions (for example some scale insects), but no larvae do. Simple eyes, or ocelli, are present in larvae and in scale insects, but they are also present in insects that have compound eyes, though they are often very inconspicuous. They have no focusing mechanism and can detect no detail, but they are sensitive to light levels. Their function in adult insects is uncertain, and may be more or less obsolete, though they are more prominent in some groups such as the Hymenoptera. They are usually placed somewhere near the top of the head.

Insect **mouthparts** could be the subject of a whole book in themselves. They are highly variable in structure and function, and different components of the mouthparts may be greatly modified and enlarged or reduced according to requirements. Insects like cockroaches or some beetles demonstrate the basic mouthpart pattern, from which other types have evolved.

There is no internal jaw in insects, as there is in mammals, so any preparation of food for ingestion is performed by the external mouthparts. The mouthparts are located at the front of the head, and made up essentially of four parts. The top is formed by the hardened upper lip (labrum), which is actually part of the

The ferocious biting mouthparts of the Green Tiger Beetle.

Various insect mouthparts

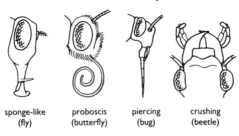

| sponge-like | proboscis | piercing | crushing |
| (fly) | (butterfly) | (bug) | (beetle) |

head capsule. Below this lie the paired mandibles, or upper jaws, which are heavily sclerotized and provided with powerful muscles; it is the mandibles that equate most closely with the idea of 'jaws' and they may be toothed, pointed and very strong. The mandibles move in towards each other from the sides, and are concerned with crushing and cutting the food.

Below the mandibles lie the paired maxillae, or lower jaws, to which are attached some segmented antenna-like appendages known as the maxillary palps. The maxillae themselves help to hold the food, while the palps have a sensory function, detecting taste and acceptability as food. The lowest part of the mouthparts is made up by the labium, or lower lip, which may carry appendages known as the labial palps.

Mouthparts such as those described above are of the biting type. However, some insects have sucking and piercing mouthparts, or various modifications and combinations of these. For example, butterflies and moths have long proboces, curled when not in use, which are used to suck either nectar from flowers or nutrient-rich liquids from other sources. Bugs, and some 'biting' flies like mosquitoes, have piercing mouthparts for taking in sap or blood, both of which flow out under pressure, obviating the need for a sucking capability. Many flies, such as hoverflies, have 'suction pads', with which they soak up liquids.

THE THORAX

Behind the head lies the thorax, usually clearly separated by a 'neck' or joint. The thorax is made up of three underlying segments, named (starting from the head end) as the prothorax, the mesothorax and the metathorax. Each of these segments carries a pair of legs, if all three pairs are present. Wings are borne on the mesothorax and metathorax. The shape and size of the segments varies considerably, depending to some extent on the tasks they perform. For example in flies, whose hindwings are reduced virtually to nothing, the metathorax is very small. The shape and markings of the various segments may be useful for identification.

The hardened plates, or sclerites, of the thorax all have names, though only two need concern us here. Grasshoppers (p.66) have a strongly developed pronotum, which forms a sort of shield over the thorax, extending down the sides and back to the abdomen. In the groundhoppers (p.74), the pronotum is extended back over the abdomen, or beyond it in some species and its shape is a useful aid to identification. In some bugs, especially shieldbugs (p.87), a protective plate over the mesothorax, known as the scutellum, is enlarged, forming the triangular patch between the wings, and even extending to the tip of the abdomen in some species, such as the European Tortoise Bug, *Eurygaster maura*.

THE ABDOMEN

The abdomen forms the remainder of the insect body. It is basically made up of 11 segments, but segment 11 is usually small or absent, and segment one is often much reduced. In many species, the other segments are clearly visible as divisions, though in some groups they are combined to form fewer divisions. Segments 8 and 9 usually bear the genitalia, which may be either inconspicuous or readily visible. In some groups, such as bush-crickets or ichneumons, there is an ovipositor, shaped according to the egg-laying requirements.

The abdomen may also possess projections from the terminal segment known as cerci. These may take the form of slender 'tails', as in mayflies (see p.42) or stoneflies (see p.64), or be short and more robust, as in grasshoppers, or be modified into 'pincers', as in some dragonflies and damselflies, or earwigs (see p.84). Their function seems to be mainly sensory, rather like antennae. In a few groups, the dorsal sclerite is projected backwards as an additional tail between the two cerci; this is especially noticeable in the three-tailed bristletails (see p.38) and some mayflies (see p.42).

THE LEGS

The legs of insects are borne on the thorax, in three pairs. This is one of the distinguishing characteristics of insects as a group. As with other insect parts, there is great variation in leg structure, and some or all of the legs may be absent in some species or groups (though there are never more than three pairs). The simple basic structure, as seen in fast-running species, such as cockroaches or ground beetles, is as shown in the diagram. Some typical variations include the

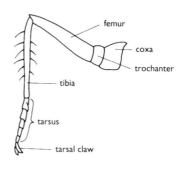

enlargement of the hind femora in grasshoppers and bush-crickets, for jumping; or the enlarged and powerful front legs of the Mole Cricket, used for digging. Grasshoppers use their legs as part of the system for producing their characteristic calls.

THE WINGS

More important, from several points of view, are the wings. The possession of wings is one of the features that distinguishes insects from other invertebrates, and one of the key factors in their success (see p.14). They are also a useful aid to identification, especially in groups like the Lepidoptera, where the pattern and colour of the wings is all-important.

Structurally, wings are not limbs, but outgrowths of the thorax. Most insects, such as Lepidoptera, Hymenoptera, and Hemiptera habitually have two pairs of wings, though they are not necessarily both conspicuous nor equal in size and

A Cardinal Beetle about to take off, giving a clear view of the difference between its forewings and hindwings.

shape. The true flies (Diptera) have only one pair of wings, on the mesothorax; the hindwings have been reduced to two projections known as the halteres, which aid in balance. Groups such as the fleas are known to have had a winged stage at some point in their evolution, but gradually lost them as they became irrelevant to their life-style. The small group of Apterygota (wingless insects, see pp.38–41), by contrast, are believed never to have been winged.

Insect wings can vary considerably in texture and appearance. The commonest type, found in the Hymenoptera, flies, dragonflies and other groups, is the membranous wing – the typical 'bee's-wing' – transparent or translucent and very delicate. Membranous wings may be completely transparent, or they may have varying degrees of suffusion with deeper colours, such as in the Banded Agrion damselfly. In some groups, such as the scorpion flies (see p.116), the pattern of darker marking is very useful in identification.

Membranous wings have patterns of veins within them, which may vary from highly complex to quite simple. The probable evolution of these vein patterns has been worked out in great detail, and every vein and cross-vein has been given a name or symbol. For identifying some groups and species, this pattern is crucial, but the technique is too detailed for this type of book. The only veins or cells (the blocks enclosed by veins) mentioned in the text as being useful for identification are the costa, which is effectively the leading edge of the wing, and the pterostigma (see p.46) which can be a useful aid to dragonfly and damselfly identification.

Some groups of insects have rather different wings. For example, butterflies and moths have wings that are wholly covered with scales. The colour and pattern produced by these scales is critical for their identification.

A few groups of insects, notably dragonflies and damselflies, move their wings independently during flight. This is viewed as a primitive characteristic, and more advanced insects have developed various ways of linking the wings together. This does not, however, mean that dragonflies are poor fliers; they are among the most

Swallowtail butterfly wing detail.

agile of insects. The degree and the method of coupling varies in other insects, from simple overlap to complex lines of hooks like an early version of velcro.

Insects fold their wings in various different ways when at rest. This can be a useful feature in deciding which group an insect belongs to. They may be held roof-wise over the abdomen, as in the Alder Fly and some caddis-flies, or parallel and adjacent to the abdomen, as in stoneflies and most damselflies. Butterflies, mayflies and a few others hold them vertically erect, while dragonflies and some hoverflies hold them out at right angles to the abdomen (though hoverflies hold them at varying angles, or fold them away along the abdomen, depending on conditions). Some insects like the skipper butterflies or the emerald damselflies (*Lestes* spp.) have an in-between system, which does not fall into any of the above categories.

Insect wings at rest

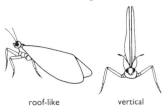

roof-like   vertical

How an Insect Works

This is not the place for a detailed exposition of insect biology, but a brief summary of the internal workings of an insect may be useful.

Although the body structure of insects is very different from the more familiar structure and physiology of mammals, there are many points of similarity, or features that can be readily compared, even if they have developed in a different way.

THE DIGESTIVE SYSTEM

The digestive system of insects is broadly similar to our own, with a tube that runs from the mouth to the anus. Generally, this is much less convoluted than those of mammals, but it is separated into parts which break up the food, store it, digest it, and then excrete it, in a relatively simple way.

BLOOD AND BREATHING

Insects have a blood system which accounts for much of the weight of the insect body, though it operates in a rather different way from ours. There is a heart and main artery, but most of the organs are bathed in blood which circulates freely in the body cavity, aided by additional pumps in the extremities in larger or more active insects. Its function is rather like the oil in a car engine, providing a continuous lubricating, cleaning and antiseptic system for the internal organs. It plays virtually no part in the distribution of oxygen, in contrast to ours, and is not laden with haemoglobin. (The red blood that may appear from a squashed mosquito is most likely to be your own!)

Breathing (respiration) is accomplished by a system of tubes called tracheae, which are open to the air and penetrate all parts of the body. The openings are known as spiracles, and the tubes are essentially ingrowths of the body wall, being lined with chitin. Air moves into the body by diffusion, which is adequate for small insects, and for larger ones when at rest. Larger insects require additional air-sacs, rather like lungs, which are alternately filled with air and emptied, and this pumping can be readily seen on some insects at rest as a rhythmic 'breathing'. Even aquatic insects breathe air, and most carry a bubble of air underwater with them, which gradually becomes exhausted. A few have a system that allows oxygen to diffuse into the bubble from the water, so that it acts like an external gill.

This method of tracheal respiration, which depends heavily on diffusion rather than an efficient carrier system, is one of the primary factors that limit the size which insects can reach. Because of the inherent inefficiencies of the system, no part of the body can be very far from the surface, or it will become starved of oxygen. Very few insects in this part of the world have bodies that are more than about 20mm across the narrowest dimension, excluding the wings.

TEMPERATURE CONTROL

Insects do not possess the precise temperature control mechanism of mammals, and are therefore very dependent on the temperature of their surroundings. Groups of insects vary considerably in their dependence on warmth, and there are species that manage to remain active at quite low temperatures, especially nocturnal insects such as some moths, and powerful insects like bumble bees and some dragonflies. By contrast butterflies and many other insects are greatly affected by warmth; some butterflies will not fly when the temperature falls below about 25°C, and for others flight becomes slow and short as the temperature falls. Very few species of butterfly fly at all if the temperature falls below 14°C.

Male Common Blue butterfly warming itself in the early morning.

Although these insects have no internal control of body temperature, they have certain behavioural mechanisms that allow them to warm themselves up, or cope with cold. In cooler, but sunny, weather, many species bask in the sun, frequently angling their wings to receive maximum radiation, by holding them at right angles to the sun's rays. Early in the morning, after a cool night, this is particularly helpful to them in allowing them to get moving before the air temperature has reached the critical level. For the naturalist, early on sunny mornings can be an excellent time to go out looking for insects, as they are still slow-moving, but often quite conspicuous as they spread themselves in the first rays of the sun.

FLIGHT AND BALANCE

Flight is of enormous importance to most insects, and is undoubtedly one of the keys to their success and wide distribution. Most insects fly by means of muscles in the thorax wall which do not directly move the wings but deform the thorax wall, causing the wings to rise and fall accordingly. In particularly strong fliers like dragonflies, the flight muscles make up about a quarter of the body weight, though in other species it is usually 10–20 per cent. The speed of the wing beat varies widely according to the weight of the insect and its manner of flight.

Insects maintain balance by constantly altering the angle of their wings as necessary. In the true flies, many of which have a poorly balanced shape, the halteres (see p.204) are highly developed balancing organs, well supplied with sensory facilities. Other insects receive the information to maintain their balance by a combination of keeping the highest light intensity on their back, general visual pattern, and information from tactile hairs on the head. Many insects are extremely agile fliers, and clearly the system is very effective.

Male Southern Hawker dragonfly in flight.

The Life History of Insects

Because of the limitations of their skeletal structure, insects are unable simply to grow steadily from being small to being fully grown, as we do. To achieve this growth, they have evolved a number of techniques, and as a result they tend to have rather complex life-cycles, with a number of different stages.

Most insects have an essentially annual life-cycle. Although some adults hibernate, they will not normally live long into their second season, and their total life-span is usually well under a year, as an adult. Almost all insects begin life as an egg (a few insects, particularly aphids, can give birth to live young, but this is a special adaptation, and is the exception rather than the rule). Eggs come in many forms and sizes, but essentially they represent a way of protecting the tiny embryo against a wide range of unfavourable conditions (such as winter cold, or drought), and they therefore have tough, resistant outer coatings. Many insect eggs have beautiful shapes and textures when seen under magnification.

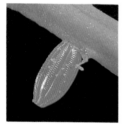
Orange-tip butterfly egg.

Common Shieldbug eggs.

Large White butterfly eggs.

METAMORPHOSIS

The young insect eats or splits its way out of the egg-case and emerges into the harsh outside world. In virtually all cases, except for a few primitive or specialized insects, the young bear little resemblance to the adults of the same species, and will undergo profound changes known collectively as metamorphosis. From this point onwards, the development of insects falls into two groups, each with a distinctive pattern of development from young stages to adult. One group, considered to be the more primitive, begins to develop wings on the outside of the body from a very early stage. Each time the insect moults (see below), it gets larger, and the wings develop slightly more. In these stages, the young resemble the adults in many respects (becoming increasingly

Common Shield Bug eggs and mass of newly hatched nymphs.

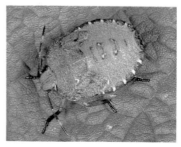
Green Shield Bug nymph. The yellowish triangular undeveloped wings are clearly visible.

A group of immature Meadow Grasshoppers, an exopterygote insect.

Exopterygote life cycle   **Endopterygote life cycle**

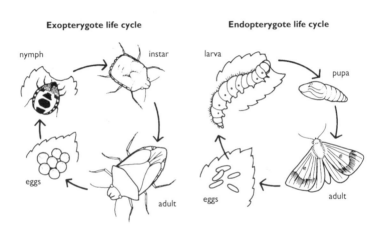

nymph   instar   larva   pupa

eggs   adult   eggs   adult

like them after successive moults), and usually live in the same places and eat similar food, albeit smaller, softer or easier to catch. Insects in these stages are known as nymphs, and the insects that undergo this type of life-cycle are called **exopterygote** insects (*exo* – outside, and *pterygote* – winged). The whole process is known as incomplete metamorphosis, because there is not a total change as seen in the following group; the adults differ from the young in size, and in the possession of fully formed wings and sexual organs.

Some aquatic insects, such as dragonflies, give the impression of a greater change because the young stages are aquatic while the adult is a totally different winged terrestrial insect. Certainly the transformation is rather more dramatic here than in, for example, the last two development stages (instars) of a grasshopper, but it is still the same process. Strictly speaking, therefore, dragonflies in their young stages should be known as nymphs, though they are often referred to as larvae.

Insects in the other group are known as **endopterygote** insects, and they undergo complete metamorphosis, as exemplified by butterflies. In these insects, the young are totally unlike the adults. These larvae will almost certainly have quite different feeding habits from the adults, and may occupy a wholly different ecological niche. Many longhorn beetle larvae, for example, live in rotting wood, whilst the adults are pollen-feeders, visiting roses and other flowers. The larva grows steadily, constantly shedding its skin, often changing gradually in colour, but retaining the same general form. When the larva has reached its full size, it ceases feeding and turns into a pupa (sometimes

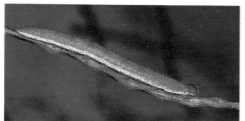

The larva (caterpillar) of the Orange-tip butterfly, an endopterygote insect.

Pupa of an Orange-tip, just before emerging.

known as a chrysalis). This is essentially a protected resting phase, during which the insect undergoes a total internal re-organization in readiness for appearing as an adult. It is protected against desiccation, and to some extent against predation or parasitism, by a tough outer skin, and possibly by good camouflage. Many species pupate in the soil. The pupal stage may also serve as a means of surviving the winter, though different groups have different strategies for this.

The adult Orange-tip butterfly.

Typical exopterygote insects with nymphal stages include bugs, grasshoppers and crickets, cockroaches, and dragonflies and damselflies. Typical endopterygote insects, with larval and pupal stages, include butterflies and moths, flies, Hymenoptera and beetles.

MOULTING

All insects from both groups, as well as the primitive wingless insects, have to undergo a process of moulting. Their chitinous external skeleton cannot simply grow with them, so insects grow a new covering under the old one, which is then split by virtue of the insect enlarging itself with the aid of air or water; the insect remains enlarged until the new skin hardens in the air, and then contracts again, leaving itself some new space for growth.

Each phase between moults is known as an instar, and the process of moulting is known as ecdysis. Some species moult numerous times, while most moult somewhere between 5 and 10 times. In species that moult only a few times, the individual phases are usually recognizable to an expert, and can be called 'third instar', 'final instar' (before adulthood), and so on.

Speckled Bush Cricket just emerged from a cast skin.

ADULTHOOD

When the fully winged adult emerges from the pupa or last nymphal instar, it usually needs to 'pump up' its crumpled wings to their full size and allow them to dry. Different groups do this in different ways and at different speeds, according to their

Four-spotted Chaser dragonfly emerging as an adult from its nymphal skin.

particular life-style, though for almost all of them it is a vulnerable phase, and they need to do it as inconspicuously as possible. Species that emerge more or less synchronously from a limited breeding area, such as dragonflies, are especially vulnerable: once a predator such as a blackbird discovers what is happening, it can kill and eat a considerable number of insects in quite a short time. Studies have shown that this is easily the most dangerous stage of the life-cycle for many insects. Dragonflies tend to emerge at night for protection, to be ready to fly at daybreak, but they can only do this if the nights and early mornings are warm.

The adult winged insect is known as the imago. It is generally true to say that only adult insects can fly, though the mayflies (see p.42) are a curious exception. In this group, the final-instar aquatic nymph crawls out of the water on to some vegetation, and a winged insect emerges. This sub-imago can fly almost immediately (though rather weakly), and it soon reaches a sheltered place where it settles. This phase is dull in colour, owing to a downy covering, and it is known to fishermen as the 'dun'. After settling, the mayfly moults again to produce a shinier, more strongly coloured fully mature adult (known as the 'spinner'). Apart from this exception, and some of the wingless insects, adults do not moult or grow any more once they have become adult.

TIMING

The life-cycles of insects all follow one or other of these patterns, though they may differ in the way in which they do it. For example, some insects simply produce one generation of adults each year, and there is an exact annual cycle, varying only slightly according to weather conditions. Other species may have larvae that live, steadily growing, for many years, such as many wood-feeding beetles, or some of the larger dragonflies, though the length of time as a larva is influenced by temperature and food quality or availability. Many species may produce several generations in a year; for some, this is simply a matter of producing as many generations as possible whilst conditions are good. For others, it is a more tightly regulated system, depending on the availability of a particular food-plant, for instance. The Holly Blue butterfly has two regular generations per year; the first-generation adults emerge from the pupa in spring, and eggs are laid on the flowers of Holly. These develop, and finally emerge later in the summer as second-generation adults, which lay their eggs in the young flowers of Ivy. In many butterflies, the two generations can be rather different in colouring, and in one species, the European Map, the two generations are so different that they were originally thought to be different species.

Different insects also differ in the way in which they overwinter. Most insects overwinter as eggs or pupae, but others overwinter as larvae or nymphs, whilst quite a few hibernate in the adult phase. It depends partly on habitat, but in other cases there is no obvious reason why one or other strategy should have been adopted.

The Ecology of Insects

In recent decades, especially the last two, there has been a great upsurge in the study of insect ecology. For one thing, many of the basic anatomical and taxonomic features have by now been well worked out; secondly, study of the economic role of insects has continued apace using more sophisticated techniques; and thirdly, the great decline in some of our more conspicuous and familiar insects (and, no doubt, in many less conspicuous ones, too) has led to a need to find out what is going on in insect populations, and why it is happening.

These latter conservation-orientated studies have tended, not surprisingly, to concentrate on obvious species such as butterflies, though our knowledge of other groups has increased considerably, too. Despite their uneven nature, such studies have shown that many of these better-known insects have remarkably complex life-cycles and requirements, and many old and rather simplistic ideas about insect ecology have had to be discarded. Some generalizations about other groups of insects and their ecology can be made from specific studies, too.

EXACTING REQUIREMENTS

The Large Blue butterfly is a well-known, but nevertheless excellent, example of just how surprising an insect's requirements and life-cycle can be. Large Blues occur in rough, grassy, flowery places, and it was well known that the larvae fed on wild thyme. Many such places exist (though they are declining), yet the butterfly was declining to the point of extinction in many areas, and more information was clearly needed. Subsequent studies revealed a remarkable story: during the first three instars, the larvae feed on wild thyme, like any ordinary caterpillar (apart from the fact that they have well-developed cannibalistic tendencies, and will quickly finish off any smaller larvae of their own species!). When they moult to the fourth instar, however, their behaviour changes; they cease feeding on the thyme, and fall to the ground, where they wait patiently until discovered by ants. This does not usually take long, as ants are abundant in such habitats, though normally only one or two species of ant are involved successfully.

The ants carry the larva into their nest, helped by the larva which makes itself as easy to carry as possible. The larva produces a sugary 'nectar' which the ants consume. Once in the nest, the butterfly larva begins to eat the ant larvae, whilst continuing to secrete 'nectar' and ant-friendly pheromones. It spends the rest of its larval life eating the ant brood, unmolested, then finally pupates in the ant's nest in spring; the adult emerges from the pupa in the nest, and crawls to the surface, untouched by the ants. Because of its carnivorous habits, any one ant nest can only support one or two larvae, and the nests of some ant species are quite unsuitable. This means that there has to be a substantial population of ants just to support a small population of the butterfly, so it is hardly surprising that the species is rare and declining. Many other species of blue butterfly have similar relationships with ants, to an equivalent or lesser degree.

A wholly different example is provided by the Stag Beetle, or some of the longhorn beetles (see p.290). In these species, the eggs are laid on old wood, and the larva feeds on the decaying wood. The larger species may spend up to five years in the wood (wood is not very nutritious!), which means that successful larval sites are quite uncommon; the wood has to be decayed and soft enough to be edible (living trees are not suitable), yet not so decayed that it falls apart during the period, leaving the larvae exposed to predators. Man often plays a part here, too, by removing much dead and decaying timber. The most suitable larval sites tend to be old, but stable, boles of large trees, and

A male Stag Beetle. Its membranous hindwings are just being unfurled ready for flight.

most of these beetles, when they emerge as adults, also need flowers, where they collect pollen or nectar. Sites that meet both these habitat requirements are increasingly uncommon, as are the beetles that they support.

INSECT NUMBERS

Insects may be small, but this is more than made up for by their enormous variety and huge numbers. It is often said that plants are the basis of any ecological system, as indeed they are, but insects run a close second in many ways, forming vital links in all parts of the chain. The numbers involved where insects are concerned are so large as to be almost inconceivable. In Europe alone, there are almost 100,000 different named species of insect, with the expectation that there are many more still to be described. In the world as a whole, about a million insects have been described so far, and it is certain that there are as many again waiting to be described. In France alone, there are more species of fly than there are species of mammal in the world. Generally speaking, the differences between species of insect are just as great, scale for scale, as between species of mammals and birds, and in some cases much greater.

Obviously the number of species of insect is only one aspect of their total numbers, but it gives an idea of the range of ecological niches and climatic zones that insects can occupy, as every species requires at least slightly different conditions, if only on the smallest of scales. There is also the question of total numbers. Insects vary in this respect in the same way that mammals and birds do, in that – as a general rule – the larger they are, the fewer there are of them, and the higher up the food chain they are, the lower their numbers. In addition, there are obviously insects that are 'doing well' in our present-day man-influenced environment, such as the House-fly or the Large White butterfly, and others that are declining, such as the Large Blue butterfly, or the Goat Moth with their demanding requirements for a declining combination of habitats.

Even the bigger insects are sometimes found together in large numbers. These are roosting 4-spotted Chaser dragonflies in an exceptionally good year for them.

If you pick up a current edition of a detailed book on birds, you will find statements to the effect that there are '420 pairs of Golden Eagle in Britain', or '441 pairs of Dartford Warbler in Hampshire'. Even allowing for the fact that such estimates may be over-precise, there is simply no possibility of doing the same for insects, and in all but the case of extreme and attractive rarities, total insect populations are unknown. However, there are estimates for individual species or groups expressed in terms of the numbers per square metre or, for large species, in terms of the numbers on particular sites. For example, it is estimated that there are 2–3 million ants in a large colony, including up to 5,000 sexually active queens. Springtails may reach huge numbers, with estimates per square metre (to a depth of 30cm) varying up to 400,000 individuals. By contrast, a population of an uncommon butterfly, even in a good site, may number only 50–100 individuals, varying from year to year.

Looking at the insect world as a whole, it is clear that insect numbers are enormous and that insects pervade every aspect of ecology. Their feeding habits, and their role as prey for other animals, should be viewed in this light.

FEEDING HABITS

The range of feeding habits amongst insects is almost as diverse as the range of insects themselves, especially if you bear in mind that larvae and young nymphs may feed quite differently from adults.

The great majority of insects are **plant-feeders** at some stage in their lives, though this simple statement masks a great variety of feeding strategies. For example, some insects (such as aphids and many other bugs) suck the sap from the leaves or stems of plants. Some insects, such as sawfly larvae, eat virtually all of the leaf material directly, perhaps just leaving the harder veins. Other insects, such as many beetles and some hoverflies, eat rotten wood in their larval stages. Many adult insects (such as butterflies, hoverflies and longhorn beetles) visit flowers to consume either nectar or pollen as their

The Currant Gall, caused by a small wasp, is one of several galls found on Oak trees.

A female Snipe Fly eats her prey while mating. The male has orchid pollinia stuck to its face.

main food source; other insects, whether larval or adult, eat mainly developing seeds and fruits. Some adult insects, such as mayflies, do not feed at all. Their feeding is all done by the nymphs or larvae.

One interesting and unusual group of plant-feeders is the gall-formers (see pp. 302–11). These insects inject growth substances into a host plant, causing it to react by forming a swelling of some sort, often in a highly distinctive shape. The insect larvae feed on the plant within their specially protected cell (though they are not protected against everything – see p.23), and the effects are clearly visible and identifiable on the outside. Gall-formers are usually viewed as plant parasites rather than simply plant-feeders, though the distinction can become blurred. There are also various species which specialize in laying their eggs in the tissues already produced as a result of the original gall-former; they do not damage the original inhabitants, and are known as inquilines.

The effect of many millions of insects and their larvae feeding on plants is clearly enormous. In some cases it is very obvious, especially when it takes place in a garden or on a crop, as, for example, when sawflies feed on Solomon's Seal, or gooseberry bushes, or when Codling Moth larvae have damaged apples. In other cases, it is clear enough to the experienced eye, but not so visible as to be normally noticed; for example, a skilled butterfly surveyor can detect the presence of most species as easily by seeing the effects of larval feeding as by seeing the adults. In many other cases, we barely notice the effects, but cumulatively it must be considerable, slowing the rate of growth of all plants that are affected.

A smaller number of insects are **predators**, feeding on living animal matter which will almost certainly include other insects. Many species are partially predatory; for example many bugs are vegetarian in their earlier nymphal stages, and gradually become carnivorous as they mature. Other species, such as some bush-crickets, are omnivorous, feeding partly as predators, partly on plant material. Social wasps, such as the Common Wasp, are well known for their habit of feeding on fruit, jam, lemonade etc. in late summer, but earlier in the year the workers spend most of their time collecting insects for the developing young wasps.

Insects such as tiger beetles and ground beetles (see p.270) are wholly predatory, both as adults and as larvae. Ground beetle adults actively hunt prey, mainly at night, whilst the larvae are moderately mobile, and seek out slow-moving invertebrate prey such as slugs and worms. Tiger beetle adults behave rather similarly, though they are mainly diurnal, but the larvae have their own method of feeding: they live in vertical shafts up to 30cm deep, where they wait near the top with their jaws at the surface; if an unfortunate insect, such as an ant, stumbles into the wrong place, it is grabbed then taken to the bottom of the shaft and eaten. This feeding habit tends to confine tiger beetles to particular habitats, especially where there is sandy soil for burrowing in. Other predatory groups include ladybirds (see p.286), lacewings (see p.114) and many bugs, such as the assassin bugs (see p.94).

Many insects feed at some stage as **parasites**; that is, they live within the body of their host and feed on it from the inside. Most insect parasites come from within the orders of Diptera or Hymenoptera, though there are other examples. Amongst the best known are the ichneumons (see p.244), a division of the Hymenoptera. Most of them parasitize other insects, especially the larvae of moths and butterflies. The adult females are highly active, and spend their time moving rapidly amongst vegetation, antennae waving furiously, looking for potential candidates. When they find a larva of the right type, they lay their eggs either into it, using their long ovipositors, or – with some species – on it. In either

A female parasitic wasp, *Pteromalus puparum*, about to lay her eggs in the pupa of a Large White butterfly.

case, the larvae eventually find their way into the host and commence feeding, beginning with non-essential organs so that the caterpillar remains alive as long as possible. Eventually, they kill the host and pupate, either within its body shell or outside it, and this may be before or after it has pupated. Parasitized larvae can often be recognized because they become slower-moving (not surprisingly!) and less well concealed, so they probably also suffer a higher rate of predation, in which case both host and parasite will be killed.

Some sand wasps (see p.252) catch their chosen hosts, which may be moth larvae, young grasshoppers or crickets, or spiders – depending on the species – and paralyse them. They are then dragged to a nest-hole (which may be either pre-constructed, or constructed after the host is caught, depending on the species), placed inside, and eggs laid into them. This obviously affords a greater degree of protection to the developing sand wasp young than if the larval hosts were left in their original position. It does, however, tend to limit them to sites where suitable burrows can be dug, mainly on sandy heathland.

As mentioned previously, gall-forming insects are not protected against everything, and there are a number of insects, especially among the chalchid wasps and ichneumons (both members of the Hymenoptera), which specialize in parasitizing the inhabitants of galls. They lay their eggs into the larvae within the gall, using their long and sensitive ovipositors, and the parasite larvae gradually eat the gall-former from the inside. Thus a mixture of parasites and gall-formers – or even all parasites – may emerge from a gall eventually.

Apart from plant-feeders, predators and parasites, there are also the **scavengers** of the insect world. These feed largely on dead animal matter, though they may stray into predation especially with easily caught prey. Pond-skaters (see p.98) are a sort of mixture of predator and scavenger, catching insects that have fallen into the water and are either struggling or dead. Scorpion flies (see p.116) feed mainly on scavenged animal matter, including the discarded remains of prey from spiders' webs, which they stealthily remove without attracting the attention of the spider. They also feed on easily caught live invertebrates, and on some vegetable matter, such as ripe fruit.

INSECT ENEMIES

Apart from predation and parasitism of insect on insect, all insects may fall victim to many other organisms. Insects provide the food for many other creatures, and their role in the food-chains of most habitats is crucial.

Birds are probably the greatest consumers of insects. A large percentage of birds are insectivorous to a greater or lesser degree, and most feed their young on at least some insect food. Some, such as House Sparrows, are simply opportunistic feeders on insects, taking insects where they present themselves; occasionally, their effect can be quite significant, such as when they discover a synchronized hatch of damselflies and consume most of them. Blackbirds, which will eat almost everything, have been known to consume a high proportion of emerging Emperor Dragonflies when they have discovered them at the crucial moment. Many other birds, such as the tits, most warblers, and the flycatchers, are more specialized insect-feeders. They consume vast quantities of insects, in both larval and adult phases, especially when they are rearing their young. Waders, such as Dunlin or Golden Plover, feed mainly on intertidal invertebrates for much of the year, but they rear their young on huge quantities of mosquitoes, black-flies, midges and other insects that are abundant at breeding time in their nesting habitats. Birds such as swallows, martins and flycatchers feed almost exclusively on flying insects, of which they consume enormous numbers.

Mammals are less well adapted to feeding on insects, though many will take a proportion of insect prey. Small carnivores such as shrews depend mainly on invertebrate prey, which can include a high proportion of insects, especially larvae. Foxes and other large carnivores or omnivores will eat ground beetles and any other nocturnal insects that they come across. Their droppings are often laden with beetle wings (elytra). In north Europe, bats have specialized particularly in eating insects – mainly nocturnal or crepuscular ones, especially moths. These are mainly taken from the air, but some species will catch insects from leaves, too.

Insects have many enemies amongst **other invertebrates**, too. Some are relatively casual consumers of insects, such as slugs and snails, which will eat insect eggs, young larvae, and small insects such as aphids, as part of their general vegetation consumption. Harvestmen will eat almost anything that they can catch (see photograph below of a harvestman attacking a live Vapourer Moth). More specialized are the spiders, which, as a group, depend heavily on insect prey. Most construct webs, typified by the orb-webs of such species as the Garden Spider, into which insects fly. Stronger insects such as bumble bees and wasps can usually escape, but other species are quickly caught, paralysed and subsequently eaten. Some spiders, such as the wolf spiders, actively chase their prey and therefore consume mainly ground-dwellers. Others, such as the crab

A harvestman eating a live female Vapourer Moth.

A Drone-fly caught in a spider's web.

spiders, sit motionless on flowers and grab any insect that happens along, quickly paralysing it with a venom injection. Not infrequently, one comes across an apparently tame butterfly on a flower, only to discover that it has been caught by a crab spider.

Insects may also fall victim to **plants** or **fungi**, though on a rather more limited scale. Fungi, in particular species of *Enteromophthora*, attack insects, gradually killing them and rotting them away. They probably mainly infect unhealthy individuals, and it is not uncommon to find dead or dying hoverflies and other flies hanging from vegetation, infected with this fungus. The extent of the attacks varies considerably from year to year, depending on the weather. There is also a small group of insectivorous flowering plants in north Europe, comprising the sundews, butterworts and bladderworts. Bladderworts catch mainly small aquatic organisms, drawn mainly from groups other than insects. Butterworts have sticky leaves which are capable only of holding small insects, such as midges. Sundews, however, can catch a wider range of insects by virtue of their very sticky hairy leaves, and victims can include almost any insect up to the size of a damselfly. All three groups of plants are virtually confined to acid boggy areas (where insects become a means of supplementing their nutrient intake), and are never abundant, so their effect on insect populations is very limited.

A hoverfly killed by the fungus *Enteromophthora*.

A Green Leaf-hopper bug caught on the sticky leafs of sundew.

Finally, and perhaps most significantly, we should mention **man**. This is covered in more detail in the section on conservation (see p.29), but in summary man has had huge effects on insect populations in a large number of ways. The most far-reaching has been the enormous changes in habitat, especially over the last 50 years, which have made so much of our countryside unsuitable for most insects. The introduction of insecticides, which are now used very widely, has also wrought dramatic changes in insect populations, not only by controlling those pests at which they are aimed, but also by influencing both the species that depended on them, and other susceptible species that come into contact with the insecticides. No insecticide is totally specific to one species, and some are very damaging to insects as a group. Even other pesticides such as fungicides can kill insects, or may at the very least affect their breeding success.

By contrast, man has also provided new habitats, or extended existing habitats, for insects, and many depend on man to a greater or lesser degree. The list should include not only obvious groups like cockroaches or house-flies, but also those that depend on essentially man-maintained habitats like chalk downland or coppiced woodland. Such species as Adonis Blue or Pearl-bordered Fritillary butterflies are actually very dependent on man to maintain their numbers in parts of north Europe.

COLOUR: CAMOUFLAGE, WARNING AND MIMICRY

Colour is very important in the insect world, and insects – and many animals that prey on them – are sensitive to it. Colour in insects seems to serve two main functions: it provides concealment or camouflage; and it can act as a warning. It must also play some role in interspecific recognition.

Insects, as we have seen, are constantly under attack – from each other, from mammals and birds, and from other invertebrates. In most cases (except, for example, in the case of fungal attack and insecticide sprays), an insect is better protected from its enemies if it cannot be seen. It follows, therefore, that a colour pattern which will conceal the insect is likely to be favoured, as more such individuals will survive. There are many ways in which insects conceal themselves, of which colour is but one; immobility and choosing good hiding places are two others. Even within the concept of camouflage, there are different ways of achieving the same aim, depending on the shape of the insect, its habits and, to a degree, chance.

Many insects simply match the colour of their usual background, such as green grasshoppers or shieldbugs, or brown groundhoppers. This is a straightforward means of camouflage, nicely illustrated in the famous studies of the Peppered Moth, which showed that the colour of these moths could change by evolution, over generations, as the colour of the bark of trees upon which they rested had changed. In this instance, airborne pollution was the cause of the changing background colour, which allowed scientists to observe the change as it happened; more commonly, the insects have adapted to an existing colour, such as that of grass, and remained the same since long before we began to study them.

In other cases, the camouflage is more subtle. The larvae of some moths look strikingly like parts of the habitat in which they live. For example, the Swallowtailed Moth has caterpillars that look just like the twigs of Ivy, its food-plant. Adult moths, too, can be extremely well camouflaged; for example, the Merveille-du-jour looks very like a

The colour of many larvae is simply plain green to match the foliage on which they feed. This is the larva of the Narrow-bordered Bee Hawk-moth.

Larvae of the Cinnabar Moth on Ragwort. Their coloration warns of their poisonous taste.

The larva of a Swallowtailed Moth mimicking Ivy stems.

piece of lichen-covered bark, on which it often rests motionless; the Buff-tip looks remarkably like a broken Birch twig complete with leaf scars and lenticels.

In one way or another, most insects are reasonably successful at concealing themselves. Other insects, however, have adopted a totally different strategy. The basis of this is to taste as unpleasant as possible and to advertise the fact! Yellows and reds, in bold patterns combined with black, tend to indicate unpleasant taste in nature, and many predators soon learn this fact, avoiding such insects on subsequent occasions. Thus unpleasant-tasting or poisonous insects avoid being heavily predated, and survive. Good examples include burnet moths, which are red and black, and taste highly unpleasant (it is said), and wasps, which are aggressive and dangerous. Clearly, though, this opens up other possibilities for different groups, which are neither dangerous nor unpleasant-tasting, to evolve the same colours, and thus avoid being predated, by proxy. This general strand of evolution is known as mimicry, and it occurs widely amongst insects.

In fact, two broad types of mimicry have been distinguished, though only one type is widespread in the northern European insect fauna. The first type, known as Müllerian mimicry, involves several equally unpleasant or dangerous insects mimicking each other. They avoid predation more successfully because predators learn the single pattern more quickly. This type is rare or absent in our fauna. (Apparent examples, such as the various wasps, are different in that these have all evolved from a common form, rather than separately imitating each other.) The common form of mimicry in our insect fauna is Batesian mimicry, in which harmless insects come to resemble unpleasant or dangerous ones, 'borrowing' their warning signals. It is easy to see how this evolves, once the process has started, as the least successful mimics will be caught, while the most successful ones survive to reproduce. Thus the mimic will gradually come to resemble its pattern ever more closely. Good examples include the hoverfly *Volucella bombylans* which resembles a bumble bee (in fact, there are several distinct forms, resembling different species of bumble bee); several hoverflies which have the bold black-and-yellow colouring of wasps; and the Wasp Beetle, which resembles a wasp.

The Wasp Beetle, imitating its namesake, is an example of Batesian mimicry.

MIGRATION

The concept of bird migration is a familiar enough one, but that of insect migration is much less so. In fact many of our insects habitually migrate over remarkably long distances, sometimes on an annual basis, or sometimes in response to a particular set of conditions. Regular migrants into the UK include a number of **butterflies**. For example, Painted Lady butterflies cannot overwinter here, and our populations invariably migrate from S Europe or N Africa (which involves a huge distance including two sea crossings), though the earlier arrivals will breed here during the summer. The Red Admiral has a broadly similar migration pattern, but it is known that some stay on to hibernate, and a small number of these survive to appear early the following year. In both species, there is a degree of southward migration at the end of the summer, though it is not a complete migration, and many individuals simply die here in the north. Other butterflies, such as the Large White, have resident populations that are augmented by immigrants from further south, followed by a visible return migration in some years.

A mass of 7-spot Ladybirds on a telegraph pole – part of the 1994 invasion in East Anglia.

Dragonflies regularly migrate, too. Some simply arrive here as occasional vagrants, such as the Red-winged Darter, but others are regular migrants, coming northwards or westwards in variable numbers almost every year. A good example is the Migrant Hawker, which regularly arrives here from further south in Europe. This species also demonstrates one of the advantages of migration; at first it might seem odd that insects swarm into an area, year after year, in which they are simply going to die. However, there is always the possibility that the habitat or climate of any new area may change to become more suitable, or that the migrants may find some niche within it that is suitable for them. In the case of the Migrant Hawker this is what seems to have happened, as increasing numbers are now becoming resident in Britain.

Other, smaller insects migrate, too. Mass immigrations of ladybirds have become well known recently: huge numbers reached Britain and elsewhere in N Europe in 1976, 1994 and other years. In such cases, there is an exceptional build-up of numbers in a favourable area, due to a particular combination of circumstances such as a series of mild winters and an abundance of food. This large population and the corresponding decline in its food supply in turn trigger an outward mass movement, which may be heavily dependent on weather conditions, and huge numbers of insects will ultimately arrive somewhere else, where food may be available. Other large-scale migrants include the small hoverfly *Episyrphus balteatus*, an aphid-feeder which may become very abundant, thanks to inward migration, in some years. These masses of insects may travel many hundreds of kilometres.

The Conservation of Insects

The more that insects have been studied, the clearer it has become that many species are in considerable decline at present. At the same time, most studies seem to show that the requirements of an insect are not as simple as was once thought. For example, in the case of plant-feeders, the presence of the larval food-plant is by no means the only requirement. Gradually, insect life has become more prominent in the world of nature conservation, hitherto dominated by birds, mammals and plants, and much more is being done to cater specifically for their needs.

There is an inherent problem in insect conservation. There are so many species that some, even among the rarer ones, may have conflicting requirements which are hard to reconcile. In this case, the more knowledge we acquire, the more difficult the problem can become! For example, at the nature reserve of Castle Hill, in southern England, the managers have had to deal with the conflicting requirements of three rare and attractive insects. This is a site for the Wart-Biter, an extremely rare insect in Britain; the Adonis Blue butterfly, which is very attractive and uncommon, and the Scarce Forester moth, which is also extremely rare in Britain. The Adonis Blue needs sunny, south-facing, unimproved downland swards with very short turf, grazed right down to ground level. The Scarce Forester is a day-flying moth that needs abundant tall flowers and grasses and is highly sensitive to over-grazing. The Wart-Biter is more demanding than either, needing bare ground where its eggs can be laid, short, flowery grass for the early nymphal stages, and long grass in which adults and later nymphs can hide from predators; the whole has to be warm and sunny. Researchers looking for potential reintroduction sites for the Wart-Biter found only two out of a short-list of 100 were suitable! Clearly it is difficult to reconcile the conflicting needs of such species, let alone the hundreds of lesser-known species, in one site, and it can only be achieved either by careful management or by an exceptionally diverse site. Castle Hill has both, and the combination of controlled grazing by cattle (which produce a more uneven effect than sheep), and a terraced hillside provides for all these species and many more.

Apart from exceptionally rare insects, and the more emotive species such as butterflies and dragonflies, we simply have to work on an average 'highest common denominator' basis, and conserve, in an ecologically sound state, as many habitats and niches as possible. Some habitats, such as shaded dead wood, ancient woodland, clear fresh water, and permanent flowery grassland, are known to be exceptionally rich insect habitats, and it makes sense to conserve them wherever possible. Insect-rich habitats are generally good for other creatures and plants anyway. Also, some plants, such as oak trees, are especially good for insects, so this has to be borne in mind. There is a problem in that many species of insect may occur in niches that are not generally insect-rich, or fashionable to conserve, so care must be taken (wherever we have the knowledge) to ensure that these are provided for, too.

It is a daunting task, and effectively an endless one – given the pressures on the countryside and the number of insects to be catered for – but it is a worthwhile one as insects have great intrinsic value and are vital to the survival of many other species. There are now specialist butterfly and dragonfly conservation groups, and other groups of specialists are beginning to see the need for conservation in their own groups. The first 'butterfly reserves' and 'dragonfly reserves' are beginning to be declared, and it may not be long before we see more general insect nature reserves, or even 'Diptera reserves' or 'Hymenoptera reserves'!

Finding Insects

Insects are so varied and widespread that it may sound perverse to suggest ways of finding them – they are everywhere. It is surprising, however, how much one can increase the number and variety of insects seen by following some simple guidelines.

The first, and most obvious, is to seek out good insect-rich habitats. These are usually flowery, sheltered places, which may often be nature reserves or managed in some way with conservation in mind.

Woodlands are especially rich insect habitats. The best ones tend to be ancient, i.e. to have had woodland on the site for at least several hundred years. Usually such places have a diverse mixture of trees, shrubs and herbs, plenty of old stumps and coppice stools, and a good mixture of microhabitats. Woods like this which also have flowery clearings or rides are even better, and such places are ideal for seeing a range of insects. Conifer plantations on ancient woodland or grassland sites, though detrimental in the long term, can be exceptionally rich insect sites for a while, when the rides remain open and sunny. As the conifers mature and the ground vegetation is shaded out, they will steadily lose their insect fauna. Coppiced woods can be very good for insects; the mosaic of open clearings, semi-shade and heavy shade, especially if coupled with a scattering of old trees, is excellent for insects. Ancient pasture-woodland, such as in an old deer park, where there are many very old trees in a matrix of pasture, can be very good for particular groups of insects, especially flies and beetles, though they may be hard to find. If the pasture is flowery and agriculturally unimproved, the chances of seeing insects are greater.

Flowery grassland is another good insect habitat. Hay meadows, even if flowery, tend to be less rich because the annual midsummer cutting is detrimental to many species. Much depends, however, on the quality of the surroundings and the general ambient temperature – a warm hay meadow surrounded by other rich habitats can be superb. Pastures can be good, as long as they are flowery and agriculturally unimproved. Heavily grazed pastures may have a limited fauna, though the insects that are present may be special. Lightly grazed or temporarily ungrazed pastures will often have an abundance of species, all present in large numbers. Damp pastures have a different fauna from dry ones, and there are many subtle differences between sites.

Water is potentially an excellent insect habitat, and it will benefit even non-aquatic species. Fast-flowing, slow-flowing and still waters have different species associated with them, though there is much overlap. Generally, still and slow-flowing waters have the widest range of species, but areas around faster-flowing waters are always worth looking at for caddis-flies, stoneflies and specialized Odonata such as the Golden-ringed Dragonfly and the Demoiselle Agrion.

A flowery clearing in a deciduous wood; a rich insect habitat.

The best waters are clean and clear, without strong algal growths, yet with plenty of oxygenating plants, emergent plants and floating-leaved species. These are used for emergence, as food-plants, as platforms for courtship and so on, and they directly improve the habitat by oxygenation and by providing light and shade or warm and cool areas. Generally sunny waters have the most species, though shaded waters have their own specialities (such as mosquitoes!).

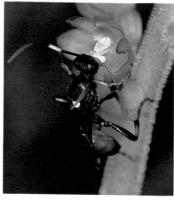

An ichneumon wasp unintentionally pollinates a Twayblade orchid. It has pollinia attached to its head.

Wetlands other than open water – i.e. vegetated wet places such as bogs and fens – are all likely to be highly productive, though access may be difficult. Acid wetlands have their own specialized species, and are often especially good for dragonflies. The best wetland sites have open water as well as vegetated wetland.

Heathlands can also be very productive insect habitats, especially on sandy soil. Such places tend to be warm, which suits many insects, and the sandy soil is ideal for a number of groups that burrow at some stage of their lives, such as tiger beetles, sand wasps, solitary bees and the Minotaur Beetle. If the heathland has a diverse mixture of plants other than heathers – such as Birch, Bracken, gorse and various herbs – it will be better still. Sand-dunes offer some of the same niches, and share some species, though they have their own specialized fauna in addition.

In general, the very best places have a combination of these habitats all close together. In such places, the sum is often greater than the total of the parts, because there are many insects that particularly like edges between habitats, or which need two or more habitats to do well.

To find insects in these habitats, other than the very obvious species, you need to move slowly, look hard, and listen. Look carefully under leaves and flower heads, or on the trunks of trees, or at the base of grass tussocks. By listening, you can detect grasshoppers, bush-crickets, Wood Crickets, cicadas, and even the flying sounds of larger insects such as dragonflies.

For more detailed investigations, the technique of beating can be useful. This consists of setting out something like a white sheet (depending on the scale you are working on) below a branch, then banging the branch hard several times. All kinds of creatures that you might otherwise not have seen will fall out from the tree. This is not a particularly ecologically friendly method, for many of the insects will not find their way back to their feeding sites, so it is only recommended where there is a good reason for it. Other more active techniques for seeing insects include using pond-nets and a tray, and setting up moth traps. These traps can be bought, or made roughly from a light, with a funnel below it leading into a closed box containing egg-boxes or other loose packing material. Moths are attracted to the light, and gradually spiral towards it, eventually dropping down into the box. They can then be observed the following morning and released. If you trap regularly, take care how you release the moths, as birds soon learn to recognize the actions as 'feeding-time'. The light and trap should be covered if there is any likelihood of rain.

Photographing Insects

The development of single-lens reflex cameras, macro lenses and flashguns has made the photography of insects a simpler and more rewarding business in recent years.

The first problem lies in finding and approaching suitable insects. The previous section should help you to find insects; this just leaves the problem of getting close to them. Insects are most sensitive to movement, especially lateral movement (see p.9), and the best way to approach them is slowly and in as straight a line as possible; they react least to this sort of approach. Some insects, such as bumble bees, will only spend a few seconds at each flower, so the slow approach rarely works – they have gone by the time you get there. For this type of insect, it is often better simply to wait at a suitable place to see what turns up. With other insects, if you fail the first few times, try again, moving more slowly, but remember that insects do vary in their responses. Eventually you will find one that does not fly away.

As far as the purely photographic techniques go, there are two basic approaches to photographing insects – using flash or using daylight – though they need not be mutually exclusive. Whichever method you choose, it is best to use a single lens reflex camera, equipped with a lens of about 100mm which can be focused at least as close as 30cm. The ideal lenses are macro lenses, designed for this very purpose.

If the insect is reasonably large (such as a dragonfly or butterfly) and well lit, then using natural light is a very effective way of photographing it. The camera can be hand-held or tripod-mounted (though it can be quite a slow process manoeuvring a tripod into position), and the picture composed as desired. Unless the main subject differs markedly in brightness from the background, then the camera's light meter should cope well enough with the exposure. In more difficult situations (for example, a white butterfly with a shaded area behind it), it is worth pointing the camera at something similar in tone but less complex nearby (such as a pale flower, with a well-lit background), and following that meter reading. Generally speaking, photographing insects in natural light offers a good opportunity to show the insect in its habitat, rather than trying for highly detailed portraits which show every feature.

For detailed close-ups, electronic flash gives better results. Electronic flash produces a burst of light which only lasts for about 1/5000th of a second, and which, for this brief period, is brighter than the ambient light (if set up correctly). This means that the effective shutter speed on the camera is not the shutter speed setting, but the duration of the flash: the existing daylight should not record at all during the period when the flash is lit, but only the light from the flash. So by using flash, you immediately have the power to 'freeze' any movement in the subject or camera. If you use the right power of flash, you can also take pictures at a very small aperture, such as f22, which gives you considerable depth of field in the final picture. Virtually all of the pictures in this book were taken in this way. Those taken with natural light only include those on pp.18 and 173 (top right).

There are various different ways of setting up flashguns. Most insect photographers prefer to use two flashguns, one on either side of the camera, to give a good even light. The worst method is to have one flashgun mounted on top of the camera, but many people take excellent pictures with a single flashgun mounted or held obliquely above the front of the lens. When two flashguns are used, it is simplest to mount them on a bar that runs along under the camera (see diagram). There are also various proprietary makes of flash holder, such as those from Novoflex, James Dean and others. A few manufacturers, such as Nikon and Canon, offer a flashgun unit which has two separate flash tubes mounted on either side of the front of the lens. These are excellent for close-

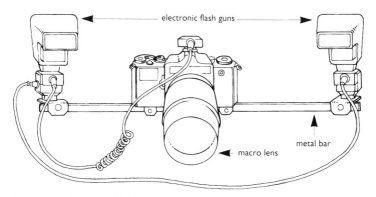

Camera set-up for photographing insects.

ups of small insects, but much less good for larger insects since the light is too frontal, which causes strong reflections. There is plenty of scope for experimentation with such a set-up, and there is no single perfect solution. In general, insects look most attractive if the lighting is oblique, but this is not essential (except for insects on water, or very reflective species like dragonflies with open wings).

Whatever system of flashguns is used, you need some method of assessing the correct exposure. Many cameras nowadays have automatic through-the-lens (TTL) metering of flash, so – as long as the flashguns are the correct type for the camera, and are both connected to it – this makes life relatively simple. The only problem with TTL metering is that the flash will light the area very close to the lens (which will be the area in which your subject is placed) but it will not light the background adequately if it is much further away. For example, if you take a close-up of a small butterfly on a tall flower from 15cm away, and the nearest piece of visible background is about 1m away, then the background will appear black. Not only can this look unattractive, but it can also fool the meter into giving you the wrong exposure. The meter will be operating *during* the exposure and will 'see' that the background is dark, so may respond by trying to give additional exposure. Thus the actual subject will be too brightly lit (overexposed). The combination of an overlit subject and a nearly-dark background is not an attractive one. The answer is to recognize this situation where it occurs, and either alter the exposure compensation on the camera to give about two-thirds of a stop less exposure, or try to take photographs of insects where the background is immediately behind them.

If your camera does not have TTL flash-metering, you need a different technique. Set the flashguns up in the way in which you intend to use them, and do some calibration tests. Photograph an insect-sized, mid-toned subject (such as a green leaf or a red flower) at several apertures, such as f8, f11, f16 and f22, and make careful notes. Then scan the processed results and pick out the one with the best exposure. Use this aperture for any future pictures. As long as you maintain the same lens and film speed, and do not significantly alter the positions of the flashguns, this aperture will give satisfactory exposures over quite a distance range. It will not be fooled by black backgrounds, as it is effectively a pre-set system, and you only need cheap flashguns which need not be specially geared to your camera make. It is a simple but surprisingly effective method.

The Classification of Insects

This is not the place for a detailed look at the basis for the classification of insects, but it may be helpful to give a quick summary of insect taxonomy, followed by an illustrated key to the main groups of insects.

Insects are part of the huge biological tribe (phylum) known as the arthropods, as described on page 7. Within this phylum, they are one of a number of **classes**. Insects themselves are divided into two **sub-classes** – the winged insects, sub-class Pterygota; and the wingless insects, sub-class Apterygota. Classes or sub-classes are subdivided into **orders**, such as the Odonata (dragonflies and damselflies) or Lepidoptera (butterflies and moths). Orders may be split into **sub-orders**, where there are two distinct lines within an order, not different enough to be separate orders, yet not homogeneous enough to be families (see below). For example, the huge order of bugs Hemiptera is split into the two sub-orders of Heteroptera and Homoptera (see p.86 for the distinction).

Orders or sub-orders are sub-divided into **families**, which contain a number of species that are closely related to each other. Families usually have a name ending in -idae, such as the Gryllidae (crickets) or Lestidae (one family of damselflies). Families may be split into sub-families, with names ending in -inae, though this is not commonly used. Within families, there are a number of **genera** (singular **genus**). All members of a genus are broadly similar, though not as similar as members of the same species, and they do not normally breed with each other. All members of the same genus have the same first scientific name (the generic name), such as *Aeshna* which applies to a number of closely related hawker dragonflies.

Each genus is composed of a number of **species**. This is the basic unit of insect classification (and all other life forms). Species may be further subdivided into subspecies, varieties or races. These are distinctive forms within the species, possibly produced by geographical separation, yet probably still able to interbreed, and still very similar to the main species in most respects.

It should, in passing, be mentioned that taxonomy is not a precise science, agreed by all. There are frequent disagreements about whether subspecies should be separate species, whether sub-orders should be separated as orders, and so on, and new information may cause existing names to be revised.

An example of the full classification of one species of insect is as follows:

Species:	Green Shieldbug *Palomena prasina*
Genus:	*Palomena*
Family:	Pentatomidae
Sub-order:	Heteroptera
Order:	Hemiptera, the bugs
Sub-class:	Pterygota, the winged insects
Class:	Insecta, the insects
Phylum:	Arthropoda, the arthropods

An Illustrated Key to the Main Groups of Adult Insects

This is a dichotomous key. It is designed as a series of 'questions', each with two possible 'answers'. With the insect to hand, or a very clear photograph, start at question one and read each of the two descriptions carefully; then proceed to the question whose number follows the description that best fits. Sooner or later, the insect in question will 'key out' to an order.

Note: This key covers the main orders of insects, though it leaves out a very few small orders. (The scorpion flies should key out under '**Neuroptera agg**'.)

1. Insects wingless, very small, with caudal appendages (tails) or a folded springing organ . . . . **Apterygota** (p.38)

   Insects winged, or – if wingless – then not as above . . . 2

2. Insects with only 1 pair of wings, the hindwings reduced to tiny knob-like structures . . . . **Diptera** (p.204)

   Insects with 2 pairs of wings 3

3. Both pairs of wings membranous, with veins, with or without coloured scales 4

   Front wings opaque, hard and leathery in texture 12

4. Wings covered with coloured scales . . . .
   . . . . **Lepidoptera** (p.118)

   Wings not covered with scales (but may be hairy), usually transparent. 5

5. Wings hairless; longitudinal veins connected by numerous cross-veins 6

   Wings hairy or hairless; very few cross-veins present . . 9

6. Long tail-like appendages present on the end of the abdomen 7

    Abdomen without long tail-like appendages (though shorter pincer-like appendages may be present) 8

7. Wings held vertically over body at rest; front wings much larger than hindwings; two or three tails present . . . .
    . . . . **Ephemeroptera** (p.42)

    Wings held flat over body at rest; front wings and hind-wings roughly equal in size; tails always 2 . . . .
    . . . . **Plecoptera** (p.64)

8. Body long and thin, often brightly coloured; antennae very short . . . . **Odonata** (p.44)

    Body variable, antennae long . . **Neuroptera agg.** (p.112)

9. Wings hairy . . . . **Trichoptera** (p.202)

    Wings not hairy, variable in other characteristics 10

10. Insects with piercing beak-like mouthparts, broad head and short antennae . . . . **Hemiptera** (p.86)

    Insects with various types of mouthparts; antennae longer than width of head 11

11. Small, squat insects, with piercing, beak-like mouthparts and 2 tubular appendages on abdomen . . . .
    . . . . **Hemiptera** (p.86)

Insects with hindwings much smaller than front wings; tubular appendages absent, but females have abdominal ovipositor or sting; mouthparts usually adapted for biting. . . . . **Hymenoptera** (p.240)

12. Front wings leathery in texture, but with distinct membranous tips. Piercing mouthparts . . . . . . **Hemiptera** (p.86)

Front wings wholly hard or leathery 13

13. Front wings hard, with no obvious veins, meeting along the centre of the back. 14

Front wings distinctly veined, overlapping and held roofwise over the body 15

14. Front wings very short, only covering a small part of the abdomen; abdominal pincers present . . . .
. . . . **Dermaptera** (p. 84)

Front wings usually long enough to cover abdomen; rarely short, but pincers never present . . . **Coleoptera** (p.268)

15. Mouthparts obviously adapted for piercing, in the form of a beak . . . . **Hemiptera** (p.86)

Mouthparts adapted for biting, no 'beak' present 16

16. Hind legs greatly enlarged and modified for jumping. . . . .
. . . . **Orthoptera** (p.66)

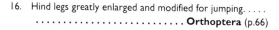

Hind legs not adapted for jumping . . **Dictyoptera** (p.82)

Apterygota Wingless Insects

A little-known group of insects that share the characteristic of having no wings. They are a primitive group, and little metamorphosis takes place during their life-cycle. They are dependent on humid situations, and are most likely to be found in leaf litter, under bark, in the soil or, in a few cases, in water.

3-PRONGED BRISTLETAILS ORDER THYSANURA

A small order, all the members of which have 3 'tails', comprising 2 cerci and a central projection known as the epiproct.

Petrobius maritimus
A slender brown insect, up to 15mm long, with antennae that are almost as long as the body. Central 'tail' distinctly longer than the 2 side tails.
Habitat Close to high water mark on rocky coasts, and short distance inland in crevices.
Status and distribution Widespread and locally common throughout in suitable habitats.
Season All year.

Silverfish
Lepisma saccharina
The most familiar of the 3-pronged bristletails. It has a flattened, tapering silvery body, up to 18mm long, with antennae rather shorter than the body. Feeds on spilt food, paper and other carbohydrate-rich materials. Active mainly at night or in dark places.
Habitat In houses and other protected, slightly humid environments.
Status and distribution Common and widespread throughout.
Season All year.

Similar species
Firebrat *Thermobia domestica* is very similar in shape, but brown rather than silver, and bristly rather than scaly. Common and widespread in warm places such as hearths, heating ducts and bakeries. Visible all year.

Heath Silverfish
Dilta littoralis
Similar in general structure to Silverfish, though generally brown in colour rather than silver and slightly larger.
Habitat Heathlands and similar habitats, where they can be found amongst the leaf litter.
Status and distribution A local, mainly southern species.
Season May be active all year, though most likely to be seen from 6–9.

2-PRONGED BRISTLETAILS ORDER DIPLURA

A small group, with about 12 species in the area. Distinguishable from the 3-pronged bristletails by the absence of a central epiproct (though the 2 cerci are still present), and by their small size, always less than 6mm long.

Campodea staphylinus
One of several very similar species that are slender-bodied, about 5mm long, white, with antennae and cerci all about half the length of the body.
Habitat In compost, under fallen leaves or under stones.
Status and distribution Common and widespread throughout, though rarely noticed because of its small size.
Season All year in most areas.

Campodea staphylinus

Petrobius maritimus

Heath Silverfish

Silverfish

SPRINGTAILS
ORDER COLLEMBOLA

Easily the largest group of apterygote insects, with about 300 species in the area, and at least 1,500 worldwide. All species are small, usually less than 5mm, distinguished by the small number of body segments, and the distinctive springing organ (furcula), which is held under the body normally, but may be released when danger threatens, to catapult the insect to safety. They occur throughout in damp, often dark places, feeding on live or decaying vegetation.

Lipura maritima

A small, bristly, greyish, bullet-shaped insect, up to 3mm long, tapering to a blunt point at the rear, and with 2 short antennae; it lacks the springing organ. Though small, it becomes more conspicuous by its habit of clustering in large groups.

Habitat Upper parts of rocky shores; often visible on the surface of rock-pools, or on seaweed.

Status and distribution Widespread and common throughout in its habitat.

Season All year.

Podura aquatica

A very small, greyish-black insect, usually about 1–2mm long, bluntly cylindrical in shape, with 2 short antennae.

Podura aquatica

Habitat In still water, especially where there is abundant surface vegetation such as duckweed.

Status and distribution Locally abundant throughout (though easily overlooked).

Season All year.

Lucerne Flea
Sminthurus viridis

Very small, bright green insect, with antennae about half the length of the body, a distinct 'waist' behind the head, and a broad rhomboidal body.

Habitat On clovers and other legumes in summer, transferring later to grasses or mosses.

Status and distribution Abundant throughout, becoming a pest in warmer parts of the world.

Season All year.

Tomocerus longicornis

A small but distinctive species, about 5mm long (including the antennae), and white in colour. The antennae are longer than the rest of the body, which distinguishes it from other related species of springtails.

Habitat Under bark, or amongst leaf litter in humid places, especially woodland.

Status and distribution Widespread and locally common throughout.

Season All year.

Lipura maritima

Tomocerus longicornis

Pterygota
Winged Insects

MAYFLIES
ORDER EPHEMEROPTERA

A small and distinctive group, with an unusual life-cycle. Unique among insects, they have 2 adult phases, moulting again after they attain the winged state. A sub-adult emerges from the aquatic nymph and takes flight, usually hiding among vegetation; this phase is dull-coloured, with opaque wings, and is known to anglers as the 'dun'. Within hours the dun moults into the sexually mature adult, which has brighter colours, translucent wings, and longer tails – the 'spinner'.

Mayflies are recognizable by the wings,

 which are held vertically above the body, always unfolded; the very short antennae; and the 2 or 3 long tails. The nymphs always have 3 tails, even if the adult has 2. Despite their name, the short-lived adults may be found in most months of the year. There are about 50 species in Britain, and 200 throughout Europe.

nymph

Green Drake or Common Mayfly
Ephemera danica
A large, beautiful species, up to 50mm long including the length of its 3 tails. The wings are broadly triangular, with dark spots, and there are numerous dark marks on the greyish-white abdomen.
Habitat Around unpolluted streams, gravelly lakes and rivers.
Status and distribution Frequent and widespread throughout.
Season 4–11.
Similar species
E. lineata is similar, but with longitudinal stripes on some abdomen segments.
E. vulgata has double triangles on most abdominal segments; occurs in summer.

Potamanthus luteus has yellowish unspotted wings, and abdomen barely marked. Local.

Chloeon dipterum
A small species, 10–15mm long, but distinctive in having only 2 wings and 2 tails. The females have yellowish front margins. Known to fishermen as 'pond olives'.
Habitat Still and slow-flowing waters.
Status and distribution Common and widespread throughout.
Season 5–10.

Ephemerella ignita
A medium-sized species, about 20mm long, with a reddish-brown body, reddish-tinged wings, and 3 tails. The hindwings are small but clearly visible.
Habitat Around fast-flowing, well-oxygenated, well-vegetated streams.
Status and distribution Widespread and locally frequent in suitable habitat.
Season 4–9.
Similar species
E. notata is yellowish-brown not red, with dark stripes and dots under the abdomen.

Baetis fuscatus
There are several very similar *Baetis* species; they tend to have clear forewings, and very small hindwings with only 2 or 3 main veins. They are 2-tailed. The body length (excluding tails) is about 10mm.
Habitat Small, fast-moving streams.
Status and distribution Widespread and frequent.
Season 5–10.

Siphlonorus lacustris
Body length of 12–15mm. Long tails and antennae. Body greenish-brown, 2-tailed. Forewings long and narrow, clear; hindwings relatively large, with numerous veins. There are several very similar species.
Habitat In lakes and slower-flowing parts of rivers and streams, especially hilly areas.
Status and distribution Widespread and locally common.
Season 5–9.

Green Drake

Baetis fuscatus

Siphlonorus lacustris

DRAGONFLIES AND DAMSELFLIES
ORDER ODONATA

Distinctive long-bodied predatory insects, with very short antennae and 2 roughly equal pairs of wings. They are separated into 2 sub-orders: Damselflies (Zygoptera) and Dragonflies (Anisoptera). Damselflies are generally smaller and more delicate, with a weaker, more fluttery flight; when at

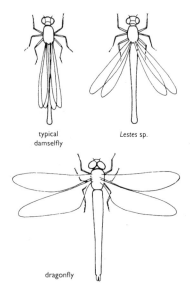

typical
damselfly

Lestes sp.

dragonfly

rest, they hold their wings together above the abdomen (see diagram), with the exception of *Lestes* species, which look otherwise similar, but normally hold their wings at about 45° to the abdomen. Their eyes are widely spaced, on each side of the head.

Dragonflies are large, robust, strong-flying insects, unlikely to be confused with anything else, except possibly ascalaphids (see p.112) which are not widespread in this area. At rest, they hold their wings out at right angles to the body (see diagram). With the exception of the club-tailed dragonflies (*Gomphus* and allies), the eyes are set very close together and are extremely large.

The nymphs all live in water, and adults therefore start their life close to water. Damselflies tend to remain close to their breeding site throughout their life, while most dragonflies will travel considerable distances. Some, such as the Scarce Hawker, are wide-ranging migrants. For a period after they emerge, both damselflies and dragonflies have a phase when their colours are not fully developed – the teneral phase. The wings have an oily appearance, which gradually disappears, and males often have the colouring of females. It is better to try to identify fully adult insects rather than teneral ones. The teneral phase may last from 2 days to 2 weeks, depending on species and temperature.

Damselflies
Suborder Zygoptera

Demoiselle Agrion
Calopteryx virgo
A beautiful insect, with strongly coloured wings, greenish-blue in the male and bronze in the female. The abdomen is about 35mm long, blue-green in the male and green or bronze in the female.
Habitat Close to faster-flowing, acid to neutral, well-vegetated streams.
Status and distribution Widespread and locally common; mainly western in Britain.
Season 5–8.

Banded Agrion
Calopteryx splendens
Resembles the Demoiselle Agrion in structure and size. The male has a blue abdomen, and the wings have large rectangular dark patches which are clearly visible even in flight. The female has a green to bronze body and greenish wings – similar to Demoiselle Agrion but greener overall.
Habitat Almost always close to slow-flowing neutral to calcareous streams and rivers, with plenty of sun and vegetation.
Status and distribution Locally common in S Britain, widespread in Europe.
Season 5–9, most abundant 6–7.

Calopteryx sp. nymph

Demoiselle Agrion, female

Banded Agrion, female

Banded Agrion, male

★ *Sympecma fusca*
An inconspicuous species, with a brown and cream abdomen, 27–29mm long, which has a dark interrupted stripe down its upper surface. The pterostigmas (see diagram) are at different positions, clearly noticeable when the wings are closed.

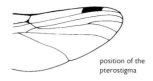

position of the pterostigma

Habitat Around sheltered still water bodies, especially near woodland.
Status and distribution Widespread and moderately common on the Continent.
Season Unusual among damselflies in that the adults hibernate; on the wing 7–10, and 3–5, and occasionally on warm winter days.

Emerald Damselfly
Lestes sponsa
A rather robust damselfly, with an abdomen length of about 30mm, predominantly emerald green, with blue at either end of the abdomen; females usually lack the blue colour. Species of *Lestes* generally hold their wings away from the body at about 45° at rest.
Habitat Occurs around a wide range of aquatic habitats, usually still, but also slow-moving, and occasionally brackish.
Status and distribution Common and widespread virtually throughout the area.
Season 6–10.
Similar species
Four rather similar species of *Lestes* occur in the area.

★ *L. viridis* has distinctive white claspers on the male's abdomen; it is widespread on the Continent.
★ *L. barbarus* has distinctive bicoloured pterostigmas.
★ *L. virens* is very similar to the Emerald Damselfly, and is best distinguished by the abdominal appendages ('claspers'), as in the illustration below. It is locally common on the Continent, though absent from many western areas.
Scarce Emerald *L. dryas* is very similar to the Emerald, differing in the appendages (see illustration), and the pterostigma, which is 2–2½ times as long as broad (cf. 3 times in Emerald). The Scarce Emerald is rare in SE England and W Ireland, but widespread in Europe.

White-legged Damselfly
Platycnemis pennipes
A medium to large species, with an abdomen length of 27–31mm. Abdomen, in males, is pale blue with a black line across all segments, broadening in the last 4. A distinctive feature is the white legs with broad hind tibia.
Habitat Most frequent around slow-moving, clean, well-vegetated streams, though may also occur in still waters.
Status and distribution Strongly southern and rather local in Britain; widespread and frequent on the Continent.
Season 5–8.
Similar species
★ *P. acutipennis* is similar in structure and size, but the males are a distinctive non-metallic orange, while the females are pale orange. Frequent around slow-moving waters from N France southwards.

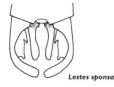

Lestes sponsa

Lestes virens

Lestes dryas

Emerald Damselfly, male

Lestes viridis, male

Lestes virens, female

Scarce Emerald, female

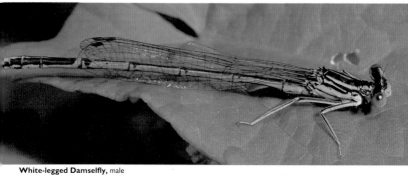

White-legged Damselfly, male

Platycnemis acutipennis, male

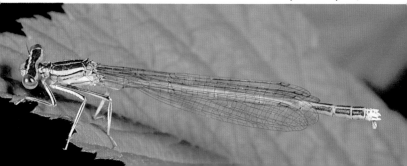

Large Red Damselfly
Pyrrhosoma nymphula
A medium-sized damselfly, with an abdomen length of 25–29mm. Predominantly red in colour, with black legs, black stripes on the thorax, and black markings towards the end of the 'tail'; females are more robust, with more abdominal markings.
Habitat Around a wide variety of still and slow-moving water-bodies, including brackish ditches and acid bogs.
Status and distribution Widespread and common throughout.
Season 4–9; an early species.

Small Red Damselfly
Ceriagrion tenellum
Similar in general appearance to the Large Red, but slightly smaller, and both sexes have red legs. Males are almost entirely red, and females have the last few segments of the abdomen black above. Both have a weak, rather fluttering flight.
Habitat Mainly an acid water and bog species in Britain; less fussy in Europe.
Status and distribution Very local in Britain, only in the south; widespread over most of Europe.
Season 5–9.

Blue-tailed Damselfly
Ischnura elegans
A medium to small species, with an abdomen length of 22–29mm. Distinctive by virtue of the male's blackish abdomen, tipped with bright blue on the penultimate segment. The pterostigmas are distinctive bicoloured pointed ovals.
Habitat Still and slow-moving waters of all types, including brackish and slightly polluted ones.
Status and distribution Very common and widespread throughout.
Season 5–9.
Similar species
Scarce Blue-tailed Damselfly *I. pumilio* is very similar, but smaller (abdomen 22–25mm long), and with the blue 'tail' extending over about 1½ segments (the segment

dividing line is clearly visible within the blue band). An uncommon species, strongly south-western in Britain, and absent from many parts of the Continent.

Common Blue Damselfly
Enallagma cyathigera
A typical blue damselfly, differing from *Coenagrion* species (see p.50) in having no additional stripe on the thorax, and by the distinctive 'stalked ball' mark on segment 2 of males. Females are duller greenish or brownish, with a conspicuous spine under segment 8.
Habitat Occurs around a very wide variety of wetlands, mainly still or slow-moving, and including brackish and nutrient-poor waters.
Status and distribution Common and widespread throughout, including upland and northern areas (where it may be confused with Northern Damselfly).
Season 5–10.

Red-eyed Damselfly
Erythromma najas
An attractive, robust species, with an abdomen length of 25–30mm. The male has a distinctive combination of red eyes, no thoracic stripes, and a blackish abdomen tipped with blue on segments 9–10. Females are paler, without the blue 'tail'.
Habitat Still and slow-moving larger water-bodies, with ample floating vegetation such as water-lilies or pondweeds.
Status and distribution Local in the UK, where it is virtually confined to England; widespread on the Continent.
Season 5–9.
Similar species
★ *E. viridulum* is shorter and more slender, with fine thoracic stripes, and a black 'x' on segment 10. Local and rather eastern, from N Germany southwards.
★ *Nehalennia speciosa* is a tiny species, with an abdomen length of up to 20mm, greenish-blue, with blue eyes. It is rare and local in scattered sites from Belgium and Holland eastwards.

Large Red Damselfly

Small Red Damselfly, male

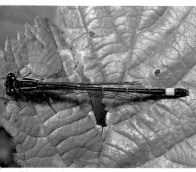

Blue-tailed Damselfly, male

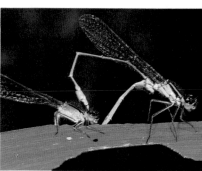

Blue-tailed Damselflies, mating

Common Blue Damselfly, male

Red-eyed Damselfly, male

Scarce Blue-tailed Damselfly, male

Erythromma viridulum, male

COENAGRION A genus including most of the blue damselflies in the area. They can be distinguished from *Enallagma* (see illustration) by the additional line on the thorax.

Coenagrion sp.   Enallagma sp.

★ *Coenagrion (Cercion) lindeni*

A robust species, with an abdomen length of 30mm. The abdomen is blue in the male (green-blue to yellowish in female), boldly marked with black, and the male has a clearly visible pair of claspers.

Habitat In moving or still water.

Status and distribution Locally abundant from central France southwards, very local further N.

Season 4–9.

Similar species

★ *C. armatum* is the only other species with marked anal claspers, but it has a mainly black abdomen except for segments 2 and 8. Confined to the N and E of the region.

Azure Damselfly
Coenagrion puella

A small to medium species, with an abdomen 23–30mm long. The males are predominantly blue with black markings, of which the 'U' shape on segment 2 and the crown on 9 are the most useful in identification; the blue stripes on the thorax are unbroken.

Habitat Usually close to well-vegetated, still or slow-moving water-bodies, though often found well away from water.

Status and distribution Abundant almost throughout except for some northern and upland areas.

Season 5–9.

Similar species

C. lunulatum also has a 'U' on segment 2, but it is interrupted, and there is no crown on segment 9. Local in Ireland, or more frequently north and east from Holland.

Southern Damselfly
Coenagrion mercuriale

Small, with abdomen only 22–24mm long. Broadly similar in pattern to most of the group, though the small size and the 'mercury' mark on segment 2 are useful features.

Southern Damselfly, abdominal segment 2

Habitat Most frequent in well-vegetated flushed areas such as bogs, fens and water-meadows.

Status and distribution Rare and strongly south-western in the UK, local and mainly southern on the Continent.

Season 5–8.

Similar species

★ *C. scitulum* has same build, with variable abdominal markings. The long brownish pterostigmas are a key feature. Rare.

Variable Damselfly
Coenagrion pulchellum

A medium-sized, highly variable species, with an abdomen length of 25–30mm. Similar to most other 'blue' damselflies, but the fine, interrupted (and occasionally absent) blue thoracic stripes and the markings on segment 2 are more or less diagnostic.

Variable Damselfly, abdominal segment 2

Habitat Well-vegetated still or slow-moving waters, such as fens and water meadows.

Status and distribution Local but widespread in Britain (absent from Scotland), more common on the Continent.

Season 5–8.

Northern Damselfly
Coenagrion hastulatum

Abdomen length 23–26mm. Males are blue and black, but there is a distinctive spearhead with 2 lines above it on segment 2, and both segments 8 and 9 are clear blue.

Habitat In still, acid waters.

Status and distribution Confined to NE Scotland in Britain; more frequent from NE Germany northwards.

Season 5–8.

Coenagrion lindeni

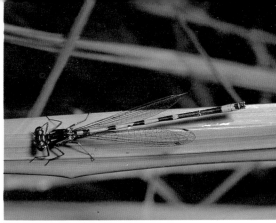

Variable Damselfly, male

Southern Damselfly, male

Azure Damselfly, male

Northern Damselfly, male

Dragonflies
Suborder Anisoptera

Club-tailed Dragonflies, Family Gomphidae

A distinctive small group, unique within European dragonflies in that they have widely separated eyes. Five species occur in the area.

eyes of a typical Gomphid dragonfly

Club-tailed Dragonfly
Gomphus vulgatissimus
A medium-sized dragonfly, abdomen length about 35mm. Both sexes are boldly black and yellow, but the male has a distinctly clubbed tail and more black coloration. Legs entirely black.
Habitat Breeds in large slow-flowing rivers, or occasionally still water, and rarely moves far from these habitats.
Status and distribution Uncommon in the UK, where it is found from the Midlands southwards; widespread on the Continent.
Season 5–6 in UK, 4–8 elsewhere.
Similar species
★ *G. pulchellus* is a more slender species, more yellow in colour, with black and yellow legs. Very local in N Europe, from Germany southwards. Common in SW Europe.
★ *G. flavipes* resembles Club-tailed in colouring, but has black and yellow legs. An eastern species, occurring very sparingly from Holland eastwards. Most frequent in E Europe.

★ *Onychogomphus forcipatus*
A boldly marked black and yellow insect, with an abdomen length of about 36mm, tipped with distinctive large, inwardly curved, yellowish claspers on the male. Characteristically seen resting on gravel or sand by rivers.
Habitat Around rivers or canals, usually where there are bare banks.
Status and distribution Frequent from central France southwards and in S Scandinavia, very local elsewhere.
Season 6–9.
Similar species
★ *Ophiogomphus cecilia* is rather similar, but has a green ground colour rather than yellow; the male lacks the strong pincers, and the female has 2 small 'horns' on the head. An eastern species, local from Germany and Denmark eastwards.

Hairy Hawker
Brachytron pratense
A medium-large species, with an abdomen length of about 45mm. Males are predominantly black, with paired blue spots on almost all abdomen segments, and yellow thoracic stripes. Females are browner, lacking the stripes, and are conspicuously hairy.
Habitat Associated with slow-moving or still water, such as ditches, canals, ponds and lakes.
Status and distribution Local in S England and Eire, widespread on the Continent. Particularly associated with coastal 'levels' in the UK.
Season 5–7. One of the earliest dragonflies to appear.

Club-tailed Dragonfly, female

Gomphus pulchellus, male

Onychogomphus forcipatus, male

Hairy Hawker, mal

Common Hawker
Aeshna juncea

A large species, with an abdomen length of about 55mm. Males are predominantly brownish-black, with short yellow thoracic stripes, and blue markings on all abdominal segments. Females are browner, with greenish-yellow abdominal markings, and no thoracic stripes. Both sexes have yellow leading edges to the wings.

Habitat Mainly in acid to neutral still waters, especially in the uplands.

Status and distribution Widespread and frequent in Britain, very local in France and the Low Countries, but more frequent in Germany and Scandinavia.

Season 6–10.

Similar species

Azure Hawker *A. caerulea* is a bluer species, with 2 small blue thoracic stripes, and eyes that only just meet. A rare species, confined to the Scottish Highlands, the Alps and N Scandinavia.

Southern Hawker
Aeshna cyanea

A very large species, with an abdomen length of up to 60mm. Males have a blackish ground colour, with broad apple-green thoracic stripes, paired green markings on the abdomen, becoming blue towards the tip, and coalescing into one spot on the last 2 segments. Females are paler, with all spots greenish.

Habitat Breeds in a wide variety of still or slow-moving acid-neutral waters, though also travels widely.

Status and distribution Common and widespread throughout, except in upland areas.

Season 6–10.

Similar species

★ *A. viridis* is rather similar, but about 10mm shorter, with yellowish-brown wings, and the abdominal spots are all paired, not joined. Rare, from Holland and N Germany northwards.

Brown Hawker
Aeshna grandis

A large species, with abdomen up to 60mm long (rather shorter in females). Distinctive, with a predominantly brown colour, marked with a few blue spots in the male; both sexes have strongly amber-suffused wings. The male has a distinct 'waist' at the top of the abdomen.

Habitat Around well-vegetated, unpolluted larger water-bodies, which may be mildly calcareous.

Status and distribution A northern and eastern species, rare in upland Britain, and absent from W France, generally common elsewhere.

Season 6/7–10.

Similar species

Norfolk Hawker *A. isosceles* is rather similar in being predominantly brown, but is paler, lacking blue, and has a yellow triangle at the top of the abdomen; the wings are more or less clear. It usually flies much earlier than the Brown Hawker, 5–7. A southern species, confined in UK to E Anglia.

Migrant Hawker
Aeshna mixta

A relatively small hawker, with abdomen up to 50mm long. The ground colour is brown, with no thoracic stripes, a yellow triangle on segment 2, and paired bluish spots down the abdomen. Both sexes have a dull brown costa (leading edge of the wing). It tends to be a more sociable species than other hawkers, several insects often flying together.

Habitat Breeds in a wide variety of still waters, including brackish ones, but travels very widely so may turn up anywhere.

Status and distribution A southern species, reaching as far north as Denmark and N England; regular migrant.

Season 7–10.

Similar species

★ *A. affinis* is very similar, but males, in particular, are much brighter blue, with a blue mark in place of the yellow triangle. A southern species, migrating northwards just into the area in good years.

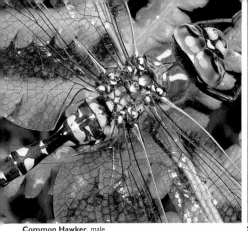

Common Hawker, male

Southern Hawker, male

Southern Hawker, female

Brown Hawker, female

Norfolk Hawker, male

Migrant Hawker, male

Emperor Dragonfly
Anax imperator

The Emperor is a very large dragonfly, with an abdomen length of up to 61mm. The male is predominantly bright blue, with a green thorax and segment 1 of the abdomen, and a black line along the whole abdomen. Females are duller, with similar markings but a greenish ground colour. The males hunt more frequently over water than the hawkers.

Habitat A species of still water, occurring in a wide variety of sites including new water-bodies.

Status and distribution A common species throughout the S of the area, becoming rare or absent from central England and Holland northwards.

Season 5–9.

Similar species

★ *A. parthenope* is similar in shape and size, but has a brown thorax, is blue on the first few abdominal segments, and is then pale greenish-blue on the rest of the abdomen. A southern species that only just reaches into central Europe where it is uncommon.

Downy Emerald
Cordulia aenea

A medium to small dragonfly, with an abdomen length of about 35mm. In both sexes, the thorax is bronze-green and very downy, while the abdomen is metallic dark green. The eyes are green, and the wings are clear except for an amber patch at the base.

Habitat Still waters of various types, especially if slightly acid and partially wooded. They disperse into woodland, but do not usually travel far.

Status and distribution Very local in Britain, mainly southern, but with outposts in N England, Scotland and Eire; widespread and quite common on the Continent.

Season 5–8.

Similar species

★ **Orange-spotted Emerald** *Oxygastra curtisii* is similar in shape and size, but distinguished by the band of single orange spots down the abdomen. A southern species, reasonably common in France, but very rare elsewhere. Extinct in the UK since 1951.

Brilliant Emerald
Somatochlora metallica

Similar in size to Downy Emerald. Both male and female have brilliant emerald-green thorax and abdomen, though the thorax is covered with yellowish down. Distinguishable from Downy Emerald by the more brilliant metallic coloration, and the longer male appendages; Downy Emerald has no yellow on its face.

Habitat Very similar to those of the Downy Emerald.

Status and distribution Rare in the UK, where it is confined (curiously) to SE England and N Scotland; frequent and widespread on the Continent.

Season 6–9.

Similar species

Northern Emerald *S. arctica* is very similar, differing in the curved calliper-like male appendages, the slightly darker colour, and the orange-yellow spots on the sides of segment 3 of the female's abdomen. Very local in boggy places, N Scotland, and scattered through central and N Europe.

★ *S. flavomaculata* is very similar structurally to the Brilliant Emerald, but has much more yellow on the top of the abdomen, and yellow all down the sides. It is widespread on the Continent, though absent from large areas.

Emperor Dragonfly, newly emerged

Orange-spotted Emerald, female

Downy Emerald

Brilliant Emerald, male

Somatochlora flavomaculata, male

Golden-ringed Dragonfly
Cordulegaster boltonii

A very large and conspicuous dragonfly; the female has an abdomen up to 65mm long (slightly shorter in the male). Distinctively patterned, primarily blackish-green, with yellow thoracic stripes and yellow rings down the whole abdomen. Eyes green in both sexes. The female has a prominent ovipositor which she uses to stab into the substrate of the river bottom.

Habitat Usually breeds in faster-flowing, well-oxygenated streams and rivers, though adults travel widely.

Status and distribution Widespread, though most frequent in upland areas; a northern and western species in Britain.

Season 5–9.

Similar species

* *C. bidentata* is extremely similar, but is less strongly marked with yellow, has a black (not yellow) occipital triangle (between the eyes), and the female has a wholly black ovipositor. An uncommon species, in hilly areas from Belgium southwards, although it is probably underrecorded.

Broad-bodied Chaser
Libellula depressa

A short, broad dragonfly, with an abdomen length of about 25mm. Male has a brown thorax with 2 yellowish stripes, and a blue abdomen which has yellow lateral spots for most of the insect's life. Female is very broad, with a brown, yellow-edged abdomen. All 4 wings have triangular dark patches at the base. Newly emerged males look very like females, but are slightly less broad-bodied.

Habitat Occurs around a very wide variety of still and slow-flowing waters, including small ponds. Also wanders widely and can be found almost anywhere.

Status and distribution A common species throughout.

Season 5–8. One of the earliest dragonflies to appear.

Scarce Chaser
Libellula fulva

This species is similar in size to the Broad-bodied Chaser but is more slender. The male has a brown unstriped hairy thorax; the abdomen is pale blue, except for dark colour on segments 1–2 and a diamond-shaped patch towards the tip. Only the hindwings have a dark patch; compare the Broad-bodied Chaser, where all 4 wings have dark patches.

Habitat Breeds in many types of still and slow-moving waters.

Status and distribution Very local in S England, but widespread and quite common on the Continent.

Season 5–8.

4-spotted Chaser
Libellula quadrimaculata

Abdomen length about 30mm. A distinctive species: both sexes are similar, brown in colour overall, but with black on the tapering abdomen from segment 7 onwards. The wings each have a spot on the centre of the leading edge, in addition to the dark pterostigmata, and the triangular patch at the base of the hindwings.

Habitat Most frequently found around still, acid waters, although it is not confined to them.

Status and distribution Widespread and common throughout in suitable habitats, sometimes becoming very abundant. Large numbers may occasionally migrate, although this has become less frequent in recent decades due to the destruction of suitable habitat.

Season 5–8.

Golden-ringed Dragonfly, male

Broad-bodied Chaser, male

Broad-bodied Chaser, female

Scarce Chaser, male

4-spotted Chaser

Black-tailed Skimmer
Orthetrum cancellatum
A small dragonfly, with abdomen 30–35mm long. Male has a brown thorax, and a blue abdomen, except for the tip which has black suffusing up as far as the seventh segment. Females are overall dull brown, with paired dark curved markings on each abdominal segment.

Habitat Most frequently seen around still water-bodies of varying acidity, especially those with a hard bottom. Adults travel widely and quickly find new habitats, such as flooded gravel pits.

Status and distribution Virtually confined to S England within the UK; widespread on the Continent north to S Scandinavia.

Season 5–9.

Similar species
★ *O. albistylum* is similar in general appearance, but the black tip to the abdomen is much more clearly defined, as though the tip of the tail had been dipped in ink, and the anal appendages are white. A southern species, reaching as far as central France and S Germany.

Keeled Skimmer
Orthetrum coerulescens
Abdomen length 27–30mm. A rather small species, with the abdomen wholly pale·blue in males. The thorax in both sexes is brown, with 2 creamy-yellow stripes, and the female's abdomen is golden-brown. Typically, the wings are held forward and downwards at rest.

Habitat Most frequently a bog species in Britain, though more catholic on the Continent. Adults tend to remain close to the larval habitat.

Status and distribution A local species in the UK, where it is strongly south-western; common on the Continent from N France southwards, scattered and rare further N.

Season 5–9.

Similar species
★ *O. brunneum* is similar, but slightly larger, and males are wholly pale blue. A southern species, common from central France southwards, rare and local further north.

★ *Crocothemis erythraea*
A small dragonfly, abdomen length up to 29mm, though often less. Males are, however, strikingly conspicuous by their 'nail-varnish' red colouring throughout. Females are dull brown. Both sexes have long, narrow brown pterostigmas, outlined with black nerves.

Habitat Most frequent around still or very slow-flowing waters of about neutral pH, though the adults are highly mobile in warm conditions.

Status and distribution A southern species, common from central France southwards, rare and scattered further N. There is an old record for the Channel Islands.

Season 5–10.

Similar species
This dragonfly can be separated from the similar red *Sympetrum* species by the broader, shorter abdomen, lacking any 'waist', and the redder thorax. The pterostigmas described above are a helpful distinguishing feature.

Black-tailed Skimmer, male

Orthetrum albistylum, male

Keeled Skimmer, male

Keeled Skimmer, nymph

Orthetrum brunneum, male

Crocothemis erythraea, male

Common Darter
Sympetrum striolatum
A small to medium dragonfly, with abdomen length of 25–30mm. Males have a brown thorax and a dull red abdomen with thin black median stripes on the last 2 segments. There is a slight 'waist' between abdominal segments 3 and 5. The legs are black and yellow.

Habitat A wide variety of still, slow-flowing, and brackish water-bodies.

Status and distribution Common and widespread throughout the area.

Season 6–11.

Common Darter   Vagrant Darter

Similar species
Vagrant Darter *S. vulgatum* is very similar, distinguishable by the slightly deeper red colour of the males, the longer black mark on the face (see illustration), and the black abdominal segment 1. An eastern upland species, occasionally recorded in Britain. **Highland Darter** *S. nigrescens* is very closely related to Common Darter, and its status as a separate species is still uncertain. It is a darker insect, with more extensive black markings, though intermediates may occur. Confined to W Ireland, W Scotland and W Norway.

Ruddy Darter
Sympetrum sanguineum
Very similar to Common Darter, but differing in that males are brighter red, there is a marked constriction of the abdomen between segments 3 and 5, and the legs are wholly black in both sexes.

Habitat Well-vegetated small to medium ponds, occasionally in slow-flowing water.

Status and distribution In the UK, virtually confined to the southern half of the country; widespread and frequent on the Continent north to S Scandinavia.

Season 6–10.

Similar species
★ *S. depressiusculum* is *very* similar, and cannot be separated in the field with certainty. The abdomen is dorso-ventrally compressed, and there is no marked waist. Local, in central Europe, probably under-recorded.

Yellow-winged Darter
Sympetrum flaveolum
Very similar in general shape and size to the other darters. The distinctive feature, readily visible in the field, is the large amber wing patches which occupy roughly the basal third of the wings, in both sexes. The legs are yellow and black.

Habitat In well-vegetated ponds and other still or slow-moving waters.

Status and distribution A rare vagrant to Britain, not generally breeding; widespread and frequent on the Continent.

Season 7–10.

Similar species
★ **Red-veined Darter** *S. fonscolombei* males have bright red abdomen and conspicuously red-veined wings; female wings are yellow-veined, and there are yellowish basal patches on the wings of both sexes. A southern species, from central France southwards, migrating further north.

Black Darter
Sympetrum danae
Small dragonfly, with abdomen length up to 24mm. Males black, with variable amounts of yellow, fading with age, on the thorax and abdomen. Females are yellowish-brown, with a dark triangle on the first abdominal segment. Legs black in both sexes.

Habitat Mainly associated with boggy pools and flushes.

Status and distribution A northern species, common throughout the UK and much of N Europe.

Season 6–10.

Common Darter, male

Ruddy Darter, male

Sympetrum depressiusculum, male

Yellow-winged Darter, male
Red-veined Darter, male

Black Darter, female

White-faced Darter
Leucorrhinia dubia

A small dragonfly, with abdomen length of about 25mm. Its most distinctive feature is the white face, present in both sexes. Males are predominantly black, with red stripes on the thorax, and red marks down the abdomen; females are marked with yellow in place of red.

Habitat Specific requirements in the UK of shallow peaty pools, usually with an active bog margin, and often with surrounding heathland. On the Continent, it is also found in acid lakes and marshes.

Status and distribution Rare and local in Britain, with a disjunct distribution in Surrey, the Midlands and Scotland; it is a northern species on the Continent, becoming increasingly common from N France northwards.

Season 5–8.

Similar species

★ *L. rubicunda* is very similar, but is larger and with more red markings. Very local in Europe from N France northwards.

★ *L. pectoralis* is larger and more robust, well marked with red, with an expanded abdomen around segment 6. Distribution similar to *L. rubicunda*.

★ *Leucorrhinia caudalis*

A small dragonfly, with an abdomen length of about 25mm. The males are distinctive, with a blue and black, strongly clubbed abdomen; females are also clubbed, but more yellow and black in colour.

Habitat Around boggy pools, especially if well vegetated.

Status and distribution Mainly an eastern species that extends patchily into W Europe as far as NE France, but very local here.

Season 5–7, a very short flying period in any one locality.

Similar species

★ *L. albifrons* is very similar in size and colour, but lacks the clubbed abdomen. Distribution similar to *L. caudalis*, though rarer still.

STONEFLIES
ORDER PLECOPTERA

A little-known group of insects, with about 150 species in Europe. They have soft, often flattened bodies, moderately long antennae, often 2 'tails' (cerci), and 2 pairs of clear, strongly veined, wings. Male stoneflies may have reduced wings. The nymphs are wholly aquatic, and resemble wingless adults, with 2 cerci. Larger ones are predatory, smaller ones are mainly vegetarian.

Dinocras cephalotes

A large stonefly, one of the few species that tends to be noticed. Males are 15–19mm long, females up to 25mm. The body is greyish-black, and both antennae and cerci are about 10mm long; the latter extend well beyond the wings when the insect is at rest.

Habitat In and around stony and gravelly fast-flowing rivers, especially in upland regions up to at least 2,000m.

Status and distribution Widespread and locally common.

Season 5–9.

Similar species

Perla bipunctata is almost identical in size, but has a paler, yellowish body. Common in broadly similar habitats to *Dinocras*, less confined to uplands.

Needle-fly
Leuctra fusca

One of a group of stoneflies known as needle-flies because of their habit of folding the wings tightly around the body to form a narrow tube. Antennae long, 'tails' very short, barely visible.

Habitat Stony streams.

Status and distribution Widespread and common throughout.

Season 6–11.

Similar species

Several other *Leuctra* species are very similar. *L. geniculata* is distinctive, when seen through a lens, as it has rings of hairs on each segment of the antennae. Widespread, though local, mainly in larger rivers.

White-faced Darter, male

Dinocras cephalotes, nymph

Perla bipunctata

Needle-fly

GRASSHOPPERS AND CRICKETS
ORDER ORTHOPTERA

A well-known and well-defined order, one of the most conspicuous of our insect groups. Of the 600 or so European species, only about 80 are found in N Europe.

They have greatly enlarged hind legs for jumping. Immediately behind the head is a prominent saddle-shaped structure known as the pronotum. The wings are very variable, though in general the forewings are larger than, and often different from, the hindwings. Wing length can be useful in identification, but only when looking at fully mature insects.

A key feature of this group is that most of them 'sing' and can be recognized by their song. True grasshoppers usually sing by rubbing the hind legs against the forewings. Bush-crickets usually sing by raising their forewings and rubbing the bases together.

Within the order Orthoptera, there are 4 main groups: true grasshoppers, ground-hoppers, bush-crickets and true crickets. The distinguishing features are described under each group.

True Grasshoppers, Family Acrididae

Diurnal insects, with relatively short antennae (cf. bush-crickets which all have long antennae). The pronotum does not extend over the abdomen (see illustration and compare groundhoppers on p.74).

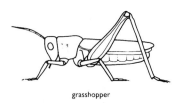

grasshopper

Males are usually smaller than females, and the tip of the male abdomen is turned up like the prow of a boat. Females do not have long dagger-like ovipositors.

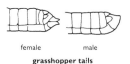

female   male
grasshopper tails

Large Marsh Grasshopper
Stethophyma grossum

A very large insect when fully grown, with males up to 25mm and females up to 40mm long. The basic colour is greenish-brown, but both sexes have red stripes on their legs, and sometimes elsewhere. The song is an audible 'ticking'.

Habitat In the UK, it is confined to wet boggy areas, but on the Continent it inhabits a wider range of wet habitats.

Status and distribution Very local in S Britain; widespread on the Continent.

Season 7–10.

Similar species
★ **Large Banded Grasshopper** *Arcyptera fusca* is similar in size and general colouring, but has more boldly banded legs, more extensive red, especially on the tibia, and occurs in dry montane pastures.

Lesser Marsh Grasshopper
Chorthippus albomarginatus

A medium-small species, with a body length of up to 15mm (male), and 20mm (female). Generally brownish to greenish, and the female has a prominent white stripe on the wing. The song is 3–4 short chirps, separated by 1–2 seconds.

Habitat Mainly coastal pastures and upper saltmarshes in Britain; in similar habitats and any damp meadows in Europe.

Status and distribution Local in S Britain only; widespread on the Continent.

Season 7–10.

Similar species
★ *C. dorsatus* is similar in shape and colour, but the female has no wing stripe, and the tip of the male abdomen is usually red. Widespread on the Continent in similar habitats.

Large Marsh Grasshopper, female

Large Banded Grasshopper, male

Lesser Marsh Grasshopper, female

Common Field Grasshopper
Chorthippus brunneus

A medium-sized species, up to 18mm long (male) and 25mm long (female). Generally dull brown, though very variable in colour, and the top of the male abdomen is usually reddish. Flies more readily than most species. The song is a very short single buzz, repeated up to 10 times at intervals of about 2 seconds.

Habitat Most frequent in dry short grassland with open areas.

Status and distribution Abundant through most of the UK, widespread and frequent on the Continent.

Season 6–10.

Similar species

* **Bow-winged Grasshopper** *C. biguttulus* is very similar in size and colour, but the males have strongly curved front edges to the forewings (the 'bow-wing'), less marked in females. Song louder, increasing in rapidity as it progresses. Widespread and common on the Continent.

* *C. mollis* is roughly intermediate between the foregoing two, most easily distinguished by its song, which is a curious mixture of whirring and clicking, lasting about 20 seconds. Local, in very dry grasslands.

Meadow Grasshopper
Chorthippus parallelus

A medium-small species, with the males reaching 16mm, and females up to 23mm. Generally greenish in ground colour, distinctive (when adult) in having very short wings, reaching to barely half-way along the abdomen in the female, about two-thirds in the male. It is flightless. The song consists of bursts of quickly repeated scraping sounds.

Habitat Most types of grassland, except very damp and very dry areas.

Status and distribution An abundant species throughout, except for Ireland and high mountain areas.

Season 6–10.

Similar species

* *C. montanus* is very similar. Both sexes have slightly longer wings, and the call is louder and slower. Widespread on the Continent but local, in wet meadows and fens.

Heath Grasshopper
Chorthippus vagans

A smallish, undistinguished species, in which males reach 15mm, females 20mm. Generally brown, though both sexes have a red-tipped abdomen. The wings of the male reach just to the tip of the abdomen, or just short of it in females (shorter than those of Field Grasshopper). The song is a slower version of Meadow Grasshopper, resembling the (quiet) quacking of a duck.

Habitat Confined to warm, dry heaths in Britain; more widespread and also on dunes or in heathy woods on the continent.

Status and distribution Very rare in Britain, only around the Hampshire-Dorset border; widespread on the Continent from Denmark southwards.

Season 7–10.

Similar species

* *C. apricarius* is similar, but has more transparent hindwings and usually lacks the red abdomen. Widespread in dry heathy or chalky areas.

Mottled Grasshopper
Myrmeleotettix maculatus

A very small but rather attractive grasshopper. Males reach only 12mm long, females about 17mm. Very variable in colour, but usually mottled with green, brown, black and white. The male has clubbed antennae which are usually bent outwards. The call sounds like a clock being wound, lasting about 10 seconds.

Habitat Most frequently in dry acid places, occasionally on limestone grassland.

Status and distribution Local but very widespread both in the UK and on the Continent.

Season 6–10.

Common Field Grasshopper, male

Meadow Grasshopper, male

Meadow Grasshopper, female

Heath Grasshopper, female

Chorthippus montanus, male

Mottled Grasshopper, male

Rufous Grasshopper
Gomphocerippus rufus
A medium-sized grasshopper: males reach 16mm, females 24mm. Although generally brown in colour, it is distinctive by virtue of the male's clubbed, white-tipped antennae, which are surprisingly conspicuous in good light; the abdomen may be red-tipped, and the females are sometimes purplish. The song is a soft purring, like a clockwork toy, lasting about 5 seconds.
Habitat Most frequently found in dry woodland clearings and margins, also on dry grassland.
Status and distribution An uncommon species in the UK, very local only in the south; widespread and moderately common on the Continent.
Season 7–10.
Similar species
★ *Gomphocerus sibiricus* is rather similar, and also has clubbed antennae, but these are dark; the males have conspicuously swollen front tibiae. A montane species, occurring only above about 1,000m. Most frequent in the Alps.

Common Green Grasshopper
Omocestus viridulus
A medium-sized species, with males up to 17mm, and females up to 24mm. Variable in colouring, but usually green, and abdomen never red-tipped. Males usually have conspicuously dark sides to the forewings. The song is a loud ticking, increasing in volume then dying away, lasting 10–20 seconds.
Habitat In most types of grassland except very wet or dry areas.
Status and distribution Widespread and common throughout, even in mountains.
Season 6–9, one of the earliest grasshoppers to mature.

Woodland Grasshopper
Omocestus rufipes
A very attractive small to medium grasshopper, males reaching 17mm, females 21mm. The male has white-tipped palps and a conspicuous red-tipped abdomen; females are greenish and less distinguished. The song resembles *O. viridulus* but is shorter, and stops as soon as full volume is reached.
Habitat Woodland clearings, heaths and dry grassland; confined to sheltered areas in the UK.
Status and distribution Uncommon and strongly southern in Britain; widespread and moderately frequent on the Continent, becoming rarer northwards.
Similar species
★ *O. haemorrhoidalis* is smaller (males only reaching 14mm), with abdomen duller orange-tipped. Local in dry grasslands, from S Scandinavia southwards.

★ Small Gold Grasshopper
Chrysochraon brachypterus
An attractive grasshopper; males much smaller than females (maximum length 17mm and 26mm respectively). Both sexes are metallic pale green, with very short wings, distinctively pink and widely separated in the female.
Habitat In most forms of grassland, from dry and short to lush and damp.
Status and distribution Widespread and locally abundant from central Germany southwards.
Season 6–9.
Similar species
★ **Large Gold Grasshopper** *C. dispar* is larger, up to 30mm in females. Males are greenish-gold, with wings reaching two-thirds of the way along the abdomen; females are brown, with short brown wings. Widespread on the Continent, most frequently in damp grassland.

Gomphocerus sibiricus

Common Green Grasshopper, male   **Woodland Grasshopper,** male

Small Gold Grasshopper, female

Stripe-winged Grasshopper
Stenobothrus lineatus

A medium-large grasshopper: males reach 19mm and females 26mm long. They are basically green, often mottled, and the males usually have a red tip to the abdomen. Both sexes have a curved white mark on the forewing, and the female has a white stripe along the edge. The song is a distinctive wheezy buzzing that rises and falls in pitch, lasting 10–20 seconds.

Habitat Dry grassland and heathland areas.

Status and distribution Locally common in the UK in S and E England; widespread and generally common on the Continent, from S Scandinavia southwards.

Season 7–10.

Similar species

Lesser Mottled Grasshopper S. *stigmaticus* resembles a small version of S. *lineatus*, with females reaching 20mm long. The white 'comma' on the wing is less well marked. Restricted in Britain to the Isle of Man, but more widespread in Europe from S Scandinavia southwards.

★ Green Mountain Grasshopper
Miramella alpina

An attractive medium-large grasshopper; females reach about 30mm, males up to 23mm. The colour is bright green, strongly marked with black, especially in male, and the hind legs are partly red. The wings are very small, brownish and widely separated.

Habitat Montane grasslands from about 1,000m upwards.

Status and distribution Widespread in suitable habitats from Germany southwards.

Season 6–9.

Similar species

★ *Podisma pedestris* occurs in similar habitats, but is basically brown, marked with yellow and black. Its distribution is broadly similar, though it is found at lower altitudes.

★ Rattle Grasshopper
Psophus stridulus

A largish species; males reach 25mm long, but females may be up to 40mm. They are dull mottled brownish, with a distinct keel on the pronotum (see p.66). In flight, the hindwings are bright orange-red with a narrow dark margin, and the insects make a distinct rattling sound as they fly. This and the Blue-winged Grasshopper, below, belong to a group of grasshoppers with coloured wings, visible as 'flash coloration' in flight.

Habitat Rough, warm, grassy areas, including the uplands.

Status and distribution Local, from S Scandinavia southwards.

Season 7–10.

Similar species

★ **Red-winged Grasshopper** *Oedipoda germanica* is very similar, but differs in having the pronotum keel broken by a distinct notch; the forewings are more striped, and the hindwings have a broader dark margin. A local, mainly southern species.

★ Blue-winged Grasshopper
Oedipoda caerulescens

This species is very similar in size and structure to the red-winged species above, especially O. *germanica*, but differs in having bright blue hindwings, broadly edged with black, and ending in a clear tip. The overall body colour can vary according to the habitat in which the insect lives.

Habitat Occurs in dry, sunny, partly bare places, such as rocky grassland and old quarries.

Status and distribution Locally abundant, from S Scandinavia southwards.

Season 7–10.

Similar species

★ *Sphingonotus caerulans* is more slender, with longer wings. The hindwings are pale blue, without a dark margin. Widespread but local in dry places on the Continent.

Stripe-winged Grasshopper, male

Green Mountain Grasshopper

Podisma pedestris, female

Blue-winged Grasshopper, female

Groundhoppers, Family Tetrigidae

A small group of rather inconspicuous insects that have a pronotum which extends back over the whole abdomen, and is sometimes prolonged beyond it. The forewings are reduced to scales, but the hindwings are well developed. They are all vegetarian, and overwinter as adults or nymphs. They have no discernible song. They are closely related to the grasshoppers, Acrididae, and resemble them superficially, but close examination reveals the very different pronotum structure (see illustration below and on p.66).

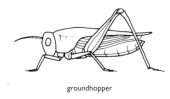

groundhopper

Common Groundhopper
Tetrix undulata
A small brown insect, with a body length of about 10mm. In this species, the pronotum reaches to about the end of the abdomen, and is strongly arched; the wings are shorter than the pronotum.

Habitat Damp, but not usually wet places such as woodland clearings, margins of lakes and old pasture, where there is plenty of moss.

Status and distribution Widespread and locally frequent throughout the UK and mainland W Europe.

Season All year, in suitable weather.
Similar species
★ *T. tenuicornis* is more thick-set and has slender antennae; there are usually 2 dark spots on the pronotum. In dry habitats through continental Europe, rarest in the west.
★ *T. bipunctata* is very similar to *T. tenuicornis*, but has shorter, thicker antennae, and the 2 pronotum spots are especially well marked. Widespread, especially in dry places.

Slender Groundhopper
Tetrix subulata
A slightly longer insect than the Common Groundhopper, reaching about 15mm to the tip of the pronotum. In this species, the pronotum extends well beyond the end of the abdomen, and the hindwings reach only to the end of the pronotum. The pronotum is less strongly keeled than in the above species. They can fly readily, and will also swim.

Habitat Damp places, often close to water.

Status and distribution Local in the UK north as far as Lincolnshire; widespread throughout the area on the Continent.
Season Virtually all year.
Similar species
Cepero's Groundhopper *T. ceperoi* is hard to separate from *T. subulata* in the field. It is slightly smaller, often more mottled, and the head is parallel-sided when seen from above. Rare in the UK, only occurring close to the S coast; a southern species on the Continent, occurring patchily further north.

Common Groundhopper   Common Groundhopper

Slender Groundhopper

Cepero's Groundhopper

Bush-crickets, Family Tettigoniidae

Although similar in appearance to the true grasshoppers in some respects, the bush-crickets differ in possessing very long antennae (usually longer than the body), and the females have dagger-like ovipositors. The wings are frequently much reduced. Bush-crickets are more nocturnal than grasshoppers.

Long-winged Conehead
Conocephalus discolor

A rather small, slender bush-cricket; its body length is about 15mm, but the antennae are much longer. Colour mainly green, with brown wings and a brown stripe on the back. The female's ovipositor is virtually straight. The song consists of long bursts of gentle sewing-machine ticking, of constant tone.

Habitat Long grass, in both dry and damp sites, often in river valleys.

Status and distribution Very local in the UK, and entirely southern, but it is gradually spreading inland; on the Continent, it is widespread in N Europe, southwards from N Germany.

Season 7–10.

Similar species

Short-winged Conehead *C. dorsalis* differs in having very short wings (except for a small percentage of the population), a curved ovipositor, and a song that varies in intensity. It is local and mainly coastal in the UK, from Yorkshire southwards, but is found throughout the area on the Continent.

* *Ruspolia nitidula* is a longer insect, up to 30mm, with long green wings exceeding the abdomen in length, and a long slender ovipositor. Locally common in tall grassland from S Germany southwards.

Wart-biter
Decticus verrucivorus

A large and bulky insect, with a body length of up to 38mm (male) and 45mm (female). It is predominantly green, mottled with brown patches, and with brown eyes, though rather variable. The ovipositor is long and slightly curved. Its call consists of long bursts of ticking sounds, gradually speeding up, produced mainly in sunny conditions.

Habitat Open grassy places, especially in the uplands, and heaths.

Status and distribution Rare in the UK, confined to a few extreme southern sites; widespread on the Continent.

Season 7–10.

Similar species

* *Gampsocleis glabra* is very similar in shape, but smaller (up to 26mm, both sexes), and the ovipositor is slightly down-curved. Local in similar habitats on the Continent, absent further north.

Great Green Bush-cricket
Tettigonia viridissima

Northern Europe's largest bush-cricket, similar in body size to Wart-biter, but with longer wings. Both sexes are primarily green, with a brown stripe down the back, and green eyes. Ovipositor long, reaching the tip of the wings, slightly down-curved. The song is a loud continuous bicycle-like ticking, which continues well into the night.

Habitat Many types of rough vegetation, from long grass to trees.

Status and distribution Mainly coastal in the UK, from Norfolk to Pembrokeshire; widespread on the Continent except in the north and in mountains.

Season 7–10.

Similar species

* *T. cantans* is slightly smaller, and has much shorter wings, so the ovipositor stands out more clearly. Locally common in Europe in montane grasslands, from which the Great Green Bush-cricket is usually absent.

Long-winged Conehead, female

Short-winged Conehead, female

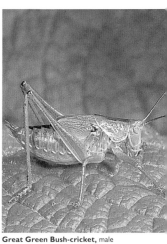

Great Green Bush-cricket, male
Tettigonia cantans, female

Wart-biter, female

Bog Bush-cricket
Metrioptera brachyptera

A bulky but quite short insect; body length 15–18mm. Colour usually dark brown with green on the pronotum and forewings, but may be almost all brown (rather like Dark Bush-cricket, see below). The ovipositor is 8–10mm long, slightly curved upwards. The song is a series of short chirrups, in long sequences.

Habitat Mainly a bog/wet heath species in the UK, but also in damp meadows on the Continent.

Status and distribution Local and mainly southern in UK, widespread and quite frequent on the Continent.

Similar species

* *M. bicolor* is similar in size, but pale green with brown on the back (rather like a squat conehead). The ovipositor is only 5–6mm long. Local in dry meadows from N Germany southwards.

Roesel's Bush-cricket
Metrioptera roeselii

A medium-sized bush-cricket, quite bulky; body length up to 18mm. The ground colour is green or brown; the forewings are always brown, and the pronotum has a broad green or yellow stripe around it. The song is a distinctive uniform high-pitched buzz, rather reminiscent of a Cicada.

Habitat Virtually confined to coastal grasslands in the UK, but occurs in almost any long grass on the Continent.

Status and distribution Local in Britain, mainly on SE coasts, but occasionally inland and north to Yorkshire; widespread and abundant on the Continent.

Season 6–11.

Dark Bush-cricket
Pholidoptera griseoaptera

A short, squat species, up to 15mm long (male), or 18mm long (female). Predominantly varying shades of brown, with a yellow underside; wings greatly reduced, to about 5mm long in the male, tiny in female. The ovipositor is about 10mm long, strongly curved upwards. The call is a single short high-pitched bleat, repeated frequently, well into the night.

Habitat Almost any rough vegetation.

Status and distribution Very common in the south of the UK, local elsewhere; widespread and common on the Continent.

Season 7–11.

Grey Bush-cricket
Platycleis albopunctata

Medium-sized, up to 22mm long. Rather similar in colouring to Dark Bush-cricket, but is not bright yellow below, and both sexes have long wings, extending beyond the abdomen. The call is a series of short buzzing sounds.

Habitat Very strongly coastal in UK, in a variety of rough dry habitats; in dry, rough habitats generally on the Continent.

Status and distribution Locally abundant along the S coast in Britain; widespread and frequent throughout the Continent.

Season 7–10.

Oak Bush-cricket
Meconema thalassinum

A small, slender bush-cricket, up to 15mm long. Predominantly pale green, with a short brown and yellow mark at the base of the pronotum. Wings well developed in both sexes, just extending beyond the abdomen. Flies readily, often coming to lights at night. No call, but male drums on leaves, and this is just audible.

Habitat A wide variety of deciduous trees, including oak.

Status and distribution Frequent in much of S England, local elsewhere. Widespread and frequent on the Continent. Mainly nocturnal.

Season 7–11.

Similar species

* *M. meridionale* differs only in the short thick wings, and the shorter ovipositor. A southern species, just reaching S Germany and Switzerland.

Bog Bush-cricket, male

Roesel's Bush-cricket, male

Dark Bush-cricket, male

Dark Bush-cricket, female

Grey Bush-cricket, male

Oak Bush-cricket, female

Speckled Bush-cricket
Leptophyes punctatissima

A short, plump species, up to 17mm long. Green, speckled with reddish-brown or black. Males have a narrow stripe down the top of the abdomen. The wings are greatly reduced, and the insect is flightless. The call is a very quiet, short click.

Habitat Rough, low vegetation, such as nettle or bramble patches.

Status and distribution Frequent in S Britain, rare or absent elsewhere. Widespread throughout the Continent.

Season 7–11.

Similar species

* Large Speckled Bush-cricket *Isophya pyrenea* is larger, up to 26mm long, and the ovipositor has a rounded, toothed tip. Frequent in dry grassy places in central Europe, including Germany.

True Crickets, Family Gryllidae

The crickets have long antennae, but are more flattened than bush-crickets, with rounded heads. Forewings, when present, are flattened closely against the abdomen.

Field Cricket
Gryllus campestris

A robust insect, up to about 25mm long. Essentially black in colour, usually with yellow wing bases. The males have strongly ribbed wings. The call is a musical chirping, repeated regularly and frequently.

Habitat Grasslands, and occasionally heaths, where it lives in burrows.

Status and distribution Very rare and local, in S England only; widespread and generally common on the Continent.

Season 5–8.

Similar species

House Cricket *Acheta domesticus* is smaller, more slender, and paler. Mainly nocturnal. Widespread in houses.

Wood Cricket
Nemobius sylvestris

A small, dark brown insect, with a body up to 10mm long, and rather longer antennae.

The forewings are short, reaching about half-way along the abdomen in males, less in females. The call is a mellifluous purring, readily audible *en masse*.

Habitat On the ground in woodland clearings and scrub.

Status and distribution Very local in S England, especially the New Forest; widespread on the Continent from N Germany southwards.

Season 6–11.

* Tree Cricket or Italian Cricket
Oecanthus pellucens

A very slender cricket, up to 15mm long. Pale brownish to yellow in colour, with long cerci. Call a far-carrying prolonged warbling, mainly at night.

Habitat Trees, scrub and and other tall herbage.

Status and distribution A southern species, reaching locally into N France and SW Germany.

Season 8–10.

Mole Crickets, Family Gryllotalpidae

Curious and distinctive, strongly built insects, with greatly enlarged front legs (for burrowing). There is only one species in N Europe.

Mole Cricket
Gryllotalpa gryllotalpa

This is a large insect, up to 50mm long, with very large front legs. It is dark brown in colour, with short forewings but long hindwings. The antennae are about the same length as the pronotum. It is able to fly, but not to jump. The song is a continuous quiet churring, rather like that of the Grasshopper Warbler.

Habitat Moist grassy places.

Status and distribution Very rare, in S England only within the UK; widespread throughout the Continent in suitable habitats.

Season Adult all year, active only in summer.

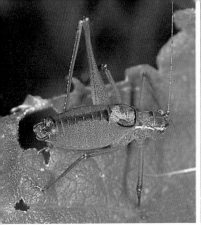

Speckled Bush-cricket, male

Speckled Bush-cricket, female

Field Cricket, male

Wood Cricket, male

Tree Cricket, male

Mole Cricket, male

COCKROACHES AND MANTIDS
ORDER DICTYOPTERA

Cockroaches are broad, flattened, robust insects, with long antennae. The broad pronotum covers the thorax and most of the head. Hindwings leathery, usually shorter in the female than the male. The mantids are closely related, but look rather different, with slender bodies, a long neck, and enlarged front legs. They are highly predatory, and females often eat the males during copulation. The eggs are laid in frothy masses which harden, and may often be found when the adults are no longer visible.

Cockroaches
Suborder Blattodea

Several tropical species have become well established in N Europe in houses and other buildings, as pests. There are also several native species, which have no association with man.

Australian Cockroach
Periplaneta australasiae
A large, highly active insect, up to 40mm long, with long antennae. Brown, with yellow markings on the wings, and a distinct yellow margin to the pronotum. Nocturnal in habits, fleeing rapidly from light.
Habitat Usually confined to warm buildings, occasionally outside.
Status and distribution Widespread in suitable places throughout. Probably originally native to Africa, despite its name.
Season Variable, depending on temperature regime.
Similar species
American Cockroach *P. americana* is usually slightly larger, up to 45mm. The yellow markings on pronotum and wings are barely visible. Probably also African in origin, but now very widespread in similar places to the Australian Cockroach.

Common Cockroach or Black Beetle
Blatta orientalis
Females are squat, blackish, about 25mm long, with greatly reduced wings. Males are similar in size, but are browner, with longer wings, although they are still flightless. The egg-case is white, darkening to black, and the female carries it for the first few days. Nocturnal.
Habitat Native to tropical Asia or Africa, but now widespread in houses, bakeries, and anywhere warm but dirty.
Status and distribution Common in suitable places throughout.
Season At any time, depending on the warmth of the habitat.
Similar species
German Cockroach *Blatella germanica* is paler and more slender, fully winged and able to fly, though rarely does so. Similar habitats and distribution.

Tawny Cockroach
Ectobius pallidus
One of the native cockroaches, which are much smaller than the introduced species. This species reaches 10mm in length, is fully winged in both of the sexes, and can fly in warm weather. It is basically pale brown, with the pronotal disc edged with yellow.
Habitat In rough grassland, woods and heaths.
Status and distribution Widespread, local and more southern in the UK, and throughout the Continent.
Season 4–10.
Similar species
Dusky Cockroach *E. lapponicus*. The females are flightless, and both sexes are more slender. In similar habitats.
Lesser Cockroach *E. panzeri* is smaller (less than 9mm long) and variable in colour but usually speckled. Males can fly, and have narrow forewings; females are flightless, squat, almost bug-like. Local and mainly coastal in the UK.

Australian Cockroach

Tawny Cockroach

Dusky Cockroach, male

Mantids
Suborder Mantodea

A southern, warmth-loving group of insects, of which only one representative reaches N Europe.

* Praying Mantis
Mantis religiosa

A predominantly green species (rarely brown), long and slender – up to 60mm long excluding antennae – yet surprisingly inconspicuous. Both sexes are winged and can fly, but the male is more slender.

Habitat Prefers rough grassy places and scrub.

Status and distribution Throughout southern Europe, reaching northwards to the latitude of N France.

Season 7–11. The frothy egg-cases may persist over winter, and indicate where adults may be found.

STICK INSECTS
ORDER PHASMIDA

A predominantly tropical group, numbering thousands of species, but only just reaching into S Europe. One species, described below, is frequently kept in homes and laboratories, and occasionally naturalizes. These are well-camouflaged, slender insects, with stick-like bodies and short to medium-length antennae.

Laboratory Stick Insect
Carausius morosus

A characteristic and well-known stick insect, almost always seen as the female, which can reproduce parthenogenetically (without the eggs being fertilized). Green or brown, up to about 10cm long.

Habitat Usually in laboratories, but may escape into gardens and waste ground, though rarely lasting long. Originally native to SE Asia.

Status and distribution Unpredictable.

Season All year indoors, surviving outside only in warm weather.

EARWIGS
ORDER DERMAPTERA

Slender, flattened cylindrical insects, with pincer-like cerci, usually markedly curved in males. Some species are wholly wingless, others have much-reduced forewings and very thin hindwings. The winged species can fly, but rarely do. Generally nocturnal. There are over 30 species in Europe.

Common Earwig
Forficula auricularia

The only earwig that is commonly seen. It is 10–13mm long, shiny brown, with reduced forewings (elytra), and hindwings that project from below the elytra. The male pincers are broad and flat at their base. Young are like miniature adults, and the female guards them until they disperse.

Habitat In many habitats, wherever there is sufficient food, and some humid hiding places.

Status and distribution Very common throughout.

Season Mainly summer, but may be seen in almost any month as the adults hibernate.

pincers of Lesser Earwig

pincers of Common Earwig

Similar species

Lesser Earwig *Labia minor* is much smaller, about 6–7mm long, with gradually curved tails. Common in rough places such as nettle patches, especially near houses. Nocturnal, occasionally coming to lights. *Apterygida media* is intermediate in size; the hindwings are completely reduced, and not visible. Widespread throughout, most commonly seen in flowers or under stones.

Praying Mantis, egg-case

Laboratory Stick Insect, female

Praying Mantis

Common Earwig

PSOCIDS OR BOOK-LICE
ORDER PSOCOPTERA

Tiny soft-bodied insects (not true lice), which live on plants or dried cellulose-based materials. Some are wingless, others winged; these hold their wings over the body in a roof-like structure, resembling aphids, but distinguishable from them by their longer antennae. Numerous species occur, with more yet to be described. Only the book-louse is at all familiar, through the damage it causes.

Book-louse
Trogium pulsatorium
One of several similar species that occur in books, stored paper, and food. They are wingless, about 2mm long, with antennae almost as long as the body. They eat the paste from the binding of books, eventually causing considerable damage.
Habitat Old books, paper, stored food, insect collections and so on.
Status and distribution Very common wherever there are suitable conditions, throughout.
Season All year indoors.

Book-louse

TRUE BUGS
ORDER HEMIPTERA

A huge family of insects, covering a wide range of forms, but generally having the shared characteristic of mouthparts modified into a beak (rostrum), with which they suck their food from plants or animals. This is usually held horizontally under the body when not in use. The antennae vary from short to quite long, but even when long, they usually only consist of a few segments which are clearly visible. There are generally 2 pairs of wings, with the forewings modified by hardening to a greater or lesser degree, though some species are wingless.

The Hemiptera are divided into two major groups on the basis of their wing characteristics, and some authors give each the status of a separate order. The **Heteropteran Bugs** have the forewings clearly divided into two separate areas – a tough, leathery basal area, and a membranous tip. The hindwings are always membranous, and both pairs are folded flat over the body at rest. The heteropterans also have their rostrum arising from the front of the head, and the antennae never have more than 5 segments. The scutellum, which is part of the thorax, is often prolonged backwards as a triangle, occasionally covering the whole body.

Heteropteran bug   Homopteran bug

Homopteran Bugs have forewings that are of the same texture throughout, whether membranous or leathery, and they are commonly held roof-wise over the body rather than flat. The antennae have at least 4 segments, sometimes many more. All homopterans are vegetarian, and many are slow-moving, passive species; in contrast, some heteropterans are animal feeders, and may be highly mobile.

All bugs pass through nymphal stages, and there is no pupal stage. The young may resemble the adults, though in many cases they are quite unlike them.

There are about 1,700 species in Britain, and 4,000 or more in N Europe.

Hawthorn Shieldbug

Heteropteran Bugs
Suborder Heteroptera

Common Flat-bug
Aradus depressus
A small flat bug, about 6–8mm long, with a very narrow 'neck' just behind the head. Thorax dark brown, abdomen reddish. The body shape is adapted for feeding under tree bark, living mainly on fungi.
Habitat Under bark of deciduous trees, on stumps, and among leaf litter.
Status and distribution Widespread and frequent in the south, absent from further north.
Season Adults visible all year.
Similar species
Pine Flat-bug *A. cinnamomeus* is more orange-coloured, with narrow forewings. Occurs mainly under the bark of conifers. Absent from the north.

SHIELDBUGS The following bugs on pages 87–91, from several families, are known collectively as shieldbugs because of their shield-like shape. Most hibernate as adults.

Hawthorn Shieldbug
Acanthosoma haemorrhoidale
A large bug, about 15–17mm long when adult, typically triangular in shape. Essentially green in colour, but with a broad triangle of red on the back.
Habitat Most common on the leaves and fruits of Hawthorn, though also on other deciduous trees.
Status and distribution A southern species, common in England and over most of the Continent, but absent further to the north.
Season Adult most of the year, most frequently seen in spring and autumn.

Parent Bug
Elasmucha grisea

A small shieldbug, less than 10mm long, greyish-brown tinged with orange. The female guards the eggs and newly hatched young against predators and parasites – hence the name.

Habitat Most frequent on Birch, but also on other deciduous trees.

Status and distribution Widespread and moderately common throughout, though easily overlooked.

Season Most visible 5–9, but adults are around all year.

Similar species

Birch Shieldbug *Elasmostethus interstinctus* is larger, green and red with yellow on the wings, and common on Birch.

Pied Shieldbug
Sehirus bicolor

A medium-sized bug, about 10mm long, very distinctive with its black head and scutellum, and piebald wings. The overall body shape is more oval than triangular.

Habitat Rough herbage, hedgerows and woodland edges, mainly on White Dead Nettle and Black Horehound.

Status and distribution A southern species, moderately common in England, but absent from Scotland and N Scandinavia.

Season Adult all year, hibernating in cold weather.

Similar species

S. dubius is a similar shape, but metallic bluish-black all over. Similar habitats and distribution.

Negro Bug
Thyreocoris scarabaeoides

A small bug, about 6mm long, roughly oval-rectangular in shape. As the name suggests, it is black in colour, and the enlarged scutellum covers most of the body.

Habitat Mainly dry grassland, occasionally open woodland.

Status and distribution A southern species, absent from northern areas.

Season 5–9.

Blue Bug
Zicronia caerulea

About 8–10mm long, dark metallic blue or green in colour. Mainly carnivorous, attacking larvae and young insects.

Habitat On dry, usually calcareous or sandy soils, in grassy places.

Status and distribution Widespread and moderately common in the south, absent from Scotland and the far north of Europe.

Season Most of the year.

Eysarcoris fabricii

An undistinguished medium-sized bug, about 8–10mm long, greenish-grey marked with brown (though variable in colour), heavily dotted.

Habitat Woodland edges and scrub, on Hedge Woundwort and other Labiates.

Status and distribution Common in the south, rare or absent in the north.

Season Most noticeable in spring and autumn.

Bishop's Mitre
Aelia acuminata

A narrowly oval brown bug, about 9mm long, with short brown wings. The body and wings are often lightly striped with yellow.

Habitat Rough dry grassland, and occasionally in cereal fields (where it may attack the grain, in southern areas).

Status and distribution A southern species, frequent in S England, rare elsewhere in the UK; widespread on the Continent.

Season All year.

Parent Bug

Blue Bug

Eysarcoris fabricii

Bishop's Mitre

★ *Graphosoma italicum*

A large, conspicuous shieldbug, up to 12mm long. Whole body boldly marked with red and black stripes, legs red or black. Its conspicuous colours warn of its unpleasant taste, and it tends to sit in the open more than other bugs.

Habitat Many types of dry grassland, scrub, and woodland edges.

Status and distribution Widespread on the Continent, except in the north; absent from the UK.

Season Most visible 5–10.

Forest Bug
Pentatoma rufipes

A large shieldbug, about 15mm long, with square pointed shoulders (see illustration below) and a short broad pronotum. Ground colour brownish, edged with yellow or brown, with a spot at the base of the pronotum.

Habitat Woodland, scrub and orchards, on various deciduous trees.

Status and distribution Widespread and frequent throughout.

Season 6–10.

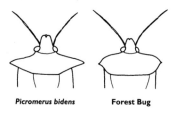

Picromerus bidens   **Forest Bug**

Similar species

Picromerus bidens is similar, but with very pointed shoulders to the pronotum (see illustration above). Widespread and common throughout.

Green Shieldbug
Palomena prasina

Probably the archetypal shieldbug, distinctly shield-shaped, about 12–14mm long. Predominantly green, apart from the membranous section of the wings, but becomes bronzey-red in autumn before hibernating, re-emerging bright green in spring. The young nymphs are more rounded.

Habitat Trees and shrubs, especially Hazel.

Status and distribution Widespread and common almost throughout, except in N Britain.

Season 4–11.

Gorse Shieldbug
Piezodorus lituratus

A typical shieldbug in shape, and about 10mm long. Varies in colour, but tends to be yellowish-green in spring, becoming darker later; young adults have a reddish tinge, especially on the wings, from their emergence until hibernation time.

Habitat Most frequent on Gorse, less often on Broom and other shrubby legumes.

Status and distribution Widespread, but local and commoner in the south of the area.

Season 4–10.

Similar species

Sloe Bug *Dolycoris baccarum* is similar in shape and size, but more yellowish-brown in colour, tinged with red, and distinctly hairy. Common on Sloe, Plums and other related trees, throughout.

Graphosoma italicum

Picromerus bidens, mating

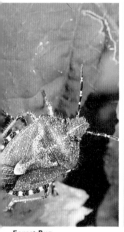
Forest Bug

Green Shieldbug, eggs
Green Shieldbug, adult

Sloe Bug
Gorse Shieldbug

Squash Bug
Coreus marginatus
A large bug, about 12mm long excluding the antennae, and uniformly brown, of varying shades. Belongs to a family of bugs known as squash bugs because in the US they are pests of squashes and other gourds.
Habitat On Dock, Rhubarb and other related plants, spreading more widely in autumn to feed on fruits.
Status and distribution A southern species, frequent in S England, and widespread on the Continent except the far north.
Season 4–10, hibernating as an adult.
Similar species
Verlusia (Syromastus) rhombeus is rather smaller and paler, local in dry sandy and chalky places in the south. Mainly coastal in UK.

★ *Philomorpha laciniata*
An extraordinary-looking bug, with a curious life history. It is about 10mm long, brown with membranous wings, but noticeable for its strongly indented and spiny appearance. The bugs frequently carry on their backs golden-yellow eggs (see photo) laid on them by other individuals seeking to have their eggs transported to new food-plants.
Habitat Dry sunny slopes; feeds on *Paronychia* and probably other plants of dry acid places.
Status and distribution A southern species, reaching to N France.
Season 5–9.

Coryzus hyoscami
An attractive and conspicuous bug, up to 10mm long, with a slender body. The whole insect is brightly patterned with red and black, with black legs. It closely resembles the *Lygaeus* ground bugs in colour and pattern, but is much hairier.
Habitat Sandy places, mainly coastal (especially sand-dunes) in the UK, but more widespread on the Continent.
Status and distribution Very local and

mainly southern in the UK, widespread elsewhere.
Season Mainly early summer and autumn.
Similar species
See Fire Bug (below) and *Lygaeus* spp. (p.94).

Alydus calcaratus
A dark slender bug, about 10mm long, that appears very undistinguished when at rest; when it takes flight, however, it reveals a bright red abdomen. An active species, flying readily, partly predatory in habits.
Habitat Dry sandy areas, especially heathland.
Status and distribution Southern and local in UK, more widespread elsewhere.
Season 6–9.

Fire Bug
Pyrrhocoris apterus
A distinctive species, 8–12mm long, with a squat body. Usually wingless or short-winged, though long-winged forms also occur. Colour bright red and black, with an inverted black triangle and 2 large black dots. Sociable, usually occurring in numbers on the ground.
Habitat A wide variety of habitats, though especially near Lime trees and mallows.
Status and distribution Very rare in UK, virtually confined to Devon; widespread throughout the Continent.
Season 3–11, occasionally in winter.

European Chinchbug
Ischnodemus sabuleti
A small dark brown insect, up to 5mm long. In any population, some are very short-winged while others have long membranous wings, as long as the body; these can fly.
Habitat In tall grass areas, including cereal crops, where they tend to congregate on the flowering heads.
Status and distribution Frequent and widespread on the Continent. locally common in the UK only in the south.
Season 5–10.

Squash Bug

Philomorpha laciniata, eggs on back

Fire Bugs, after hibernation

European Chinchbug

★ *Lygaeus saxatilis*
A brightly coloured ground bug, 10–12mm long, very similar in colouring to *Coryzus hyoscarni* (see p.92), red and black all over. This species is more likely to be found on the ground than on vegetation, though this is not a certain point of differentiation from *Coryzus*.
Habitat Dry places, meadows, woodland edges, occasionally heaths.
Status and distribution Frequent on the Continent, except in the north.
Similar species
★ *L. equestris* is very similar, but has 2 white dots on the membranous parts of the wings; similar distribution.

Heath Assassin Bug
Coranus subapterus
A slender brown bug, 9–12mm long, with a bristly-hairy appearance. Occurs in both long-winged and short-winged forms. Squeaks audibly if handled. A predatory species, attacking other insects and small spiders.
Habitat Heathland and other sandy, dry places.
Status and distribution Widespread and locally common almost throughout, except Ireland.
Season 6–10.
Similar species
Fly Bug *Reduvius personatus* is similar in size and shape, but dark brown to black, and always winged. Occurs around buildings, mainly nocturnal.

★ *Rhinocoris iracundus*
A large, conspicuous bug, up to 18mm long. It is red and black, with a narrow black head, and a slightly concave abdomen with transverse red and black stripes. Highly predatory.
Habitat Among sunny herbage, often seen on flowers.
Status and distribution Widespread on the Continent but never abundant.
Season 5–9.

Common Damsel Bug
Nabis rugosus
A slender brown bug, 6–7mm long, with wings as long as the abdomen (though short-winged forms also occur). They are active predatory insects, and can fly well.
Habitat Rough grassy places.
Status and distribution Abundant in suitable localities throughout.
Season 6–10.
Similar species
Marsh Damsel Bug *Dolichonabis limbatus* is slightly longer, almost always with very short wings. Widespread and common in damp, rough grassland, where they usually stay close to the ground; 5–11.
Ant Damsel Bug *Apterus mirmicoides* is usually darker, and the young stages are very ant-like. Dry grassy places in England and Wales, widespread in Europe.

Common Green Capsid
Lygocoris pabulinus
A predominantly green bug, with brown membranous wing-tips; body length 6–7mm, with antennae almost as long. A voracious herbivore, sometimes becoming a pest of various crops.
Habitat A variety of herbaceous and shrubby plants; undemanding in its requirements.
Status and distribution Widespread and very common throughout.
Season 5–10.
Similar species
There are a number of similar green 'capsid' bugs, hard to distinguish satisfactorily in the field.
Black-kneed Capsid *Blepharidopterus angulatus* has black 'knees' on all its legs (less marked in adults). Common throughout in deciduous trees; 6–10.
Apple Capsid *Plesiocoris rugicollis* is paler, with a yellow head. It occurs on Apple, Willow and Poplar trees, throughout.
Potato Capsid *Calocoris norvegicus* is green with black wingtips, and two black spots on the thorax. Widespread and often abundant.

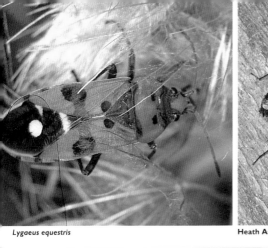

Lygaeus equestris

Heath Assassin Bug

Heath Assassin Bug, with bug *Phytocoris tiliae* as prey

Rhinocoris iracundus

Common Damsel Bug

Potato Capsid

Common Flower Bug
Anthocoris nemorum

A small slender bug, up to 5mm long at most. The head and abdomen are black, and the wings are shiny throughout, usually patterned dark brown and pale. Predatory on aphids.

Habitat Flowers and herbaceous and shrubby vegetation.

Status and distribution Very common throughout.

Season Much of the year, especially common 4–5 and 7–10.

Cyllecoris histrionicus

A small but distinctive bug. Although only 6–7mm long, it can be identified by the slender body, black and yellow pronotum and brown wings with yellowish markings.

Habitat Oak trees, being mainly vegetarian when young, carnivorous later.

Status and distribution A common species throughout.

Season 6–9.

Heterotoma merioptera

A very small bug, no more than 5–6mm long, and not conspicuous, but easily identified once seen. Brownish or dark green in colour, but the distinguishing feature is the broad, enlarged second joint of the antennae, which looks like a paddle.

Habitat Most frequent on Stinging Nettle, also on other rough herbage.

Status and distribution Common generally, but rare in the north.

Season 7–10.

Phytocoris tiliae

A distinctive bug, 8–10mm long, off-white with black markings, and membranous wing-tips; legs black and white. Unlikely to be confused with anything else.

Habitat Woodlands and other areas with trees; particularly fond of Lime trees, but not confined to them.

Status and distribution Widespread and common throughout.

Season 6–10.

Tarnished Plant Bug
Lygus rugulipennis

A small bug, about 5mm long, very variable in colour, but usually with a reddish 'tarnish' on the wings, and yellowish triangles towards the wing-tips. Finely downy if seen under a lens or microscope.

Habitat On a wide range of herbaceous plants, such as Stinging Nettle and Dock.

Status and distribution Widespread and frequently abundant throughout.

Season Mainly 4–5 and 7–10.

Miris striatus

A conspicuous bug, with a slender body, up to 12mm long. Variable in colour, but predominantly brown, black and yellow, with yellowish-orange legs, and 2 yellow-orange triangles on the wings.

Habitat Oak and other deciduous trees.

Status and distribution Widespread and common throughout.

Season 5–9.

Meadow Plant Bug
Leptoterna dolabrata

A medium-sized bug, up to 10mm long. Very variable in colour, but basically black and yellow, or black and reddish-orange, with the pronotum and scutellum strongly marked with black. Males fully winged, females usually short-winged.

Habitat Rough fertile grassy places .

Status and distribution Widespread and abundant throughout.

Season 5–10.

Capsodes gothicus

A small but reasonably conspicuous bug, up to 6 or 7mm long. The adults are boldly marked with black and yellow, while nymphs are black and red, with black hairs.

Habitat Damp herbaceous vegetation.

Status and distribution Local in the UK, absent from the north and upland areas; more widespread on the Continent.

Season 6–10.

Calocoris stysi is similar, but longer and narrower. Widespread.

Common Flower Bug, with prey

Miris striatus

Heterotoma merioptera, on nettle

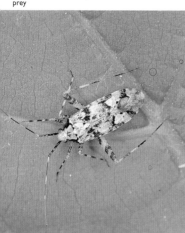
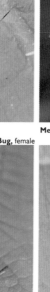

Phytocoris tiliae

Meadow Plant Bug, female

Meadow Plant Bug, male

Calocoris stysi

WATER BUGS A miscellaneous group of bugs, from various families, that have adopted an aquatic lifestyle. Some live on the surface of the water, others have developed the ability to remain submerged for long periods. A number of these bugs are distinctive enough to have attracted common names.

Water Measurer
Hydrometra stagnorum

An inconspicuous, slender bug, up to 12mm long. Brown, with a very long thin head, and usually wingless, though winged forms occur. Moves slowly over the surface of the water, usually among vegetation. Carnivorous.

Habitat Ponds, lakes and slow-moving waters, especially if well vegetated.

Status and distribution Widespread through most of the UK and continental Europe, except the north. Normally present in small numbers.

Season 6–10.

Water Cricket
Velia caprai

A small, inconspicuous insect, up to about 8mm long. Blackish-brown, with the abdomen yellow-orange, especially below. Most commonly wingless, but some have wings. A surface feeder. The 'cricket' name comes from its appearance; it has no call.

Habitat Still or slow-moving waters, especially if shaded.

Status and distribution Widespread, though local, throughout; most common in hilly areas.

Season 7–10.

Common Pondskater
Gerris lacustris

A familiar insect, with a narrow brownish body about 10–12mm long. Skates over the water surface on wide-spreading legs,

grasping prey or carrion with front legs. Wings may be present, partly developed, or absent.

Habitat Still and slow-moving water of all kinds.

Status and distribution Common and very widespread throughout.

Season 4–10.

Similar species

There are several other species of Pondskater, hard to separate without close examination.

G. thoracicus is a species of nutrient-rich and even brackish waters.

G. gibbifer occurs mainly in lowland acid waters.

Aquarius (Gerris) najas

Similar to Pondskater, but distinctly larger, up to 20mm long, usually dark grey or blackish. There are pointed projections on either side of the seventh segment of the abdomen.

Habitat Found in flowing and often well-oxygenated water.

Status and distribution Widespread and locally common, especially in hilly areas.

Season 5–9.

Saucer Bug
Ilyocoris cimicoides

A medium-sized, squat, oval bug, about 15mm long. Shiny brown in colour, and the head looks rather like a Viking helmet in close-up! A highly predatory species (which may pierce human skin if handled) that swims underwater, carrying an air bubble.

Habitat Well-vegetated ponds, where it may be quite abundant.

Status and distribution Confined to southern Britain, though more widespread on the Continent. Locally common.

Season May be active all year, but most often seen 4–5 and 8–10.

Water Cricket

Common Pondskater

Saucer Bug

Water Stick Insect
Ranatra linearis

A curious and distinctive brown insect, up to 40mm long or more, with a long 'tail' half the length of the body. The 'tail' is hollow, and allows the insect to draw air from the surface when submerged. The front legs are modified for grasping prey, and look rather like antennae. Able to fly, but only rarely does so.

Habitat Clean, well-vegetated ponds.
Status and distribution Local and southern in the UK; widespread on the Continent.
Season May be seen all year, except in very cold weather.

Water Scorpion
Nepa cinerea

Rather similar in structure to Water Stick Insect, but broader, more flattened and shorter overall. The 'tail' is more distinct, as the body tapers sharply to it, though it is used for the same purpose as in the Water Stick Insect. The front legs are more robust than those of Water Stick Insect, and more obviously predatory.

Habitat Shallow well-vegetated water bodies.
Status and distribution Widespread throughout lowland areas, though rarely common.
Season active all year.

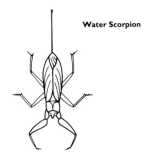
Water Scorpion

Water Boatman or Backswimmer
Notonecta glauca

A highly active, medium-sized bug, about 15mm long. Belongs to a distinctive group whose members swim upside down, carrying a large air bubble. The fully formed wings are pale greyish in this species. A powerful predator, also able to fly.

Habitat Various types of still and slow-moving water.
Status and distribution Widespread and frequent throughout.
Season All year.
Similar species
N. maculata is the same size, but has the forewings mottled with orange, and an orange patch on the abdomen.
N. obliqua has striped wings, and is a less common bog species.

Sigara dorsalis

A small group of species belonging to the genera *Sigara* and *Corixa* are often called Lesser Water Boatmen. This one is 6–8mm long, brown, often speckled with yellow. They are active insects, swimming the 'right' way up, and able to fly.

Habitat Various types of water-bodies, including ponds, slow-flowing waters and slightly brackish ditches.
Status and distribution Common and widespread.
Season All year, most conspicuous in 4–5 and 7–10.
Similar species
A number of other species occur, usually requiring magnified examination to distinguish them. In general, *Corixa* species are slightly larger and more bristly than *Sigara* species.

Water Stick Insect

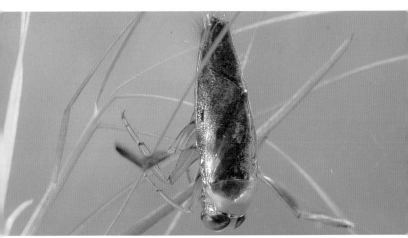

Water Boatman

Sigara dorsalis   *Corixa punctata*

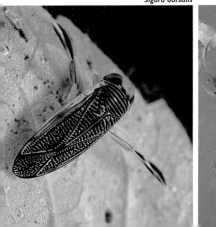 

Homopteran Bugs
Suborder Homoptera

See p.86 for the distinction from heteropteran bugs.

New Forest Cicada
Cicadetta montana
A small cicada, up to 20mm long, the only representative of the group in the UK or N Europe. Body brown, wings clear except for brown veins. Call quieter than most cicadas, and easily missed.
Habitat In woodland, especially along the edges or in sunny clearings. Often associated with Lime trees.
Status and distribution Very rare in Britain, occurring only in the New Forest; local on the Continent, becoming more frequent southwards.
Season 6–8.

Horned Treehopper
Centrotus cornutus
Distinctive brown insects, about 10mm long, with a leathery pronotum that extends down the back and is horned on each side.
Habitat In woodland, especially in clearings and along rides where there are abundant herbs.
Status and distribution Local, and rarely common, but widespread almost throughout.
Season 4–8.

* Buffalo Treehopper
Stictocephalus bisonia
Another distinctive species, about 10mm long, resembling *Centrotus* but green, and with a broad horned pronotum that looks rather bison-like from the front.
Habitat In various wooded habitats, including orchards; introduced from N America.

Status and distribution Not persistent in the UK; widespread and locally common on the Continent, mainly southern.
Season 6–9.

Common Froghopper or Cuckoo Spit
Philaenus spumarius
A familiar insect, in its nymphal stage, by the frothy mass produced to protect the developing nymphs. Adults are much less conspicuous, about 6mm long, variably brown with stripes.
Habitat Many sheltered habitats, such as woodland, scrub and rough grassland.
Status and distribution Abundant throughout.
Season 'Cuckoo spit' mainly 4–6, adults 6–9.

Aphrophora alni
A froghopper that resembles the above species in its adult form (but has a less obvious 'cuckoo spit' phase). Adults are rather larger, up to 10mm long, with a distinctly keeled pronotum.
Habitat Woodland and scrub.
Status and distribution Widespread and common throughout.
Season 5–10.

Cercopis vulnerata
The most conspicuous and just the largest of the froghoppers, reaching 12mm in length. Boldly marked with red and black, which serves as a warning of its unpleasant taste.
Habitat Many species-rich sheltered habitats, such as woodland rides, verges and clearings.
Status and distribution Commonest in the south in the UK; widespread on the Continent.
Season 4–7.

Horned Treehopper   **Buffalo Treehopper**

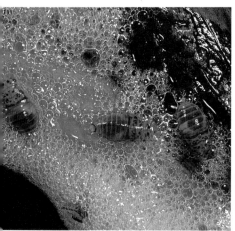

Common Froghoppers, cuckoo spit and nymphs

Common Froghopper, adult

Aphrophora alni

Cercopis vulnerata

Cixius nervosus

Body length about 7–9mm. Wings all membranous, like a tiny cicada, with brown transverse stripes and conspicuous veins. Scutellum dark brown with 3 prominent keels.

Habitat Woodland, in association with various broadleaved trees.

Status and distribution Widespread and common.

Season 5–10.

Ditropis pteridis

A distinctive little froghopper, 7–9mm long, transversely striped with dark brown and yellow. Females are larger, more swollen and more brightly coloured, and have shorter wings (see photo).

Habitat Strongly associated with Bracken, in which the eggs are laid; occurs on heaths and in open acid woodlands.

Status and distribution Local and mainly southern.

Season 6–9.

Iassus lanio

One of the larger leafhoppers, up to 8.5mm long. Head and thorax brown, wings brown or greenish.

Habitat Woodland, usually associated with oaks.

Status and distribution Widespread and common throughout, though easily overlooked.

Season 6–10.

Eupteryx aurata

A small but distinctive species, only 4–6mm long, but boldly marked with brown and yellow in a rather squared pattern.

Habitat Rough vegetation, where it is most commonly associated with Stinging Nettle, also on various labiates; occasionally on crops.

Status and distribution Widespread and common throughout.

Season 6–11.

Cicadella viridis

A distinctive and attractive leafhopper, up to just under 10mm long. Overall green or greenish-blue in colour, but with pronotum partly yellow, and head yellowish; males generally darker than females.

Habitat Bogs, marshes and wet meadows.

Status and distribution Common throughout, often becoming abundant.

Season 7–10.

Evacanthus interruptus

A medium-sized leafhopper, up to 7mm long. The pronotum is usually black, sometimes marked with yellow, and the wings are brown-and-yellow striped – a reasonably recognizable pattern.

Habitat On grass and other herbaceous plants; formerly a pest of hops.

Status and distribution Widespread and common throughout.

Season 6–10.

Rhododendron Leafhopper
Graphocephala fennahi (coccinea)

A distinctive largish leafhopper, up to 8mm long, striped green and red. Not as conspicuous as its colouring suggests, but quickly located by looking at the upper surface midribs of Rhododendron leaves.

Habitat On Rhododendron bushes, wherever they occur.

Status and distribution North American in origin, but spreading through S Britain.

Season 5–10.

Ditropis pteridis, swollen with eggs

Iassus lanio

Eupteryx aurata

Cicadella viridis

Evacanthus interruptus
Rhododendron Leafhoppers

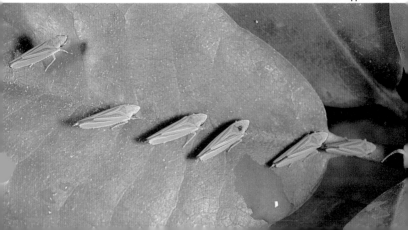

Aphids, Family Aphididae and others

All-too-familiar small homopteran bugs with or without wings. They are usually roughly pear-shaped, and wings, if present, are held over the body like a roof. The abdomen has two 'horns' (cornicles) towards the tip, which produce a waxy secretion. These insects have complex life-cycles, generally beginning with wingless females in spring, which give birth to young parthenogenetically (without fertilization being necessary); winged forms, including males, build up through the summer. Many are pests of cultivated crops. There are hundreds of species within the area, and most are difficult to identify without close examination.

Phylloxera quercus
Small aphids, up to 2mm long. most often seen in groups of yellow wingless females, darker winged individuals, and white cast skins. In spring, eggs are present – they do not give birth to live young.
Habitat Oak trees, under the leaves, where they cause yellowish feeding spots around the colony.
Status and distribution A common species throughout.
Season 4–10.

Woolly Aphid or American Blight
Eriosoma lanigerum
The aphids themselves are small and dark, but the white waxy fluff that they produce for concealment and protection makes them quite conspicuous as a group.
Habitat In crevices and depressions of tree bark, especially Apple and Pear.
Status and distribution Widespread and common throughout, often being considered a pest of apples.
Season 5–10.

Blackfly or Black Bean Aphid
Aphis fabae
Usually black, sometimes green. They spend the winter, as eggs, on Spindle and other wild shrubs; winged forms then spread and colonize various herbaceous plants.
Habitat A wide range of herbaceous plants, especially beans, docks and other species. Can be a nuisance on garden plants.
Status and distribution An abundant species throughout.
Season 5–9.

Greenfly or Rose Aphid
Macrosiphum rosae
A largish aphid, up to 3mm long, pink or green in colour, with distinctive long black cornicles. Well known as a pest of roses in spring.

Rose Aphid

Habitat Wherever roses occur, or other herbaceous plants such as teasels and scabious.
Status and distribution An abundant species throughout, reaching huge numbers in mild springs.
Season 4–6 on roses, 6–9 on other plants.
Similar species
Rose-grain Aphid *Metopolophium dirhodum* is usually green, with a darker stripe on its back. Overwinters on roses, as eggs, then spreads to grasses and cereals. Abundant and widespread.

Phylloxera quercus, females, young and cast skins

Blackfly

Greenfly

Blackfly

Greenfly

Jumping Plant Lice or Psyllids, Family Psyllidae

Inconspicuous, small bugs, rather like aphids but with much more strongly developed legs; the long antennae distinguish them from small leafhoppers.

Apple Sucker or Apple Psyllid
Psylla mali

A predominantly green species, becoming brown later in the summer; about 3mm long, with wings much longer than the body. Can cause significant damage to apples when present in abundance, causing buds and leaves to shrivel.

Habitat Apple trees, and occasionally other deciduous trees.

Status and distribution A common species throughout, often abundant.

Season 4–10.

Similar species

There are many similar species, often host-specific, requiring close examination to separate them.

Whiteflies, Family Aleyrodidae

Tiny homopteran bugs, usually no more than 2mm long, with waxy white wings. In close-up they resemble tiny moths, though they are not related to them. There are numerous species, most of which for the non-specialist are impossible to identify. Two species are often noticed because of their effect in the garden.

Cabbage White Fly or Snowy Fly
Aleyrodes proletella

A typical whitefly, approximately 2mm long, and conspicuously white in colour. They are common enough to occur in swarms on suitable food-plants, and are therefore very noticeable. They breed through the summer, becoming increasingly common.

Habitat On varieties of *Brassica*, causing noticeable damage when abundant.

Status and distribution Common in the south, becoming rarer further north.

Season 4–10.

Similar species

Greenhouse Whitefly *Trialeurodes vaporariorum* is similar in size, but less brightly white. It attacks a wide range of plants in greenhouses, especially crops, but cannot survive winters outside in N Europe. Local.

Scale Insects, Family Coccidae and others

There are numerous species of scale insect, in several families, brought together because of the hard or waxy scale-like structure under which the females live. Many females are legless, wingless and lacking in antennae, and remain on the one food-plant throughout their life. Males are winged but inconspicuous. In quantity, they can be very damaging to crops.

Parthenolecanium corni

A conspicuous species, with brown shell-like convex structures, 7–10mm across, with white scaly material visible underneath.

Habitat On the trunks and branches of various trees and shrubs, wild and cultivated.

Status and distribution Widespread and common, often abundant where it occurs.

Season 6–11.

Mussel Scale
Lepidosaphes ulmi

These resemble small mussels – elongated, slightly curved, brownish shell-like structures, 3–5mm long, occurring in dense groups.

Habitat On various trees, especially Apple, and they may become a pest of orchards.

Status and distribution Widespread and common throughout.

Season 6–10.

Apple Sucker

Jumping Plant Louse, *Psylla* sp.

Mussel Scale

Cabbage White Fly

THRIPS
ORDER THYSANOPTERA

Tiny dark-coloured insects, with a narrow flattened body, rarely more than 3mm long; usually with 2 pairs of feathery fringed wings, though some forms are wingless or short-winged. They are abundant almost everywhere on plants, and there are about 200 species in the area, yet they are little known generally. In warm, sultry weather, large numbers of some species may take flight and become more conspicuous as tiny, dark 'thunder-flies'. Identification of thrips species is a matter for the specialist, and only one species is featured here, as an example.

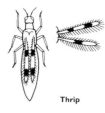

Thrip

Aeolothrips intermedius
Tiny, dark, narrowly cylindrical insect, 2–3mm long, with wings banded brown and cream (just visible to the naked eye, but best observed under a lens); antennae about 0.5mm long.

Habitat Rough flowery places; mainly associated with dandelions and other yellow composites, occasionally other yellow flowers.

Status and distribution Abundant throughout.

Season 5–9.

FLEAS
ORDER SIPHONAPTERA

All-too-familiar insects, with a distinctive flattened appearance. They are brown to black in colour, wingless, flattened from side to side, and have enlarged legs for jumping. All the adults are parasitic bloodsuckers, mainly on mammals. About 60 species occur in Britain, though not all are original natives. The host can be a helpful aid to identification, but does not make identification certain.

Cat Flea
Ctenocephalides felis
An average-sized flea, 3–4mm long, mid- to dark brown in colour, and strongly flattened. Frequently bites man as well as its primary hosts. The eggs are pearly-white, and the larvae are like tiny pale, bristly worms.

Habitat Common in houses, wherever cats occur. Larvae may be on hosts or amongst general debris.

Status and distribution Widespread and common throughout the area.

Season Most frequent spring to autumn, but season may be extended in centrally heated houses.

Similar species
Human Flea *Pulex irritans* and **Dog Flea** *Ctenocephalides canis* are both very similar, and are hard to distinguish without microscopic examination. Dog fleas have more rounded heads than cat fleas. Human fleas have a rounded forehead and a longer 'face'.

Cat Flea, adult

Cat Flea, eggs and larva

ANT-LIONS, LACEWINGS AND RELATIVES ORDER NEUROPTERA

A varied group of insects, linked by having membranous net-veined wings, commonly held roof-wise over the body. Antennae thin and thread-like. Most species are carnivorous in adult and larval stages.

* Ant-lion
Myrmeleon formicarius
Body slender, brownish, about 40mm long, with a wingspan of up to 80mm. Wings membranous and virtually unmarked. Top of head dark brown or black. The larvae construct little craters, in which they sit hidden at the base with just their jaws exposed. Small invertebrates fall in and are immediately grabbed, though sometimes the larva will shower sand-grains over the victim to speed its fall. The craters are often the first sign of the presence of this species.
Habitat Dry sandy places such as heaths and dunes.
Status and distribution Local from S Scandinavia southwards, commonest in the south.
Season 5–8.
Similar species
Could be confused with duller damselflies, but the latter have much more visible abdomens, and very short antennae.
* **Ant-lion** *Acanthaclisis baetica* is larger and more robust, up to 50mm long. It occurs mainly on sand-dunes, and reaches northwards to N France.
* *Euroleon nostras* is a smaller species, about 35mm long, with lightly spotted wings. Local in scrub and open woodland from S Scandinavia southwards.

* Ascalaphid
Libelloides longicornis
Although this group only just reaches into the region, its members are highly distinctive and frequently noticed. They resemble dragonflies, holding their wings open when stopping briefly, though they fold them over the body when at rest. The wings are heavily marked with black and yellow, and the wingspan is about 60mm. The long antennae are heavily clubbed.
Habitat Sunny flowery slopes and pastures.
Status and distribution From central Europe southwards, mainly south-western, most common in S Europe.
Season 6–9.
Similar species
May be distinguished from dragonflies as a group by the clubbed long antennae, and the folding of the wings if seen at rest.
* *L. coccajus* is a very similar species, but has veins all dark (no yellow ones) and a slightly dark patch at the base of the hindwing. It is a southern species that just reaches the area.

* Mantis Fly
Mantispa styriaca
Resembles a small Praying Mantis, but is only 15–20mm long, pale brown in colour, with delicate clear wings. Carnivorous, but not aggressive.
Habitat Woodland and dry, scrubby, warm places.
Status and distribution A southern species, found from N France southwards.
Season 6–8.

Ant-lion, larva holes

Ant-lion, *Myrmeleon formicarius*

Ascalaphid, *Libelloides longicornis*

Mantis Fly

Lacewings, Families Chrysopidae and Hemerobiidae

These two families include both the green and the brown lacewings, though they are not so readily distinguished by colour as the name suggests. They have delicate membranous wings, heavily veined with numerous cross-veins, and a generally delicate appearance. Mostly green or brown in colour, with wings held roof-wise over the body.

Giant Lacewing
Osmylus fulvicephalus
The largest British species of lacewing, with a wingspan of about 50mm. The wings are mottled with brown, sometimes heavily. A slow, clumsy flier, mainly nocturnal in habits.
Habitat Along wooded and shady streams, resting under leaves or below bridges during the day.
Status and distribution A southern species, absent from N Britain and the north part of the Continent; locally common in the south.
Season 5–8.

Green Lacewing
Chrysopa carnea
A pale green insect with unspotted, delicate, membranous wings; becomes pinkish in autumn. The length from the head to the wing-tips is about 18mm. Antennae long and slender.
Habitat A wide range of habitats with trees and shrubs. Often enters houses in autumn and winter.
Status and distribution Very common throughout.
Season Most common 5–10, but individuals may be seen all winter.
Similar species
C. perla is more bluish-green in colour, strongly marked with black on the head and body. In woods and hedgerows, absent from the north.

C. septempunctata is bright green, and has a black spot (actually 7 small spots) on top of the head. Similar habitats and distribution.

All the green lacewing larvae are carnivorous. They may cover themselves with remains of their victims, or other material. The eggs are distinctive, laid in batches or singly, at the end of long stalks.

Brown Lacewing
Kimminsia subnebulosa
One of a number of rather similar insects, generally similar in shape to green lacewings, but only about 10mm long. They are brownish or greyish, with clear wings.
Habitat Sheltered woodland and scrub.
Status and distribution Widespread and common, though easily overlooked.
Season Mainly 4–10.
Similar species
Wesmaelius quadrifasciatus is slightly larger, and has wings marked with brown blotches. Mainly in coniferous woodland and scrub.

Alder Fly
Sialis lutaria
Although rather similar to the Brown Lacewing, this is a surprisingly distinctive species, with its smoky brown wings, boldly marked with dark veins, held roof-wise over the body. Body is dark brown, about 20–25mm long. Flies weakly, and settles readily on waterside vegetation.
Habitat The larvae are aquatic, and the adults are usually found near vegetated stretches of still or slow-moving water.
Status and distribution Common throughout.
Season 4–8.
Similar species
There is one other British species, *S. fuliginosa*, which is darker, less common, appears slightly later (from late June onwards), and prefers faster-flowing waters.

Green Lacewing, larva

Giant Lacewing

Green Lacewing

Chrysopa perla

Chrysopa septempunctata

Alder Fly

Alder Fly, larva

Snake Fly
Raphidia notata

As a small group of species, the Snake Flies are distinctive, looking rather like an Alder Fly with a long snake-like neck which may be raised upwards. Brown in colour, the slender body is about 15–18mm long, excluding the female's long needle-like ovipositor. Both adults and larvae are carnivorous, and they are unusual in having mobile pupae.

Habitat Mainly in old woodland, especially where old tree-stumps are present (the larvae feed on other larvae in dead wood).

Status and distribution Local but widespread. Never common.

Season 5–7.

Similar species
There are 3 other species of Snake Fly in the UK.

R. maculicollis is very similar, with a slightly narrower head, and is probably the commonest species; mainly in conifers.

R. confinis has a more triangular head.

R. xanthostigma is the smallest species, barely 10mm long.

SCORPION FLIES
ORDER MECOPTERA

A very small order of insects as far as N Europe is concerned, with just 4 species in Britain, and about 8 through the region. They are mostly quite distinctive, with a strongly defined downward-pointing beak on the head (see photo); the abdomen of the males of most species is upturned, resembling that of a scorpion. They are scavengers or weakly predatory, and the larvae resemble a moth caterpillar.

Common Scorpion Fly
Panorpa communis

This species follows the general pattern described above. The body is mainly black and yellow, about 20mm long, with a wingspan of about 30mm. The wings are spotted with black and black-tipped (though the pattern is variable).

Habitat Open woods, hedgerows and scrub.

Status and distribution Widespread and generally frequent.

Season 4–8, most frequently seen in early summer.

Similar species
P. germanica is very similar in size and shape but has lighter wing markings and parallel male 'pincers' (more calliper-shaped in Common Scorpion Fly, but not easy to separate). Similar habitats, but less common.
P. cognata is smaller, and the sixth abdominal segment is noticeably square. Similar habitats, local.
★ *P. meridionalis* is a more heavily spotted species, from central France southwards.

Snow Flea
Boreus hyemalis

Resembles the other scorpion flies in having the same 'beak' and similar body shape, but is much smaller (barely 10mm long) and very short-winged. The male has no upturned abdomen. The body is dark, and the female has a sword-like ovipositor.

Habitat Mossy places, especially where there is regular snow.

Status and distribution Locally common, mainly northern and upland.

Season Through the winter, from 10 onwards; very hardy and active even in snow.

Snow Flea

Snake Fly, *Raphidia notata*

Raphidia maculicollis

Common Scorpion Fly, female

Common Scorpion Fly, male

Panorpa meridionalis

BUTTERFLIES AND MOTHS
ORDER LEPIDOPTERA

A large and important order, with many familiar species. Collectively, they have 2 pairs of membranous wings, heavily clothed with coloured scales that give pattern and colour. A few species have wingless females. The mouthparts are usually in the form of a long slender tube, spirally coiled when not in use, used for sucking nectar and other fluids, though some species do not feed as adults, and have reduced mouthparts.

The larvae (caterpillars) are all herbivorous, and some are well known as pests. Caterpillars usually have 3 pairs of true legs at the head end, and several (usually 5) pairs of stumpy prolegs towards the rear. The number of prolegs can help to distinguish Lepidoptera caterpillars from those of sawflies (see p.240), which nearly always have 6 or more pairs of prolegs.

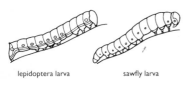

lepidoptera larva   sawfly larva

The division into butterflies and moths is not matched by an exact scientific division: both groups are drawn from a range of families. **Butterflies** are all day-flying, brightly coloured, and usually rest with the wings held together over the head, except when sunbathing. They have slender clubbed antennae, similar in males and females. **Moths** are mainly nocturnal (though there are many day-fliers), and tend to have duller colours (though there are many bright ones). The wings are usually held flat, or angled roof-like over the body. The antennae of moths are nearly always *not* clubbed, and they are usually hairy or feathery, especially in males.

Butterflies

All the regularly occurring British species are covered in the following pages, together with many of those from the rest of the region. The larvae are only described and/or illustrated where they are especially striking or frequently seen.

Swallowtail
Papilio machaon
A large distinctive butterfly, with a wingspan of 70–80mm, boldly marked with black and yellow. The hindwings have long tails, an uncommon feature in N European butterflies. Males and females are similar. Larvae are green and black striped, with red dots.
Habitat Confined to damp fens in the UK; more widespread in rough flowery places on the Continent. Various Umbelliferae are the food-plants.
Status and distribution Rare and confined to East Anglia in the UK; widespread and frequent throughout the Continent.
Season Usually 6–9.
Similar species
See Scarce Swallowtail, below.

* Scarce Swallowtail
Iphiclides podalirius
A striking species, resembling the Swallowtail, but the wings have a more striped (rather than netted) appearance, and the 'tails' are even longer. The pale areas are cream-coloured rather than yellow in fresh specimens. The larva is green, with small red dots and yellow stripes.
Habitat Warm, sheltered grassy/scrubby areas. The food-plants include Hawthorn, Blackthorn and various cultivated fruit trees.
Status and distribution A southern species, extending to N Germany but very local through most of the region.
Season 5–9, depending on latitude.

Swallowtail, male

Swallowtail

Swallowtail, larva

Scarce Swallowtail

* Black-veined White
Aporia crataegi

An attractive medium-large butterfly, with a wingspan of about 60mm. Distinguished from other 'whites' by the conspicuous black veining on the wings, especially the underside. Sexes broadly similar.

Habitat The food-plants are Blackthorn and Hawthorn, and the butterflies occur in many flowery places with these shrubs.

Status and distribution Widespread, though declining in the north; common in the south. Extinct in Britain.

Season 5–7.

Similar species
Might be confused with Black-veined Moth *Siona lineata* (see p.168), but this is only half the size.

Large White
Pieris brassicae

A familiar butterfly, easily the largest of the common 'whites', with a wingspan of 60–70mm. Basically white, with black forewing-tips. Female has black spots on upper side of forewings, and is yellower below.

Habitat Almost anywhere, especially in gardens, wherever cruciferous food plants (including *Brassica* species) occur; a very mobile butterfly.

Status and distribution Widespread and common or abundant throughout, though varying year to year.

Season 4–10.

Similar species
See Small White, below.

Small White
Pieris rapae

A medium-sized butterfly, very familiar as the archetypal 'Cabbage White'. Wingspan about 40–50mm; basically white, with blackish forewing-tips, and females have more marked black spotting. Much smaller than Large White, and less boldly marked.

Habitat Almost anywhere flowery, but especially common around gardens. Not as mobile as the Large White.

Status and distribution Very common everywhere; a frequent pest of gardens and crops.

Season 4–10.

Green-veined White
Pieris napi

An attractive butterfly, slightly smaller than the Small White, and distinguished by the lines of grey-green scales along the veins on the undersides of the hindwings; in general second-generation butterflies (in summer) are less 'green-veined' than spring ones.

Habitat A variety of flowery, damp, usually sunny habitats, less commonly in gardens and never a pest of *Brassica* species. Main food-plants are Garlic Mustard and Cuckoo Flower.

Status and distribution Common throughout, though never abundant.

Season 3–9, depending on location.

Similar species
See Bath White, below.

* Bath White
Pontia daplidice

An attractive butterfly, similar to Green-veined White in size. The undersides of the hindwings, in particular, are heavily mottled with greenish-grey, more extensively than in Green-veined White; upper surfaces of wings are spotted and mottled with black.

Habitat Rough, warm, flowery places. Food-plants include Wild Mignonette and various crucifers.

Status and distribution An occasional vagrant to the UK. A southern species that reaches north to S Scandinavia, but becomes rare north of the Alps.

Season 4–9, usually with a gap in the middle.

Similar species
See Orange-tip (female), below.

Black-veined White

Large White

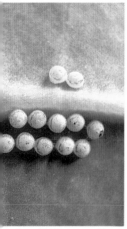

Large White, eggs on cabbage

Large White, caterpillars
Small White

Green-veined White
Bath White

Orange-tip
Anthocharis cardamines

A medium-small butterfly, with a wingspan of about 45mm. Males are very distinctive, white above with extensive orange wing-tips edged with black; females lack the orange and have a larger black tip. Below, the hindwings are marbled, rather like a Bath White, though the upper surface has much less black than that species.

Habitat Flowery, often damp places, such as wet meadows and wood borders. Its main food-plants include Cuckoo Flower and Garlic Mustard.

Status and distribution A common species throughout the area, except the extreme north, but rarely abundant.

Season 4–6.

Clouded Yellow
Colias crocea

Beautiful and distinctive butterflies (as a group), with a wingspan of about 50–55mm. The wings are bright yellow-orange above, with broad black margins; the undersides are yellow, with small black spots and a double white spot on the hind-wings, ringed with pink.

Habitat Sunny, flowery places, especially common in Lucerne fields. Food-plants include Lucerne, vetches and other legumes.

Status and distribution Widespread, occurring throughout the area; it migrates into the area from the south, breeds in good years, but does not survive the north-ern winters; very variable in abundance.

Season 4–10.

Similar species

* Pale Clouded Yellow *C. hyale* is very similar, but slightly smaller and with pale yellow upper surfaces to wings (almost white in female). Similar habitats to Clouded Yellow, though rather less com-mon or widespread. Rare vagrant in UK.

* Berger's Clouded Yellow *C. australis* is very hard to separate from Pale Clouded Yellow, though upper hindwing of Berger's is usually brighter yellow in males. Still sometimes considered as a variety of Pale. Similar habitats, though generally more southern.

Brimstone
Gonepteryx rhamni

An attractive and distinctive large butterfly; wingspan about 60mm. Both sexes have 'leaf-shaped' wings; males are bright yellow all over (the original 'butter fly') and could not easily be confused with any other species; females are greenish-white, though their shape and lack of black separates them from the 'whites'.

Habitat A very mobile species, mainly occurring in open woodland and scrub, and rough flowery places. The larval food-plants are Alder Buckthorn and Purging Buckthorn.

Status and distribution Widespread and common throughout, except N Britain.

Season 3–10, usually with a gap in mid-summer; adults hibernate and may emerge on warm winter days.

Wood White
Leptidea sinapis

A small delicate butterfly, with a wingspan of about 40mm. Basically white with grey-ish markings and males have black tips to forewings; no black spots. Flight is much more delicate and fluttery than Small White.

Habitat Sheltered flowery places such as woodland rides.

Status and distribution Widespread through most of the area, though very local in the Low Countries, and absent from N Britain; common in Ireland.

Season 5–9, usually with a gap in mid-summer in any one place.

Orange-tip, male

Orange-tip, male

Clouded Yellow, male

Clouded Yellows, mating

Brimstone, male

Wood White, male

HAIRSTREAKS Members of the large family Lycaenidae (which also includes the Blues and Coppers). The hairstreaks are quite a distinctive group, generally brownish in colour, with short 'tails' on the hindwings, and there are often white streaks on the undersides of the wings.

Brown Hairstreak
Thecla betulae

A small butterfly; wingspan about 35mm. Upper wing surfaces brown (with a large orange patch on the female's forewing), but undersurfaces essentially orange, streaked with white.

Habitat Open woodland, scrub and hedgerows; most frequently seen high in the trees, occasionally coming down to flowers. Inconspicuous. The main food-plant is Blackthorn.

Status and distribution Very local in England, north to the Midlands; widespread, though never common, on the Continent.

Season 7–9.

Purple Hairstreak
Quercusia quercus

Similar in size to Brown Hairstreak, with typical hairstreak shape, but with grey underwings and iridescent purple-blue upper surfaces (overall in males, but at base of forewings only in females).

Habitat Older woodland areas, especially where mature oaks are present. Tends to keep high in the trees, only rarely coming down. Oak is the main food-plant.

Status and distribution Widespread throughout, except for N Britain. Quite common, though easily overlooked.

Season 6–8.

* Ilex Hairstreak
Nordmannia ilicis

A predominantly brown hairstreak, though both sexes have white lines and orange dots below; the female has an orange spot on the upper surface of the forewing.

Habitat Open woodland and scrub, visiting flowers more readily than most hairstreaks.

Status and distribution Widespread north to S Scandinavia, but very local in the north of its range.

Season 6–8.

White-letter Hairstreak
Strymonidia w-album

Slightly smaller than the above hairstreaks; generally brown, with orange below, and white streaks partly in the form of a 'W' – hence the Latin and English names.

Habitat Open woodland and hedgerows, where Elm is present. The food-plant is Elm, and it rarely strays far from them. Most often seen up in the trees, but does come down to Bramble and Privet flowers.

Status and distribution Local in S Britain; more widespread on the Continent, though never common, and absent from some areas.

Season 6–8.

Similar species

See Black Hairstreak, below.

Black Hairstreak
Strymonidia pruni

A predominantly brown hairstreak, with a wingspan of about 35mm. Both sexes similar, almost always seen with their wings closed; the undersides are golden-brown, with a white line and a broad orange band towards the edge, fringed with black dots. Can resemble White-letter, but these rows of black dots are much more distinct in Black Hairstreak.

Habitat Woodland edges and clearings, or old hedges near woodland. Its main food-plant is Blackthorn (or, less often, other species of *Prunus*), and it does not move far from it.

Status and distribution Very local in the UK, only in the SE English Midlands. More widespread on the Continent, but local and absent from many western areas.

Season 6–8.

Brown Hairstreak, female

Purple Hairstreak, female

Ilex Hairstreak

White-letter Hairstreak

Black Hairstreak, female

Black Hairstreak, larva

Green Hairstreak
Callophrys rubi

A small butterfly, with a wingspan of 30–35mm; similar in shape to other hairstreaks, but with the 'tails' much reduced. The undersides of the wings are an unmistakable iridescent green, with an interrupted white streak; the dull brown upper surfaces are rarely seen.

Habitat A variety of habitats, including heathland, pastures and open woodland, reflecting its wide range of food-plants, which include Bilberry, Dyer's Greenweed, Rock-rose and various legumes.

Status and distribution Widespread throughout the area, though rather local; rare in northern Britain.

Season 4–7.

BLUES AND COPPERS The remainder of the family Lycaenidae is made up of these 2 groups which are, as their name suggests, generally blue or coppery in appearance. More extreme examples of coppers and blues are quite distinct, but some species, and especially some females, overlap. They are all small butterflies, frequently with underwings heavily dotted black, often edged with orange.

Small Copper
Lycaena phlaeas

An attractive little butterfly, with a wingspan of 30–35mm. Generally orange in appearance, with forewings above being orange, dotted and edged with black; hindwings are brown edged with orange; below, the wings are orange, dotted with black, though rather variable.

Habitat Rough, sunny, flowery places, including pastures and heaths, wherever its most frequent food-plant – Sheep's Sorrel – occurs.

Status and distribution Widespread and moderately common throughout the area, though rare or declining in intensively agricultural parts.

Season 4–9 in several generations.

Similar species
* Sooty Copper *Heodes tityrus* is similar in size and shape, but much darker brown – males are almost all dark brown. Widespread on the Continent from N Germany southwards.

Large Copper
Lycaena dispar

A distinctly larger insect; wingspan up to 45mm. Very strongly orange-coloured, with upper surfaces of wings almost entirely so, edged with black; undersides appear more greyish, because the hindwings (which are most visible) are grey, dotted black and edged with orange.

Habitat Damp grassy places such as fens, where its main food-plant, Great Water Dock, occurs.

Status and distribution Very rare, introduced, in the UK, in E Anglia only. On the Continent, mainly in central Europe; absent from much of W France and Scandinavia.

Season 6–9.

Similar species
* Scarce Copper *Heodes virgaureae* has males that look very similar above, but are brown spotted black below; females are heavily spotted with black above. Similar habitats, but more local and eastern.

* Purple-edged Copper
Palaeochrysophanus hippothoe

Broadly similar in form to Large Copper, though smaller in size and, as the name suggests, with a purple edge to the hindwing, and a broad dark edge on both wings. The undersides are pale grey-brown, with fine dark spots.

Habitat In damp fields and poor fens, feeding on species of dock and *Polygonum*.

Status and distribution Local and mainly eastern on the Continent, commonest in hilly areas.

Season 6–8.

Green Hairstreak, female

Small Copper

Small Copper

Scarce Copper
Large Copper

Purple-edged Copper

★ Short-tailed Blue
Everes argiades

A small butterfly, about 25mm across. Upper sides of wings almost wholly blue (male), edged darker, while females are brown; both sexes have a distinct short tail on the hindwings; undersides pearly-grey with fine lines of black dots, and orange on hindwings.

Habitat Flowery, grassy places, feeding on various legumes.

Status and distribution Widespread on the Continent, but absent from much of the north-west.

Season 5–8.

Similar species

★ **Long-tailed Blue** *Lampides boeticus* is rather similar, but the tails are more conspicuous, with 2 black dots on the wing close to them. Undersides have a latticed pattern. Similar habitats, from central Germany southwards.

Long-tailed Blue

Small or Little Blue
Cupido minimus

As the name suggests, a very small butterfly, with a wingspan of about 25mm, though variable in size. The upper surfaces of the wings are uniform in colour, bluish-black in males, browner in females, with a white fringe. Undersides blue with black dots, no orange.

Habitat Dry, flowery grassland, where the food-plant Kidney Vetch occurs.

Status and distribution Widespread throughout the area, but rather local, and absent from some parts.

Season 5–7.

Holly Blue
Celastrina argiolus

A medium-sized blue; wingspan about 35mm. The upper surfaces of the wings are clear blue, edged with black (narrowly in males, more broadly in females, which can look very dark); the undersides are grey-blue with black dots, no orange.

Habitat Open woods, hedges and gardens, wherever the two food-plants, Holly and Ivy, are present. The spring and summer generations alternate between these two food-plants respectively.

Status and distribution Widespread throughout, though absent from N Britain; rarely common, and prone to wide fluctuations in numbers.

Season 4–9, with a gap in the middle.

Similar species

★ **Green-underside Blue** *Glaucopsyche alexis* is slightly larger, similar in pattern but darker blue above, and the greyish underside has an iridescent greenish patch on the hindwing. Absent from the UK and much of NW Europe, widespread elsewhere.

Chalkhill Blue
Lysandra coridon

A large blue; wingspan almost 40mm. Males are very distinctive, pale silvery blue above, with a dark margin and a chequered fringe; females are brown. The underwings are paler than most species, heavily spotted with black, and orange towards the hindwing margins.

Habitat Flowery chalk or limestone hillsides, where Horseshoe Vetch or related small legumes occur.

Status and distribution In UK, confined to S England; a southern species on the Continent, from central Germany southwards.

Season 6–8.

Short-tailed Blue, male

Small Blues, mating

Holly Blue, male

Green-underside Blue, male

Chalkhill Blue, female aberrant form

Chalkhill Blue, male

Silver-studded Blue
Plebejus argus

A smallish blue; wingspan about 30mm. Upper surface of male is blue, with a broad black border on the forewing, and a white fringe; females are browner, with a band of orange spots near the edge. The undersides are pearly-grey, with orange spots; a few of these on the hindwing have blue 'studs' – a distinctive feature, shared only by the Idas Blue.

Habitat Most frequent on heaths, less common in grassy places; heather and various legumes are the food-plants.

Status and distribution Local and strongly southern in the UK, widespread throughout the Continent.

Season 6–8.

Similar species

* Idas Blue *Lycaeides idas* is almost identical, differing in tiny details such as the absence of a spine on the front tibia. Widespread in rough, flowery places, especially acid and/or upland.

* Mazarine Blue
Cyaniris semiargus

Rather similar in size and colour to the Silver-studded Blue, though the undersides of the wings are greyish-blue with dark spots, completely lacking any orange markings.

Habitat Flowery rough grasslands. The larvae feed on various legumes.

Status and distribution Became extinct in the UK at the end of the 19th century. Widespread throughout the rest of N Europe.

Season 6–8.

Brown Argus
Aricia agestis

A medium-sized blue; wingspan is about 30mm. Both sexes are similar, basically brown, very similar to females of other blues such as the Common Blue (see p.132). However, they are a clearer brown, lacking any blue tinge, with bright orange spots on both wings and a black spot in the centre of the forewing; the undersides are much paler.

Habitat Sunny, rough, flowery places, where rock-rose, storksbills or cranesbills are abundant.

Status and distribution Local and strongly southern in the UK; mainly southern on the Continent, reaching N Germany.

Season 5–8.

Similar species

Northern Brown Argus (or **Mountain Argus**) *A. artaxerxes* is very similar (and still sometimes described as a variant of Brown Argus). The orange spots are smaller, and there is usually a white spot on each forewing. A butterfly of northern and mountain areas; very local in the UK from Derbyshire northwards.

Silver-studded Blue, male

Mazarine Blue, male

Idas Blues, mating

Brown Argus, female
Northern Brown Argus, female

Northern Brown Argus, female

Large Blue
Maculinea arion

One of the largest blues, with a wingspan of 40–45mm. The upper surfaces of the wings are blue with black border and black spots; the undersides are greyish-brown, heavily dotted with black and suffused with blue, but lacking orange. The extraordinary life-history of this insect is described on p.19.

Habitat Rough, flowery places where wild thyme and the correct ant species occur.

Status and distribution Became extinct in the UK about 1979, now reintroduced very locally. More widespread on the Continent, though absent from many lowland and intensively farmed areas.

Season 6–8.

Similar species

★ **Alcon Blue** *M. alcon* is similar, but with fewer black spots on the upper surfaces; generally slightly more purplish than the Large Blue. Similar distribution and habitats, on gentians.

Adonis Blue
Lysandra bellargus

Similar in size to Chalkhill Blue. In N Europe, the males are very distinctive (though there are similar species further south in Europe), bright turquoise blue, with noticeable black lines through the white fringe; females are brown above with orange marginal spots. Very similar to Chalkhill Blue on the underside.

Habitat Warm flowery places on limestone and chalk, usually with short turf, where Horseshoe Vetch occurs.

Status and distribution Very local and strongly southern in UK; as Chalkhill on the Continent.

Season 5–9.

Similar species

Common Blue (below) is probably most similar, though females are likely to be confused with several species.

Common Blue
Polyommatus icarus

Slightly smaller than Adonis Blue, with a wingspan of about 35–37mm. Males are bright blue above (less intense than Adonis), with a wholly white fringe. Females very variable above, from brown to almost blue, with orange spots on the margins.

Habitat Flowery, sunny places, on a variety of soils. Food-plants include Bird's Foot Trefoil and other legumes.

Status and distribution Widespread and common throughout; generally the commonest blue.

Season 5–9.

Duke of Burgundy
Hamearis lucina

A small butterfly; wingspan 30mm. Related to the blues but with the markings of a fritillary. The upper surfaces are dark brown spotted with orange; females have much more orange than males. Below, there are 2 prominent white bands on the hindwings.

Habitat Open woodland, scrub and rough sheltered grassland where the food-plants, Cowslip or Primrose, occur.

Status and distribution Very local and confined to England in UK; widespread on the Continent, becoming commoner southwards from S Scandinavia.

Season 5–6 in UK, 5–9 elsewhere.

Adonis Blue, male

Adonis Blue, mating

Common Blue, male

Common Blue, mating

Duke of Burgundy, female

Tortoiseshells, Fritillaries and Admirals, Family Nymphalidae

A very large family, too broad in character to summarize satisfactorily, but containing many of our largest and most colourful butterflies. Most species, especially males, have only 2 pairs of legs fully developed, with the front pair much reduced and often furry.

Purple Emperor
Apatura iris

A beautiful, large butterfly, with a wingspan of 75–85mm (females are larger). The sexes are similar, though the male is a richer purple, visible in certain lights; there is a broad white band across the upper surface of the wings, uninterrupted on the hindwing.

Habitat Woodland, where both old trees and Broad-leaved Sallow (the larval food-plant) are present.

Status and distribution Local and confined to S England in the UK; more widespread on the Continent, but absent from most of Scandinavia.

Season 7–8.

Similar species
* **Lesser Purple Emperor** *A. ilia* is slightly smaller, with paler brown (not black) tips to the antennae, and an orange-ringed spot on the forewings. Similar distribution, though less common and more southern.

The following two species could be confused with Purple Emperors.

White Admiral
Limenitis camilla

Similar in general pattern to Purple Emperors, but smaller, 60–65mm wingspan, rather darker, without the purple sheen. There are no orange spots on the hindwings or forewings. A more conspicuous butterfly than the previous two, coming frequently to flowers and gliding around in the sunshine.

Habitat Woodland; the food-plant is Honeysuckle, and the adults love Bramble flowers.

Status and distribution Local and southern in the UK; widespread on the Continent from S Scandinavia southwards.

Season 6–8.

Similar species
* **Poplar Admiral** *L. populi* is as large as a Purple Emperor; the hindwings have a distinctive orange band near the edge on the upper side, and a bluish border below. Widespread on the Continent, though rare in the west.

* Camberwell Beauty
Nymphalis antiopa

A large, beautiful and unmistakable species, with a wingspan of 65–70mm. The combination of colours on the upper surfaces – rich deep brown, bordered by blue spots and a creamy-yellow margin (paler after hibernation) – is distinctive.

Habitat Woodland and open flowery glades – a very mobile species. Food-plants include several willow species and other broadleaved trees.

Status and distribution An occasional vagrant to the UK, never establishing. Widespread throughout the Continent, though never abundant.

Season 3–4 and 6–8.

Large Tortoiseshell
Nymphalis polychloros

A large butterfly, with a wingspan of 65–70mm, very reminiscent of the much more familiar Small Tortoiseshell (see p.136) in colouring, though duller orange and with the blue forewing marginal spots greatly reduced or absent – they are very prominent in Small Tortoiseshell. The underwings are pale brown, undistinguished.

Habitat Open woodland, glades and rides; the main food-plant is Elm, though many other broadleaved trees may be used.

Status and distribution Very rare in the UK, and highly unpredictable; widespread but not common on the Continent.

Season 2–4 and 6–8, hibernating as adults (and occasionally appearing).

Similar species
See Small Tortoiseshell, p.136.

Purple Emperor, male

Purple Emperor, male

White Admiral

White Admiral, larva

Camberwell Beauty

Large Tortoiseshell, female

Peacock
Inachis io

A conspicuous, familiar and unmistakable butterfly, with a wingspan of up to 70mm. The upperwings are boldly patterned, with a red-brown ground colour, large blue 'eye-spots' on all 4 wings, and a scalloped edge; the undersides are dark and virtually without pattern. The larvae are black and spiky, gregarious.

Habitat In many flowery places, including gardens – a mobile species. The larval food-plant is Stinging Nettle.

Status and distribution Widespread and common throughout, with strong migrations occurring in some years.

Season 3–5 and 7–9, overwintering as an adult and occasionally appearing on warm days.

Red Admiral
Vanessa atalanta

Another large, familiar, unmistakable butterfly, with a wingspan of up to 72mm. Both sexes are similar, with brown velvety wings, each with a scarlet stripe, and a black-and-white tip to the forewings.

Habitat A mobile species, occurring anywhere there are flowers (or fruit in autumn), including gardens. The larval food-plant is Stinging Nettle.

Status and distribution A migratory species, moving in from the south every year and breeding, but few survive the winter. Widespread and generally common throughout.

Season 5–10.

Painted Lady
Cynthia cardui

A large, distinctive species with wingspan of up to 70mm. Sexes similar, with a ground colour of orange on the upper surfaces, blotched with black, and tipped with black and white on the forewing; forewing underside is similar but paler, but the hindwing has a pale, intricate pattern edged with blue spots. Migrant individuals are generally paler.

Habitat Almost anywhere flowery – a very mobile species. The food-plants are usually thistles, less often nettles.

Status and distribution Migrant, moving northwards each year, occurring throughout the area in variable numbers.

Season 4–10.

Small Tortoiseshell
Aglais urticae

A familiar medium-sized butterfly, with a wingspan of 50–55mm. Generally tawny-orange above, both wings edged with a line of blue spots; undersides brown, striped paler and edged with blue. Larvae are black and yellow, spiky, and gregarious but much smaller than those of Peacock.

Habitat Almost anywhere that there are flowers – a very mobile species. The larval food-plants are Stinging Nettle and Small Nettle.

Status and distribution Widespread and abundant throughout.

Season 3–10.

Similar species
See Large Tortoiseshell (p.134).

Comma
Polygonia c-album

Another distinctive species, with a wingspan of 55–60mm. Upper surfaces of wings tawny and black, rather fritillary-like, but with very ragged edges to the wings producing a distinctive shape. Underneath the wings are dark, but with a conspicuous white 'comma' in the centre of the hindwing – the basis of the English and scientific names.

Habitat Open woods, clearings, hedgerows and gardens, but very mobile. The food-plants are Stinging Nettle, Elms and Hop.

Status and distribution Widespread and generally common throughout, decreasing northwards, where it occurs mainly as a migrant. Absent from Scotland.

Season 3–9, but adults hibernate and may be seen occasionally on warm winter days.

Peacock

Red Admiral

Red Admiral

Painted Lady

Small Tortoiseshell

Small Tortoiseshell, larva
Comma

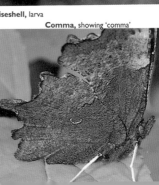

Comma, showing 'comma'

★ Map Butterfly
Araschnia levana

A curious butterfly; the 2 seasonal generations are quite different in appearance. First brood individuals resemble Wall Browns above, though with blue spots on the hindwing; the second generation resemble small White Admirals. Both generations have a striking grid pattern (the 'map') on the undersides. The wingspan of both generations is 35–40mm. The eggs are laid in strings, hanging below leaves.

Map Butterfly,
egg strings

Habitat Open woodland and scrub. The food-plant is Stinging Nettle.

Status and distribution A central European species, extending patchily westwards into France; locally common, and recently spreading.

Season 4–9.

FRITILLARIES   A broadly homogeneous group within the Nymphalids. Virtually all are tawny marked with black, but they vary considerably in size. For many species, on the Continent at least, a view of the underside of the wings is needed for certain identification.

Silver-washed Fritillary
Argynnis paphia

A beautiful butterfly, the largest of the fritillaries, with a wingspan of almost 80mm for the larger females. Upper sides are typical fritillary – tawny, mottled and streaked with black, with males being paler and more orangey. The undersides are, as the name suggests, washed with silver.

Habitat Woodland, where it particularly favours flowery rides and clearings. The food-plants are various violet species, and the eggs are laid on nearby large trees.

Status and distribution A south-western species in the UK, though more widespread in Ireland. Widespread and locally common on the Continent.

Season 6–8.

Dark Green Fritillary
Mesoacidalia (Argynnis) aglaja

Generally similar in appearance to Silver-washed, though smaller, with a wingspan of up to 70mm. The undersides of the hindwings are greenish, with large white spots.

Habitat Flowery, grassy places such as downland, dunes and undercliffs, occasionally heaths; the food-plants are various violets.

Status and distribution Scattered throughout the UK, rarest in the east; widespread and locally common on the Continent.

Season 6–8.

Similar species

High Brown Fritillary *Fabriciana (Argynnis) adippe* is very similar to the Dark Green, and is best distinguished by the hind underwing, which has a row of red dots with silver pupils towards the edge; on the forewing underside, Dark Green has a row of distinct white spots which are less distinct in High Brown. More likely to be seen in woodland than Dark Green, but the two do overlap. Rare, declining and western in UK; widespread, away from cultivated lowlands, on the Continent.

★ **Niobe Fritillary** *F. niobe* is very similar, but the hind underwings have strongly marked black veins. Widespread on the Continent, especially in the uplands.

Map Butterfly, first generation

Map Butterfly, second generation

Map Butterfly, second generation

Silver-washed Fritillary

Silver-washed Fritillary, female

Dark Green Fritillary

High Brown Fritillary

Niobe Fritillary

★ Queen of Spain Fritillary
Issoria lathonia

A medium-sized fritillary; wingspan about 45mm. Hindwing undersides have very large silver spots; overall shape slightly different from comparable fritillaries, with concave edge to forewings.

Habitat Flowery grassland and scrub, on violets.

Status and distribution Widespread throughout except in the UK, but rare and declining in the north and in agricultural lowlands. Migratory, but only rarely reaching the UK.

Season 4–9.

Similar species
★ **Lesser Marbled Fritillary** *Brenthis ino* is similar in size and colour, but has convex margins, more strongly black-fringed; below, the hindwings are marbled with yellow. Widespread on the Continent, but declining, especially in the lowlands. Prefers damp meadows.

Pearl-bordered Fritillary
Clossiana (Boloria) euphrosyne

A medium-sized fritillary, with a wingspan of about 45mm; upper sides typical fritillary-coloured; underside of hindwings boldly marked with yellow and brown, with a large white central patch, and white spots around the border (the 'pearl border').

Habitat Woodland clearings and rides, and flowery pastures.

Status and distribution Widespread but mainly western, and declining, in the UK; occurs throughout the area on the Continent, though rarely common.

Season 5–7.

Similar species
See Small Pearl-bordered Fritillary below.

Small Pearl-bordered Fritillary
Clossiana (Boloria) selene

Very similar to Pearl-bordered but slightly smaller. From above, the 2 are hard to separate, but the undersides of the hindwings of this species have many more white patches, and the general pattern is bolder and brighter.

Habitat In rather damp pastures and woodland clearings, often feeding on Marsh Violet.

Status and distribution Strongly western in the UK, though occurring as far north as N Scotland; widespread on the Continent, though declining everywhere through drainage.

Season 5–8, though slightly later than Pearl-bordered in any one site.

Similar species
★ **Weaver's Fritillary** *C. dia* is similar but slightly smaller. The hindwing undersides have 3 large white patches in a row, and small marginal white spots. Open woodland and rough grass, mainly in hilly areas; local.

Glanville Fritillary
Melitaea cinxia

Similar to Pearl-bordered in size and in its appearance from above. The undersides of the hindwings are boldly marked, with prominent white and orange alternating bands – distinctive in the UK, but less so on the Continent.

Habitat Confined in the UK to undercliffs and coastal areas; occurs more generally on the Continent, in flowery pastures. Feeds mainly on plantains.

Status and distribution Very rare in the UK, where it is found only on the Isle of Wight and in the Channel Islands; widespread and moderately frequent on the Continent.

Season 5–6 in UK, 5–9 elsewhere.

Similar species
★ **Knapweed Fritillary** *M. phoebe* is very similar in size and shape; upper side of hindwings lacks the row of spots found on the Glanville, and underside has orange dots, rather than black dots, in outermost yellow cells. Similar habitats, but more local and southern.

Queen of Spain Fritillary

Queen of Spain Fritillary

Pearl-bordered Fritillary, male

Small Pearl-bordered Fritillary

Small Pearl-bordered Fritillary

Weaver's Fritillary

Glanville Fritillary, male

Glanville Fritillary, female

★ Spotted Fritillary
Melitaea didyma
Rather similar to the Glanville, but highly variable in colouring. The undersides of the hindwings show the main differences: there is a clear row of orange patches near the margin, without dots; the upper side often looks slightly redder than the average fritillary.

Habitat Flowery pastures, on various soils. Food-plants include speedwells and plantains.

Status and distribution Widespread on the Continent from N France and S Germany southwards.

Season 5–9.

Heath Fritillary
Mellicta athalia
A very variable species; wingspan 40–45mm. The upper sides of the wings tend to be more darkly marked and evenly chequered than other species, with dark edges to the wings. Underwings very variable.

Habitat Open woods and flowery pastures, *not* usually on heaths.

Status and distribution Very rare in the UK, in a few southern sites, but beginning to increase as a result of correct management. Widespread and moderately common on the Continent.

Season 6–7 in UK; 6–9 on the Continent.

Marsh Fritillary
Eurodryas aurinia
Similar to Heath Fritillary in size. May be recognized from above by its duller colour, with more pale patches – almost like the underwings of some species. The underwings lack any silvery-white patches, and are mottled yellow and orange-brown, with yellowish margins. The larvae are black and bristly, living gregariously in loose webs, often basking openly.

Habitat Most frequent in damp rough pasture and heath, though also occurs on dry limestone grassland. The food-plant is Devil's Bit Scabious, less frequently plantains and other herbs.

Status and distribution Uncommon and declining, with a strong western tendency in the UK; widespread but local and declining on the Continent.

Marbled White
Melanargia galathea
A beautiful and distinctive butterfly, similar to no other N European species. Wingspan 53–58mm. The upper surfaces of the wings are boldly chequered black and white; the undersides are usually yellowish, marked with grey and black.

Habitat Rough ungrazed or lightly grazed flowery grassland. The food-plants are various finer grasses.

Status and distribution A southern species, absent from N Britain and Scandinavia; locally common and sometimes abundant further south.

Season 6–8.

Grayling
Hipparchia semele
A medium-large butterfly, with a wingspan of 55–60mm (though normally seen resting with wings closed). Not particularly distinctive; the visible hindwing underside is banded dark brown, pale greyish, then mid-brown; the forewings are orange below, with 2 'eye-spots'. NW European races (including British ones) are smaller than more southern ones.

Habitat Heaths and rough grassy places, especially near coasts.

Status and distribution Widespread around the coasts of the UK, less commonly inland; widespread and locally common on the Continent.

Season 6–9.

Similar species
★ **Tree Grayling** *Neohipparchia statilinus* is similar, but duller in colour, and lower 'eyespot' lacks the white pupil. In open woodland and scrub, from N France southwards.

Spotted Fritillary

Heath Fritillary

Heath Fritillary

Marsh Fritillary

Marsh Fritillary

Marbled White

Grayling

* Dryad

Minois dryas

A medium-large butterfly, with a wingspan of about 60mm. Generally mid- to dark brown in colour, with 2 'eyes' on each forewing that have orange outer rings and blue 'pupils'.

Habitat In dry grassy places, rarely fens.

Status and distribution Local, from central Germany southwards.

Season 7–9.

Mountain Ringlet

Erebia epiphron

A small butterfly; wingspan 35–40mm. Predominantly dark brown, with orange patches containing black dots; highly variable where it occurs elsewhere in Europe.

Habitat Grassy places in mountains, or moorlands. The main food-plant is Mat Grass.

Status and distribution A mountain species, occurring locally in the UK from the Lake District northwards; otherwise in mountains from the Alps southwards.

Season 6–8.

Similar species

Scotch Argus *E. aethiops* is similar in size and general appearance, though this species has bolder 'eye-spots' with white 'pupils', and more pronounced orange patches. Similar habitats, though rather more widespread on the Continent.

Meadow Brown

Maniola jurtina

A familiar medium-sized butterfly, with a wingspan of 50–58mm. Basically brown, with darker patches and orange towards the tip, in which there is a single black 'eye-spot' with I white 'pupil'. The undersides are undistinguished brown.

Habitat Rough flowery grasslands.

Status and distribution Widespread and common throughout.

Season 6–9.

Similar species

See Gatekeeper, below.

Gatekeeper

Pyronia tithonus

This species resembles a smaller version of the Meadow Brown, with a wingspan of 40–48mm. The predominant colour of the upper surfaces of the wings is orange, with a broad brown border; the forewings have single brown 'eye-spots', each with 2 white 'pupils'; these are also present on the undersides of the forewings.

Habitat Sheltered grassy places, hedgerows, woodland rides and so on.

Status and distribution Widespread and common generally, though absent from N Britain and mainland Europe north of Holland.

Season 7–9.

Ringlet

Aphantopus hyperantus

A medium-sized dark velvety brown butterfly, with a wingspan of about 50mm. The general appearance is dark brown, but the undersurfaces of both wings have several yellow-ringed 'eye-spots' with white 'pupils', also present in more subdued form on the upper surface of the hindwings. A weak flier.

Habitat Hedges, edges of grassy areas, damp meadows and occasionally bogs.

Status and distribution Widespread in UK, but local and absent from many areas. Widespread and moderately common on the Continent.

Season 6–8 (7–8 in UK).

Dryad

Mountain Ringlet

Scotch Argus, female

Meadow Brown

Gatekeeper

Gatekeeper

Ringlet

Ringlet

Large Heath
Coenonympha tullia

A medium-sized, rather greyish butterfly, with a wingspan of about 40mm. Settles with wings closed, so the hind underwings are normally seen – these are grey, irregularly banded with cream, and with 6 or so dark 'eye-spots'; northern forms (var. *scotica*) are larger and the eye-spots are much reduced, with no 'pupils'.

Habitat Bogs and moorland, where the food-plants White Beaked Sedge, Cotton Grass or various sedges occur.

Status and distribution A northern species, very local in S Britain, becoming commoner northwards; absent from most of France, but increasingly common northwards and eastwards.

Season 6–8.

Similar species

* Pearly Heath *C. arcania* is similar in size, but has a marked white band on the underside hindwing, which has a prominent ocellus to the inside of it. A widespread species in rough grassy places, especially in hilly areas.

* Chestnut Heath *C. glycerion* resembles Pearly Heath, but has a more marked orange marginal band, and less distinctive eyespots on the forewings. An eastern species, mainly in the uplands, just reaching into our area.

Small Heath
Coenonympha pamphilus

Resembles a smaller version of Large Heath, with a wingspan of only 35mm. The hindwings are greyish and furry-looking below, with a poorly defined pale band; the forewings, which are often revealed when the butterfly is resting, are orange below, edged brown, with a single 'eye-spot'.

Habitat Rough grassy places. The main food-plants are soft grasses such as fescues.

Status and distribution Widespread and common throughout.

Season 5–10.

Speckled Wood
Pararge aegeria

A medium-sized butterfly with a wingspan of 46–50mm. Northern forms (which occur over most of the area) are very distinctive mottled cream and brown above, with scalloped wing margins. Southern forms (which reach NW France) have orange in place of cream, and resemble Wall Brown (see below). It rarely visits flowers.

Habitat Shady or partially shaded places, such as woodland rides. The food-plants include various soft grasses.

Status and distribution A common species through most of the area, though very local in N Britain.

Season 3–10.

Wall Brown
Lasiommata megera

An attractive medium-sized butterfly, with a wingspan of about 45mm. They always bask with wings open, revealing the beautifully marked orange and brown upper sides, with a single large 'eye-spot' on the forewings, and 4 smaller ones on the hindwings (similar-sized fritillaries do not have these spots).

Habitat Rough grassy places, with bare ground. The food-plants include various coarse grasses such as Cocksfoot.

Status and distribution Mainly southern in Britain, where it is moderately common but declining. Widespread and quite common over most of the Continent.

Season 4–10.

Similar species

The ***** southern form of Speckled Wood (see above) looks very similar, but has scalloped wing margins and is less orange.

* Large Wall Brown *L. maera* is rather similar, very slightly larger, and with a double 'eye-spot' on each forewing. It is generally less bright in colour. In rough grassy places, widespread, though absent from many lowland areas.

Large Heath

Small Heath

Speckled Wood

Wall Brown

Skippers, Family Hesperiidae

A distinctive family of small butterflies with 40 representatives in Europe. These mostly share the habit of a darting flight, 'skipping' from flower to flower, rather than fluttering or gliding. Some of the skippers tend to hold their wings angled at about 45° when sunbathing, and the Dingy Skipper wraps its wings around the body when roosting. Skippers are generally the most moth-like of the butterflies.

Grizzled Skipper
Pyrgus malvae
A small butterfly; wingspan 25–28mm. The upper surfaces of the wings are attractively chequered white and dark brown, and the fringes are barred with brown. The undersides are similar but duller. A distinctive species in Britain, but there are increasing numbers of similar species further south.
Habitat In sheltered flowery sites, such as woodland clearings. The food-plants include Wild Strawberry, cinquefoils and other members of the rose family.
Status and distribution Only in the south of the UK, where it is local; widespread but local on the Continent.
Season 5–6 in UK, 5–8 in Europe.

★ Large Grizzled Skipper
Pyrgus alveus
Similar in general appearance to Grizzled Skipper, but distinctly larger (wingspan up to 33mm), and with much less white on the upper surfaces of the hindwings; the undersides of the hindwings have larger white patches, and a greenish tinge.
Habitat Rough flowery grassland, mainly in hilly areas.
Status and distribution Widespread on the Continent generally, though absent from much of the Low Countries.
Season 5–9.

Dingy Skipper
Erynnis tages
Similar in shape and size to Grizzled Skipper, but duller, overall brown with small blurred white and darker patches. The underwings are light greyish-orange.
Habitat Rough, warm, flowery places with bare ground. The main food-plants are Bird's-foot Trefoil and other legumes.
Status and distribution Scattered in the UK, mainly southern, becoming coastal further north. Widespread throughout on the Continent.
Season 5–8.

★ Large Chequered Skipper
Heteropterus morpheus
Slightly larger than Dingy Skipper. Upper sides of wings brown flecked with yellow; undersides conspicuous and distinctive, with numerous large oval white spots on a brownish-yellow background.
Habitat Rough, damp, grassy areas. Food-plants include various larger grasses.
Status and distribution Local in heathy and upland areas on the Continent.
Season 6–8.

Chequered Skipper
Carterocephalus palaemon
A beautiful little butterfly, with a wingspan of about 30mm. Upper wing surfaces boldly chequered with white or yellow patches on brown; the underwings are similar but duller.
Habitat Woodland clearings and sheltered scrubby grassland. Food-plants include Purple Moor Grass and other grasses.
Status and distribution In the UK, it has become extinct in England, but is very locally common in the W Highlands of Scotland. More widespread on the Continent, but local.
Season 5–7.

Grizzled Skipper

Dingy Skipper

Large Chequered Skipper

Chequered Skipper, male

Lulworth Skipper
Thymelicus acteon

One of the 'golden skippers' (as are all the following species) which rest with their wings at 45°. This is both the smallest (wingspan about 26mm) and the darkest of the group, and the females have a gold circle on the forewings (upper side). The undersides of the antennae tips are cream-coloured.

Habitat Rough grassland, where Tor Grass or bromes occur.

Status and distribution Very restricted in UK, on the Dorset and Devon coasts. Widespread on the Continent from N Germany southwards, rare in the north.

Season 6–9.

Small Skipper
Thymelicus sylvestris

A small golden-brown butterfly, with few positive distinguishing features. Brighter than Lulworth (above) and lacking the golden circles; smaller and less boldly marked than Large Skipper (see below). Essex Skipper can only be satisfactorily separated by looking at the undersides of the antennae: black in Essex, orange in Small.

Habitat Many kinds of rough grassy places with flowers. Food-plants include various coarse grasses.

Status and distribution Common in S Britain, absent from Scotland; widespread on the Continent.

Season 5–8.

Essex Skipper
Thymelicus lineola

Resembles Small Skipper very closely. It can only be reliably distinguished by the black undersides to the antennae, though with experience the slightly paler colour and the slightly shorter sex brand on the male's forewing, which runs roughly parallel to the wing margin (angled slightly towards it in the Small Skipper) can be used.

Habitat Found in rough grassy places, including fens and the upper parts of salt-marshes.

Status and distribution Locally common in south-eastern parts of Britain; absent elsewhere. Widespread throughout N Europe.

Season 5–8.

Silver-spotted Skipper
Hesperia comma

An attractive skipper; wingspan 30–35mm. Its most distinctive feature is the undersides of the wings, which are greenish-brown marked with conspicuous white spots, brighter in females. The upper surfaces are similar but less boldly marked, with more orange.

Habitat Chalk grassland and similar places with short grass and bare soil. Food-plants include fescues and other fine grasses.

Status and distribution Rare and declining in the UK, confined to S England. Widespread and locally frequent on the Continent.

Season 6–9 in Europe, 8–9 in UK.

Large Skipper
Ochlodes venatus

Rather similar to Small Skipper, but larger (to 36mm), and with upper surfaces of wings distinctly marked with squarish orange patches towards the edges, separated by dark veins. The undersides are similar but less boldly marked, though distinct from the plain undersides of Small, Essex and Lulworth.

Habitat Grassy, flowery places of all kinds. Food-plants include Cocksfoot and other coarse grasses.

Status and distribution Increasingly common southwards in England and Wales; widespread and common on the Continent.

Season 6–9.

Lulworth Skippers, male and female

Small Skipper

Essex Skipper

Large Skipper
Silver-spotted Skipper

Silver-spotted Skipper

Moths

The differences between moths and butterflies are discussed on p.118. Moths themselves constitute a very large group of insects, with over 3,000 species occurring in the area covered, and about 5,000 in Europe as a whole. Moths can be difficult to identify, partly because there are so many, but also because there are many variants, and individuals gradually lose their scales with age, causing the identification features to become blurred. Within the moths, some groups can be reasonably easily recognized, though as some groups may contain hundreds of species, this does not really solve the identification problem.

Moths are often separated into the larger ('macro-') moths and the 'micro-moths'. Many guides cover only the larger moths, partly because micro-moths are difficult to identify, and partly because there are so many of them. The selection of more conspicuous micro-moths featured on pp.196–201 includes some that are most visible in their larval stage (such as some of the leaf-miners).

The macro-moths, which include virtually all the familiar moths, are divided into 17 families, often grouped together into a smaller number of superfamilies. Some families are very small, others are difficult to characterize; but a few, such as clearwings, hawk-moths and so on, are worth knowing and are briefly described in the text.

Macro-moths

Orange Swift
Hepialus sylvina
A medium-sized moth; wingspan about 30mm (male) to 45mm (female). Males orange-red, striped with white; females browner. Larvae live on roots.
Habitat Widespread in many open and unimproved habitats, including gardens. Nocturnal.
Status and distribution Widespread and generally common throughout the area.
Season 6–9.
Similar species
Common Swift *H. lupulinus* is slightly smaller, with white markings on brown wings. Common almost throughout.
Gold Swift *H. hecta* is as small as Common Swift, with white markings on gold. Widespread.

Goat Moth
Cossus cossus
A large robust moth, with a wingspan of up to almost 10cm in the larger females. The wings are greyish striped and mottled darker, and the stout body is striped. The larvae are reddish-purple, and may reach 80mm long when fully grown.
Habitat The larvae live in dead wood (taking several years to mature), and the adults may be seen almost anywhere. Nocturnal.
Status and distribution Formerly widespread and moderately common, but declining steeply due to loss of larval habitat.
Season 6–8.

Leopard Moth
Zeuzera pyrina
Similar to the Goat Moth in shape, but much smaller (wingspan 50–75mm), with brighter white wings dotted with grey; the furry 'head' is white with 6 black dots.
Habitat The larvae feed in the wood of deciduous trees; adults may be seen almost anywhere with trees – woods, parks and gardens. Nocturnal.
Status and distribution Local and southern in the UK; widespread on the Continent.
Season 6–8.

Orange Swift, male

Orange Swift, female

Goat Moth, larva

Burnets and Foresters, Family Zygaenidae

Brightly coloured day-flying gregarious moths.

Common Forester
Adscita statices

An attractive and conspicuous moth despite its small size (wingspan 25–30mm). Bright, slightly bluish, green, with black antennae; commonly seen at flowers.

Habitat Rough, flowery grassland. The larvae feed on Common and Sheep's Sorrel.

Status and distribution Widespread and locally common throughout, though declining.

Season 5–7.

Similar species

Cistus Forester *A. geryon* is smaller (if same sexes are compared). It is local in dry, flowery habitats, mainly southern.

Scarce Forester *A. globulariae* is the same size as Common, but the males have pointed not thickened antennae tips. Very local and southern, feeding mainly on knapweeds.

6-spot Burnet
Zygaena filipendulae

Burnets are very distinctive as a group, with black forewings dotted with red, and red hindwings with a narrow dark border. Wingspan 30–40mm. This species has 6 red spots on each forewing. The papery pupal cases are a common sight attached to grasses.

Habitat Grassy, flowery places of all kinds.

Status and distribution Common and widespread, throughout the area.

Season 5–9.

Similar species

See the following two species.

5-spot Burnet
Zygaena trifolii

Very like 6-spot, though slightly smaller, with 5 red spots on each forewing, and a broad dark margin to the hindwing.

Habitat Rough grassland, often slightly damp. The food-plants are Greater and Common Bird's-foot Trefoil.

Status and distribution A southern species, extending northwards in the UK to the English Midlands; widespread on the Continent as far north as Denmark.

Season 5–8.

Narrow-bordered 5-spot Burnet   **5-spot Burnet**

Similar species

Narrow-bordered 5-spot Burnet *Z. lonicerae* differs in that the hindwing dark border is very narrow, and the red forewing spots tend to be more separate. Occurs in all kinds of grassland, widespread but local, though often overlooked.

Transparent Burnet
Zygaena purpuralis

Similar in size and general colour to the above, but the wings are thinly scaled and translucent; the forewings are streaked with 3 indistinct marks; the hindwings are red with a very thin border.

Habitat Grassy, flowery slopes, mainly in the mountains.

Status and distribution Very local in the UK, confined to Scottish W Highlands and Islands, and W Eire; confined to hilly areas on the Continent.

Season 5–8.

Cistus Forester

6-spot Burnet

Scarce Forester, male

5-spot Burnet

5-spot Burnet, larva

Transparent Burnet

Clearwings, Family Sesiidae

Small to medium-sized moths, with wings free of scales, therefore at least partly transparent – they may resemble wasps or hornets. Mostly day-flying.

Hornet Moth
Sesia apiformis
Distinctive and attractive moth, with a wingspan of 40–50mm. Body yellow striped with brown, wings clear but edged with brown. Legs brown. Day-flying.
Habitat Open woodland and damp areas with poplars. The main food-plant is Black Poplar, less commonly other poplars; the larvae feed on the wood.
Status and distribution Widespread but local; very rare in N Britain, frequent throughout the Continent.
Season 6–8.
Similar species
Lunar Hornet Moth *S. bembeciformis* is similar, but slightly smaller, with darker head and thorax, and conspicuous orange hairs on hind legs. Similar habitats and distribution; food-plant is willow.

Currant Clearwing
Synanthedon tipuliformis
A small moth, with a wingspan of about 20mm. Body dark, with 3 (female) or 4 (male) yellow rings on abdomen. Wings clear, with brown tips and margin.
Habitat Can be found in woods and gardens, wherever wild or cultivated currants occur.
Status and distribution A locally common species in S England, becoming rarer towards the north; widespread on the Continent.
Season 5–7.
Similar species
Sallow Clearwing *S. flaviventris* is almost identical, but lacks the yellow on the abdomen; it occurs in slightly different habitats, where it feeds in Sallow stems, causing a gall-like swelling. Local in SE England, widespread on the Continent.

Red-belted Clearwing
Synanthedon myopaeformis
A small moth, with a wingspan of 20–25mm. The body is black, with a single red 'belt'; wings clear, edged black.
Habitat Woods and orchards where Apple, Rowan, Pear or related trees occur.
Status and distribution Local in S Britain, widespread on the Continent from N Germany southwards.
Season 6–8.
Similar species
Large Red-belted Clearwing *S. culiciformis* is slightly larger, and has bases of forewings dusted with red scales. Feeds on Birch and Alder. Widespread and frequent.
Red-tipped Clearwing *S. formicaeformis* has red-tipped forewings. Widespread and frequent, except in Scotland.

Six-belted Clearwing
Bembecia scopigera
Wingspan about 20mm, body rather wasp-like in colouring with six yellow bands on a black ground colour.
Habitat Rough flowery grassy places, especially on limestones. May fly by day.
Status and distribution Locally common in the south of Britain, widespread on the Continent.
Season 6–9.

December Moth
Poecilocampa populi
A medium-sized moth, with a wingspan of 40–45mm. Females much larger than males. Forewings dark grey, with white streaks; hindwings paler, body very hairy.
Habitat Wooded and well-treed countryside, feeding on various deciduous trees.
Status and distribution Widely distributed and moderately common throughout.
Season 10–12 (a time when few other moths are flying).
Similar species
Small Eggar *Eriogaster lanestris* is similar in shape and colour, but has 2 white spots on each forewing, though variable. Widespread though local and declining, flying 2–3.

Red-belted Clearwing, male

Six-belted Clearwing, female

Clearwing, larvae holes

The Lackey
Malacosoma neustria

The adult is a medium-sized moth, with a wingspan of up to 40mm; dull brown, with a darker stripe. The larvae are much more conspicuous and distinctive, being large, blue-, red- and white-striped, with long dark brown hairs. They feed on Hawthorn, Blackthorn and other shrubs.

Habitat Woods, hedges and scrub.

Status and distribution Widespread and common throughout.

Season 4–6 for larvae, 7–8 for adults.

Oak Eggar
Lasiocampa quercus quercus

A large moth, with a wingspan of up to 90mm. All wings similar, deep brown near the body, paler towards the edge, and forewings have a single white spot. Males have feathered antennae, and fly by day.

Habitat Woodland and scrub, and more open habitats – very mobile.

Status and distribution Widespread and moderately common throughout.

Season 6–8.

Similar species

Northern Eggar *L quercus callunae* is relatively unusual in that 2 subspecies have different English names. Differs mainly in that the margin of the deep brown colour turns outwards on the forewing. Similar distribution, though more local, and found more in heathy and moorland areas.

Grass Eggar *L trifolii* is rather smaller, and much paler, but with a similar pattern. Widespread in heathy places.

Fox Moth
Macrothylacia rubi

Similar in size, shape and colour to Grass Eggar, with a wingspan of 50–70mm, but distinguished by the 2 pale bars across the forewings; ground colour variable, especially in males, which may be quite red. Day-flying.

Habitat Rough grassland, heathland and moorland; food-plants include heathers, Bilberry, Bramble.

Status and distribution Widespread and common throughout.

Season 5–7.

The Drinker
Philudoria potatoria

A largish moth, with a wingspan of 50–70mm. The ground colour is yellowish to red-brown; males are darker, and both sexes have a distinctive brown diagonal line across the forewings. Males fly by day. The larvae are conspicuous and distinctive, being dark and hairy, with white marks along the side.

Habitat Rough habitats, often damp, where reeds, Bush-grass and other tall grasses grow.

Status and distribution Widespread and common throughout.

Season 7–8, larvae 9–6 (most noticeable 5–6).

The Lappet
Gastropacha quercifolia

A large moth; wingspan up to 90mm. Usually reddish-brown, with 2 wavy lines across the forewing, and scalloped edges to the wings. Males have feathery antennae.

Habitat Open woods, hedges and unimproved farmland. The larvae feed on various shrubs.

Status and distribution Absent from N Britain, widespread on the Continent.

Season 6–8.

Emperor Moth
Saturnia pavonia

A large, beautiful moth; wingspan 80–90mm. All 4 wings have large colourful 'eye-spots' in the centre on both surfaces. Males are day-flying and have feathery antennae. The larvae eventually become very conspicuous, green, with red or yellow spots and clumps of black bristles.

Habitat Mainly on heaths and moors, sometimes in other rough habitats.

Status and distribution Widespread throughout, but not common.

Season 4–6, larvae 6–7.

The Lackey

Oak Eggar, male

Fox Moth, male and female

The Drinker, female

Emperor Moth, larva ready to pupate

Emperor Moth, male

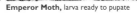

Kentish Glory
Endromis versicolora
A large, conspicuous moth; wingspan up to 90mm. The forewings are brown, marbled with white and other colours, crossed by two wavy lines. Males have feathery antennae, and fly by day. The larvae are large and green, with a point towards the hind end, resembling some hawk-moth larvae.
Habitat Moorlands and open Birch woodland. The larvae feed on Birch.
Status and distribution In the UK, now confined to the Scottish Highlands; widespread though local on the Continent.
Season 3–5.

Geometers, Family Geometridae

Small or medium-sized moths with small bodies and relatively large wings, held either spread out or in a triangular shape. Female antennae simple. Caterpillars have only 2 pairs of legs, and move in a looping fashion – they are known as 'loopers'.

Orange Underwing
Archiearis parthenias
A medium-sized moth; wingspan of 35–40mm. Forewings dark, blotched paler, but the underwings are bright orange and black. Day-flying.
Habitat Open or lightly wooded areas with Birch trees. Males may visit Sallow flowers.
Status and distribution Widespread and frequent throughout.
Season 3–4.
Similar species
Light Orange Underwing *A. notha* is slightly smaller, with paler hindwings and less variegated forewings.
   See also the underwings in the Noctuid family (p.184).

Large Emerald
Geometra papilionaria
A distinctive, medium-large moth, with a wingspan of 50–65mm. Basically greenish-blue with numerous scalloped white marks on all wings.

Habitat Woods and hedgerows. The larvae feed on Birch, Beech and other trees.
Status and distribution Widespread and moderately common throughout.
Season 6–8.
Similar species
Most other emeralds (see below) are smaller.
Light Emerald *Campaea margaritata* is almost as large, but paler yellowish-green, with an unscalloped line across the centre of the wings. It is actually in a different family. Widespread throughout.

Blotched Emerald
Comibaena pustulata
A distinctive little moth, with a wingspan of about 30mm. The emerald-green wings are blotched with brown and white, unlike any other Emerald.
Habitat Oakwoods. The larvae feed on oak.
Status and distribution Absent from N Britain, locally common further south; widespread and common on the Continent.
Season 6–7.
Similar species
Common Emerald *Hemithea aestivaria* is similar in size, but has white uneven lines across the wings, not blotches. Similar habitats and distribution.
Small Emerald *Hemistola chrysoprasaria* is larger (it is only 'small' in relation to Large Emerald!), up to 40mm across, with straight, unbroken white lines. Local on limestones, feeding on Wild Clematis.

Little Emerald
Jodis lactearia
A small moth; wingspan about 25mm. Very pale green, with only faint white lines on the wings.
Habitat Woods, hedges and anywhere with trees and shrubs. Larvae feed on various trees and shrubs.
Status and distribution Widespread and common throughout.
Season 5–7.

Kentish Glory

Orange Underwing

Large Emerald

Blotched Emerald

Birch Mocha
Cyclophora albipunctata

A small to medium moth, with a wingspan of 25–30mm. The wings are pale greyish-white, often suffused with red, and each has a central dark-edged dot.

Habitat Woodland and heathland, where Birch occurs.

Status and distribution Widespread in S Britain, general on the Continent.

Season 5–8.

Similar species

Dingy Mocha *C. pendularia* is very similar, but darker and more heavily speckled; local, mainly southern, on Sallow.

False Mocha *C. porata* is more yellowish, with darker lines across the wings. Widespread, though mainly southern.

Blood-vein
Timandra griseata

A medium-small moth; wingspan 30–35mm. The wings are pearly-grey, beautifully marked with a red stripe that runs in a single wave when the wings are held at rest. The margins of the wings are also red in colour.

Habitat A variety of open habitats, where docks, sorrels and related plants occur.

Status and distribution Widespread in the south, becoming rarer northwards.

Season 5–9.

Similar species

Small Blood-vein *Scopula imitaria* is smaller, with a yellower ground colour and less well-marked stripe. Similar distribution. The main food-plant is Privet.

Riband Wave
Idaea aversata

The wingspan of this moth is about 35mm. The ground colour is greyish-white to yellow, marked with a broad angled stripe across all four wings. Flies by day if disturbed.

Habitat In a variety of habitats, feeding on numerous herbs and shrubs.

Status and distribution Widespread and common throughout.

Season 6–9.

Silver-ground Carpet
Xanthorhoe montanata

Wingspan about 30mm. A pretty little moth, with the characteristic triangular shape of other 'carpets' when settled. The greyish-white wings have a strongly marked central black, uneven stripe.

Habitat Woods, hedgerows and other undisturbed habitats.

Status and distribution Widespread and common throughout.

Season 5–7.

Similar species

There are many other 'carpets' with a broadly similar pattern. Among the most similar are the following:

Garden Carpet *X. fluctuata* has a darker, more speckled ground colour, with the stripe less well marked. Common everywhere.

Flame Carpet *X. designata* has the black stripe replaced by red; widespread throughout.

Green Carpet *Colostygia pectinaria* has a similar pattern, but is mainly green. Widespread and frequent throughout.

Common Carpet *Epirrhoe alternata* has a reddish-grey stripe on a greyish background. Common throughout.

Purple Bar *Cosmorhoe ocellata* has a bluish-purple bar, and a dark spot towards the edge of the forewing. Common throughout.

Birch Mocha

Blood-vein

Riband Wave

Silver-ground Carpet

Garden Carpet

Green Carpet, faded specimen

Small Phoenix
Ecliptopera silaceata

A small to medium moth; wingspan 30–35mm. The forewings are dark, marbled with white and cream; the hindwings are pale, virtually unmarked.

Habitat Many open or semi-shaded habitats, where willowherbs occur.

Status and distribution Widespread and common throughout.

Season 5–8.

Similar species

Dark Marbled Carpet *Chloroclysta citrata* is similar, but has a more distinct angled pale bar across the tips of the forewings. Widespread and moderately common throughout.

Common Marbled Carpet *C. truncata* is extremely similar, usually rather darker. Widespread and common.

Argent and Sable
Rheumaptera hastata

A conspicuous medium-sized moth with a wingspan of 35–40mm. Both forewings and hindwings are boldly marked with black and white, with a clear white band crossing the middle of each wing (the northern race, *nigrescens*, has more dark markings on the wing). Partly day-flying.

Habitat A species of woodlands and moorland where Birches are present; they are the larval food-plant.

Status and distribution Widespread, but local and more frequent in upland areas.

Season 5–7.

Winter Moth
Operophtera brumata

This species has marked sexual dimorphism, as the females are flightless and virtually wingless. Males have a wingspan of about 30mm, and are pale yellowish-brown. The females are small and dark, and barely look like a moth at all. They crawl up the stems of trees to lay their eggs in crevices or on buds.

Habitat Woodlands, orchards, gardens.

Status and distribution Widespread and common throughout.

Season 10–3.

Similar species

Northern Winter Moth *O. fagata* is slightly larger, paler and shinier. Widespread, and not particularly northern.

Chimney Sweeper
Odezia atrata

A small moth; wingspan 25–30mm. Sooty-black all over, except for the margins of the wings around the tip, which are white. Day-flying.

Habitat Flowery places where the food-plant, Pignut, occurs.

Status and distribution Widespread and locally frequent throughout.

Season 5–7.

Similar species

Occasionally mistaken for a small butterfly, such as the Small Blue (see p.128). The antennae and detailed colouring are quite different.

Magpie Moth or The Magpie
Abraxas grossulariata

An attractive and distinctive moth; wingspan 42–48mm. The combination of white ground colour, heavily dotted black, with orange stripes is unmistakable. May cause damage to currant bushes.

Habitat Woods, gardens and scrub, where currants, gooseberries or Hawthorn occur.

Status and distribution Widespread and common throughout.

Season 6–8.

Similar species

Clouded Magpie *A. sylvata* is similar in size and shape, but lacks the black dots and has reduced orange and grey patches. A local woodland species.

Clouded Border *Lomaspilis marginata* is smaller, mottled deep grey and white. Common in wooded areas. See also the unrelated Small Magpie, p.198.

Small Phoenix

Chimney Sweeper

Magpie Moth

Magpie Moth, larva

Latticed Heath
Semiothisa clathrata
An attractive little moth; wingspan about 30mm. Distinctively patterned chequered brown and white wings. Male antennae not feathery. Day-flying.
Habitat Many types of open habitat, including heaths and downs. The food-plants include various legumes.
Status and distribution Widespread and common throughout.
Season 4–9.
Similar species
Netted Mountain Moth *S. carbonaria* is darker, less distinctly chequered. A moth of mountain areas, in Scotland, and widespread in N Europe.
Common Heath *Ematurga atomaria* is similar in size and colour to Latticed Heath, but lacks the strong transverse lines. Common in heathy places and open woodland throughout.

Brown Silver-line
Petrophora chlorosata
An undistinguished pale brown moth; wingspan about 35mm. Forewings are brown, with 2 darker stripes across; hindwings paler. Of interest as one of the relatively few insects to feed on Bracken.
Habitat Heaths or moors, wherever Bracken occurs.
Status and distribution Widespread and locally frequent, throughout.
Season 5–7.

Speckled Yellow
Pseudopanthera macularia
A small but unmistakable moth. Wingspan about 30mm. Wings yellow, speckled with black. Day-flying, especially in sunny weather.
Habitat Open woods, scrub and rough grassland. Food-plants include various Labiates (Mint family).
Status and distribution Widespread and locally common throughout.
Season 4–7.

Brimstone Moth
Opisthograptis luteolata
A distinctive moth, with a wingspan of 35–45mm. The wings are yellow (like a male Brimstone butterfly), and the forewings are edged with 3 red-brown blobs.
Habitat Hedges, gardens and open woods.
Status and distribution Widespread and common throughout.
Season 5–10.

Canary-shouldered Thorn
Ennomos alniaria
Wingspan 38–40mm. An attractive moth, with pinkish-yellow wings, and a furry yellow head-thorax area. The legs are furry, and the males have feathered antennae.
Habitat Woods, fens and other unimproved habitats. Food-plants include Alder and Birch.
Status and distribution Widespread and common throughout.
Season 7–10.
Similar species
Large Thorn *E. autumnaria* is larger, with thorax hairs pinkish-yellow. Forewings dark towards the tip. Common throughout.
August Thorn *E. quercinaria* is similar in size to Canary-shouldered, but duller in colour and lacking the bright yellow thorax hairs. Common throughout.

Early Thorn
Selenia dentaria
Wingspan 45–50mm, rather smaller in second-generation specimens. A greyish-brown moth, though very variable in colour, with (usually) 4 bands of deeper colour across the forewings. Rests with wings held above body, or partly raised.
Habitat Woodland, hedges and scrub.
Status and distribution Widespread and common throughout.
Season 3–9, with a gap in the middle.
Similar species
Lunar Thorn *S. lunularia* has much more jagged wing margins. Widespread but local.

Latticed Heath

Common Heath

Brown Silver-line

Speckled Yellow

Brimstone Moth

Canary-shouldered Thorn

Swallowtailed Moth
Ourapteryx sambucaria

A beautiful and distinctive moth, with a wingspan of 55–65mm. Pale yellow overall, with 2 greyish lines across each forewing, and spots of red next to the 'swallow tails' on the hindwings. The larvae closely resemble twigs, especially Ivy.

Habitat Woods, hedges and gardens. Food-plants include Ivy and Hawthorn.

Status and distribution Widespread and moderately common throughout.

Season 6–8.

Belted Beauty
Lycia zonaria

Males have a wingspan of 30–35mm, females are wingless. Males have attractive brown-grey wings striped with white, hindwings paler. Females are small and dark.

Habitat Sand-dunes and grassy areas. Food-plants include Bird's-foot Trefoil, clovers and Burnet Rose.

Status and distribution Rather local, though widespread. Mostly coastal.

Season 3–5.

Peppered Moth
Biston betularia

A largish moth; wingspan up to 62mm. Famous because of its wide variety of colour forms, shown to have evolved in relation to pollution-darkening of tree bark.

Habitat In a wide variety of wooded or lightly treed sites; a wide range of food-plants includes trees and herbs.

Status and distribution Widespread and reasonably common virtually throughout.

Season 5–8.

Scarce Umber
Agriopis aurantiaria

Males have a wingspan of about 40mm, females are wingless. Male forewings are yellowish-brown, with darker markings; the hindwings are very pale. Females dark brown.

Habitat Wooded areas and unimproved farmland.

Status and distribution Widespread and moderately common throughout, except in the far north.

Season 10–12.

Similar species

Dotted Border *A. marginaria* is similar in size and shape, but has a row of dots along the back of all wings. Similar habitats and distribution.

Mottled Umber *Erannis defoliaria* is more strongly marked and mottled, and has a spot in the centre of each forewing. Widespread and common throughout.

Great Oak Beauty
Boarmia roboraria

A large moth; wingspan up to 70mm. Variable in colour, but essentially grey mottled with white and some black, forming a lacy pattern.

Habitat Oak woodland; the larvae feed on oak.

Status and distribution Rather local and mainly southern.

Season 6–8.

Similar species

Pale Oak Beauty *Serraca punctinalis* is smaller and lighter in colour. Similar habitats and distribution.

Black-veined Moth
Siona lineata

A small to medium moth; wingspan up to 50mm. It is creamy-white in colour, and the undersides have a strongly marked pattern of black veins. The moths fly by day, with a weak fluttery flight.

Habitat Limestone and chalk grassland, where Tor Grass occurs.

Status and distribution Very rare in UK, where it is found only in Kent. More widespread on the Continent, commonest towards the south.

Season 5–7.

Similar species

Could be confused with some of the white butterflies (see p.120) but the general differences between moths and butterflies (see p.118) should distinguish them.

Swallowtailed Moth

Belted Beauty, mating

Peppered Moths, pale and dark forms

Great Oak Beauty

Scarce Umber

Hawk-moths, Family Sphingidae

Distinctive medium to large moths. Powerful fliers, generally with rather narrow, pointed forewings. Most larvae are large, striped, and have a 'horn' at the tail end.

Convolvulus Hawk-moth
Agrius convolvuli

A strikingly large moth; wingspan up to 12cm. Forewings greyish, marbled; hindwings browner. The abdomen is striped with red, white and black. The proboscis may be up to 13cm long!

Habitat A migrant into N Europe from the Mediterranean area, which may occur wherever there are flowers, especially *Petunia* and *Nicotiana*. Breeds on *Convolvulus*, but only rarely does so in N Europe.

Status and distribution Very variable in numbers, regularly reaching S England, but not necessarily going further.

Season 6–9.

Death's Head Hawk-Moth
Acherontia atropos

An extraordinary insect, unlike anything else. Wingspan up to 13cm, and body very broad. Wings beautifully marbled brown, yellow and black when fresh; skull-like ('death's head') pattern on the thorax, and abdomen boldly striped. Proboscis relatively short, and this is one of the few hawk-moths that settles to feed. Larva large, variable in colour, green or yellow, with bold diagonal stripes.

Habitat Very mobile, occurring almost anywhere.

Status and distribution A migrant from S Europe, arriving in small, but variable, numbers.

Season 6–10.

Privet Hawk-moth
Sphinx ligustri

Resembles Convolvulus Hawk, but smaller, with hindwings banded pink and brown, and forewings browner. Wings normally held roof-wise along the body when at rest. Larva green, striped with brown.

Habitat More sedentary than above species, living mainly in rough flowery places where Privet occurs.

Status and distribution Local in S Britain, widespread on the Continent.

Season 6–7.

Poplar Hawk-moth
Laothoe populi

A medium-sized hawk-moth; wingspan up to 90mm. Wings greyish to pinkish-brown, broadly banded, with a single white mark in the centre of the forewings. Hindwings orange-red at base, usually concealed, and show in front of forewings at rest. Larvae green with yellow stripes.

Habitat A variety of habitats, associated with Sallow, Poplar and Aspen.

Status and distribution Widely distributed and moderately common throughout the region.

Season 5–9.

Similar species

Pine Hawk-moth *Hyloicus pinastri* is also greyish-brown, but lacks the orange on the underwings. Occurs in association with pine, and often rests on trunks by day. Widespread but local.

Lime Hawk-moth
Mimas tiliae

Wingspan in the range 70–80mm. Forewings beautifully marbled, with a ground colour varying from pink to green or brown. Adults do not feed. Larvae green with fine yellow stripes.

Habitat In light woodland, parks and gardens, associated with limes, elms and a variety of other trees; not an especially mobile species.

Status and distribution Southern and local in the UK; more widespread on the Continent.

Season 5–7.

Convolvulus Hawk-moth

Death's Head Hawk-moth, larva

Death's Head Hawk-moth

Privet Hawk-moth

Pine Hawk-moth

Poplar Hawk-moth

Lime Hawk-moth

Eyed Hawk-moth
Smerinthus ocellata
Wingspan 80–95mm. Forewings brownish, marbled, rather like Poplar, but the hindwings are quite different – orange-red, with a large 'peacock eye' on each, which may be flashed if the insect is threatened. Larva green with yellow stripes.
Habitat Woodland, parks and gardens, associated with Apple and willows.
Status and distribution Widespread in England and Wales, rare further north. Generally distributed on the Continent.
Season 5–9.

Narrow-bordered Bee Hawk-moth
Hemaris tityus
A bumble bee-like insect, with a wingspan of about 45mm. Wings clear, except for narrow brownish border. Flies by day, and visits flowers of Bugle, Rhododendron, and others.
Habitat Woodland clearings, damp acid pastures, where Devil's Bit Scabious grows.
Status and distribution Widespread throughout, but not common.
Season 5–6.
Similar species
Broad-bordered Bee Hawk-moth *H. fuciformis* is slightly larger, and has broader brown margins to the wings. Widespread but local in woodland clearings and rides; larvae feed mainly on Honeysuckle.

Hummingbird Hawk-moth
Macroglossum stellatarum
An appropriately named and unmistakable moth which darts from flower to flower, feeding as it hovers. Wingspan 50–60mm, underwings yellow. Day-flying, visiting Red Valerian, Honeysuckle, Petunia and other nectar-rich flowers.
Habitat Entirely migrant in this area, and may occur wherever there are suitable flowers. Often seen near the top of sunny old walls.

Status and distribution Widespread, occurring virtually throughout, but highly variable in numbers.
Season 6–10 (though odd individuals may occur at almost any time).

Large Elephant Hawk-moth
Deilephila elpenor
An attractive and distinctive species, with a wingspan of 60–70mm. Forewings striped brown and pink, hindwings half pink, half brown. Larvae are impressive, large, greyish, with a snout like an elephant's trunk, and large 'eye-spots'.
Habitat Rough grassland, waste ground and gardens. Larvae feed on willowherbs, bedstraws, and sometimes *Clarkia* or *Fuchsia*.
Status and distribution Widespread and moderately common.
Season 5–7.
Similar species
Small Elephant Hawk-moth *D. porcellus* has a wingspan of 45–55mm, and is generally yellower in appearance; hindwing yellow edged with pink. Larva smaller, browner, lacking horn at tail end; feeds mainly on bedstraws. Widespread but local.

Spurge Hawk-moth
Hyles euphorbiae
Similar in size and shape to Large Elephant, but with brown and pink forewings, and pink hindwings.
Habitat Larvae feed on spurge; adults are highly mobile and may turn up anywhere.
Status and distribution A S European species which moves northwards irregularly. Rare vagrant to UK.
Season 5–9.
Similar species
Bedstraw Hawk-moth *H. gallii* looks very similar, but has bolder brown front margin to the wings, and less pink on the hindwings. A mobile species, moving northwards in some years. Very rare UK visitor.

Eyed Hawk-moth

Hummingbird Hawk-moth

Narrow-bordered Bee Hawk-moth
Large Elephant Hawk-moth, larva

Large Elephant Hawk-moth
Small Elephant Hawk-moth

Prominents, Family Notodontidae

So called because of a tuft of hairs on the hindwing which projects when the moth is at rest.

Buff-tip
Phalera bucephala
A remarkable moth, with a well-developed and unusual camouflage pattern (see p.27). Wingspan 55–65mm. Wings greyish, like Birch bark, tipped with yellow hairs, and with a yellow thorax – the overall effect can be very like a broken Birch twig. Larvae distinctive, with longitudinal yellow, black and white stripes.
Habitat Woods, heaths and lightly treed sites, where Sallow, Poplar and Birch occur.
Status and distribution Widespread and common throughout.
Season 6–8.
Similar species
Nothing looks quite similar.
Chocolate-tip *Clostera curtula* has a similar colouring pattern, with dark brown wing-tips and a brown head. Wooded areas, widespread but mainly southern in UK.

Puss Moth
Cerura vinula
A very attractive moth; wingspan 65–80mm. The overall impression is of a white 'fluffy' moth; the abdomen is white, with about 10 black dots, and the wings are pale greyish-white with darker lines; male antennae feathered. The larvae are extraordinary, as shown in the photograph opposite.
Habitat A variety of habitats, where willows occur – woods, fens, dunes and other sites.
Status and distribution Widespread and quite common.
Season 4–7.
Similar species
Leopard Moth *Zeuzera pyrina* (see p.152) is rather similar, but wings are more dotted, and there are 6 large dark dots on the thorax.

Iron Prominent
Notodonta dromedarius
A greyish-brown moth, with a wingspan of 45–50mm. There are rust-coloured patches on the forewings. As in other prominents, there is a tuft of scales on the back. The larva is more exceptional: green, with several narrow humps on its back.
Habitat Lightly wooded areas, where Birches and alders occur.
Status and distribution Widespread and reasonably common throughout.
Season 5–9.

Swallow Prominent
Pheosia tremula
An attractive moth, with a wingspan of 50–60mm. Wings longitudinally striped; dark brown towards the body, paler in the centre, and darker along the margins.
Habitat Various habitats; larvae feed on Aspen, poplars and willows.
Status and distribution Widespread and common throughout.
Season 5–8.
Similar species
Lesser Swallow Prominent *P. gnoma* is similar in pattern, but smaller, with more white on the wing, and a white triangle near the hind margin of the forewing. Similar habitats and distribution. Feeds on Birch.

Coxcomb Prominent
Ptilodon capucina
Wingspan 40–50mm. A marbled brownish moth, made distinctive by the especially prominent 'hump', the scalloped margins to the forewings, and the hairy crest.
Habitat Woodland, hedges and scrub. Larvae feed on various broadleaved trees.
Status and distribution Widespread throughout, generally the commonest Prominent.
Season 5–9.
Similar species
Maple Prominent *Ptilodontella cucullina* is very similar in shape, but this species has large pale patches on the wing-tips. Similar habitats, but more local.

Buff-tip

Puss Moths, mating

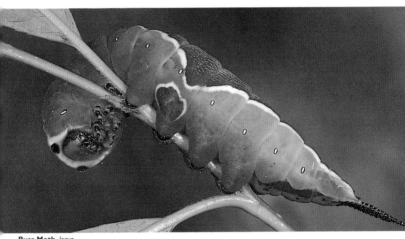

Puss Moth, larva

Iron Prominent, larva

Coxcomb Prominent

Pale Prominent
Pterostoma palpina

A curious-looking moth, with long projections in front of the head. Wingspan 45–60mm, with a long body; wings greyish, marbled with brown and white – well camouflaged when at rest.

Habitat Open woods and scrub.

Status and distribution Widespread throughout, and generally common.

Season 5–8.

Great Prominent
Peridea anceps

Rather similar to Pale Prominent, though larger (up to 65mm wingspan), generally darker in colour, and lacking the prominent duckbill-like snout. The hindwings (usually hidden at rest) are very pale greyish. The larvae are bright green, with reddish diagonal stripes.

Habitat Scrub and woodland; the larvae feed on oaks.

Status and distribution Widespread and moderately common throughout.

Season 5–7.

---

* Pine Processionary Moth
Thaumetopoea pityocampa

Adults are undistinguished, pale grey-brown moths with a wingspan of 30–35mm. Larvae, however, are very conspicuous, living communally in web 'tents' on pine branches; the tents remain visible after the larvae have left. They travel in a procession when seeking a pupation site in spring.

Habitat Wherever pine trees, of various species, occur.

Status and distribution Very common in S Europe, just reaching into central Europe.

Season Adults 5–7; larval nests visible much of the year.

Similar species

* Oak Processionary Moth *T. processionea* is very similar, but occurs on oaks.

Vapourer Moth
Orgyia antiqua

A fascinating moth, of which all stages may be noticed. Males are orangey-brown, with a white spot on each forewing; wingspan 35–40mm. Females are wingless and dark. She remains on her empty cocoon, where a male will find her, and she lays a batch of large conspicuous eggs all over it (see photo). The larvae are very distinctive, with colourful tufts of hairs.

Habitat All kinds of habitats, wherever there are trees and shrubs.

Status and distribution Widespread and common throughout.

Season 6–10.

Similar species

Scarce Vapourer *O. recens* is very similar, but males have white marks at the tips of the forewings. Very local, in SE Britain only; widespread but local on the Continent.

Pale Tussock
Callitaera pudibunda

Wingspan 50–70mm, males smaller. The wings are greyish-white, with a broad darker band; the furry front legs are held forwards at rest. The adults do not feed. The larvae are attractive and distinctive, yellow and very hairy.

Habitat In woods and areas with trees and shrubs. Food-plants include various trees and shrubs.

Status and distribution Widespread and generally common throughout, though absent from Scotland.

Season 4–7.

Similar species

Dark Tussock *Dicallomera fascelina* is slightly darker, with more brown on the wings. Widespread, but commoner in the north.

* Reed Tussock *Laelia coenosa* has a beautiful caterpillar (see photo); now extinct in UK, but locally common in N Europe.

Pale Prominent

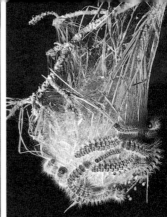

Pine Processionary Moth, 'tent'

Vapourer Moth, female egg laying

Pine Processionary Moth, larvae in procession

Vapourer Moth, larva

Pale Tussock, larva

Reed Tussock, larva

Gold-tail or **Yellow-tail**

Euproctis similis

A small to medium moth; wingspan 35–45mm. Generally white in appearance, but the abdomen is tipped with a brush of yellow hairs in both sexes. The larvae are distinctive, red and black with tufts of hairs.

Habitat Woods and hedges, occasionally gardens. The larval food-plants are mainly Hawthorn and Blackthorn.

Status and distribution Common in England and Wales, rare in Scotland; widespread on the Continent.

Season 6–8.

Similar species

Brown-tail *E. chrysorrhoea* is very similar, but slightly smaller, and with a brown tip to the abdomen. The larvae are similar, but duller, and live gregariously in webs on Hawthorn and other shrubs. Generally less common, but may become abundant at times.

Black Arches

Lymantria monacha

An attractive and distinctive moth; wingspan 45–55mm. Wings white, heavily dotted, striped and suffused with black; males have feathery antennae.

Habitat Wooded habitats. Larvae feed mainly on oak, but also on other trees including pines.

Status and distribution In S Britain only; more widespread on the Continent.

Season 7–9.

Similar species

★ **Gypsy Moth** *L. dispar* is similar in form, but lacks most of the black markings; males have a brown ground colour. Extinct in UK as resident, but occasional as immigrant. Widespread on the Continent.

Rosy Footman

Miltochrista miniata

A pretty little moth, with a wingspan of about 30mm. Forewings pinkish-yellow finely marked with black; hindwings almost white. Larvae grey and furry, feeding on lichens such as Dog Lichen on trunks.

Habitat Woodland.

Status and distribution A southern species in Britain, more widespread on the Continent.

Season 6–8.

Dotted Footman

Pelosia muscerda

Wingspan 30–35mm. Dull yellowish-brown, with 5 dark dots on the forewings.

Habitat Woods and scrub; the larvae feed on algae, and possibly lichens.

Status and distribution Now very rare in UK, local on the Continent.

Similar species

Small Dotted Footman *P. obtusa* is smaller, browner, with more rounded wings. Rare, in E Anglia only in UK, local on the Continent.

Common Footman

Eilema lurideola

Representative of a small group of distinctive moths. Wingspan 32–38mm. Forewings grey, edged yellow; hindwings creamy-yellow. The wings are folded back along the body when at rest.

Habitat Woods, hedgerows and gardens; the larvae feed on lichens on trunks.

Status and distribution Widespread and generally common, rarer in N Britain.

Season 6–8.

Common Footman   Scarce Footman

Similar species

Scarce Footman *E. complana* is almost identical but the yellow stripe at the front of the forewing does not taper (see illustration). Local, mainly southern.

Dingy Footman *E. griseola* is duller and browner in colour, and has curved front edges to the forewings. Widespread, but rare in the north.

Gold-tail, larva

Gold-tail

Black Arches, male

Rosy Footman

Dotted Footman   **Common Footman**

Garden Tiger
Arctia caja

Both adults and larvae are familiar. Wingspan 55–80mm. Forewings white with broad chocolate marbling, but very variable; hindwings yellow or orange, with black spots. The caterpillar is the 'woolly bear', covered with orange-brown hairs.

Habitat Almost everywhere, especially woods, gardens and scrub. The larvae feed on many different herbs.

Status and distribution Widespread and common throughout.

Season 6–8. Larvae most noticeable 4–6.

Similar species

See other Tiger moths, below.

Cream-spot Tiger
Arctia villica

Broadly similar to Garden Tiger but slightly smaller. Forewings basically black with large white blobs, merging together; hindwings yellow dotted with black.

Habitat Scrub and grassland, especially on limestones.

Status and distribution Local in S Britain only; widespread on the Continent, though commoner southwards.

Season 5–7.

Jersey Tiger
Euplagia quadripunctaria

Generally similar to Cream-spot Tiger, but the dark blackish-brown forewings have broad white stripes diagonally across them; hindwings orange, marked black. Day- (and night-) flying.

Habitat Grassy, flowery places or open woodland. Larvae feed on various herbs.

Status and distribution Very rare in the UK; Devon and the Channel Islands only. Widespread on the Continent.

Season 6–9.

Similar species

Wood Tiger *Parasemia plantaginis* has a rather similar stripey appearance, but is smaller, and has underwings mainly black, with yellow. Widespread and locally common throughout, not confined to woods.

Scarlet Tiger
Callimorpha dominula

Similar in general form to Cream-spot Tiger, though smaller (wingspan about 55mm). Forewings blackish-green, with large white or yellow spots; underwings normally scarlet with black marks. Flies by day, and the scarlet is readily visible. Larvae black and yellow, and bristly.

Habitat Found in damp meadows and fens. Larvae feed on various herbs, especially Comfrey.

Status and distribution Local in UK northwards only to the S Midlands; widespread throughout the Continent.

Season 6–8.

Ruby Tiger
Phragmatobia fuliginosa

A much less conspicuous moth than the other Tigers. Wingspan 30–40mm. Forewings reddish-brown with a dark dot, hindwings variable grey to pink.

Habitat Various habitats, including moors, heaths, damp grassland and scrub. Larvae feed on heathers and various herbs.

Status and distribution Widespread and common throughout.

Season 4–9.

Cinnabar Moth
Tyria jacobaeae

A familiar and distinctive moth, in both adult and larval stages. Wingspan 35–45mm. Forewings greyish, with a red stripe and 2 red dots; hindwings red. The larvae are boldly striped yellow and black. Both larvae and adults are active in the day, relying on their warning colours.

Habitat Sunny places where ragwort, especially Common Ragwort, occurs.

Status and distribution Widespread and often abundant, throughout.

Season Adults 5–7; larvae 6–8.

Similar species

Burnet moths (see p.154) may be confused with this, but the Cinnabar wing pattern, with the long broad stripe and 2 spots, is unique. Cinnabars also have thin antennae.

Garden Tiger, male

Garden Tiger, larva

Cream-spot Tiger

Jersey Tiger

Scarlet Tiger

Ruby Tiger

Cinnabar Moth, larvae on ragwort

Cinnabar Moth

Buff Ermine

Spilosoma lutea

Wingspan 35–40mm. An attractive yellow moth, with black dots; females generally paler.

Habitat Many kinds of habitat; the larvae feed on a wide range of trees and shrubs.

Status and distribution Widespread and common throughout.

Season 5–8.

Similar species

Clouded Buff *Diacrisia sannio* has yellow wings, lacking black, but with a single brownish dot; females are more orange-coloured. Males day-flying. Widespread and common throughout.

White Ermine

Spilosoma lubricipeda

An attractive moth, with white wings, liberally spotted with black dots. Wingspan 35–45mm. The abdomen is orange-yellow, dotted with black.

Habitat Open woods, gardens, scrub. Larvae feed on various herbs.

Status and distribution Widespread and common throughout.

Season 5–8.

Similar species

Puss Moth (see p.174) and Leopard Moth (see p.152) are much larger. Muslin Moth females are very similar (see below).

Muslin Moth

Diaphora mendica

Females of this species are very similar to those of White Ermine, differing in the white abdomen, and having fewer black dots on the wings. Male Muslin Moths are brown, with black dots.

Habitat In open woods, scrub and hedges; the larvae feed on various plants. Females often day-flying.

Status and distribution Widespread and common throughout.

Season 5–7.

Noctuids, Family Noctuidae

A very large and variable group. Often the forewings are dull, while the hindwings are brightly coloured. The hindwings are usually folded out of sight when the moths are at rest. Larvae plump, not hairy or bristly.

Heart and Dart

Agrotis exclamationis

Wingspan 35–45mm. The forewings vary from pale brown to deep reddish-brown, but the distinguishing features are the heart-shaped and the torpedo-shaped dark marks on each forewing – hence the common name.

Habitat A wide variety of habitats including cultivated farmland. Larvae feed on many different plants.

Status and distribution Widespread and common throughout.

Season 5–8.

Similar species

Turnip Moth *A. segetum* is similar in size and shape, but lacks the dark 'dart', and is generally paler. Widespread and common.

Garden Dart *Euxoa nigricans* is richer brown with more complex marbling on the wings. Common throughout.

Flame Shoulder

Ochropleura plecta

A small moth, with a wingspan of about 30mm. The wings are mainly inconspicuous reddish-brown, but are readily identified by the long white shoulder stripe.

Habitat May occur in almost any habitat; larvae feed on a wide range of herbaceous plants.

Status and distribution Widespread and common throughout.

Season 5–9.

Clouded Buff

White Ermine

Heart and Dart

Flame Shoulder

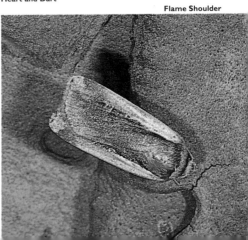

Large Yellow Underwing
Noctua pronuba

A largish moth; wingspan 50–60mm. Forewings dark brown in the male, paler reddish- or greyish-brown in the female, but both vary considerably. The underwings are a striking yellow colour, edged with black. These are flashed in flight but concealed on landing, so that as it settles the moth effectively disappears.

Habitat Many different habitats. Migrants from further south reinforce the resident population.

Status and distribution Widespread and common.

Season 6–10.

Similar species

Broad-bordered Yellow Underwing *N. fimbriata* has a much broader black margin to the underwing. Widespread, but mainly in wooded areas.

Lunar Yellow Underwing *N. pronuba* resembles Large, but is smaller, and has an additional black dot on the underwing. Widespread but local.

Lesser Yellow Underwing *N. comes* resembles Lunar in size and pattern, but has a weakly marked comma in place of the black dot. Widespread throughout.

Least Yellow Underwing
Noctua interjecta

A small species of underwing, with a wingspan of 30–35mm. Similar in overall pattern to Large Yellow Underwing, with reddish-brown forewings. Yellow underwings broadly edged with black, with no clearly defined extra spot, though there is a dark smudge towards the base.

Habitat Many different open habitats. Larvae feed on a wide range of herbs.

Status and distribution Widespread but local, throughout except the far north.

Season 6–8.

Beautiful Yellow Underwing
Anarta myrtilii

Though sharing the yellow underwings with the above species, this is a very different moth in its behaviour. Wingspan only about 25mm. Forewings reddish-brown, attractively marbled white and darker; underwings yellow edged black. An active day-flying moth, especially in hot sunny weather.

Habitat Heaths and moors; the larvae feed mainly on heather.

Status and distribution Widespread throughout, but local.

Season 4–8.

Similar species

Small Dark Yellow Underwing *A. cordigera* is similar in size, but has darker forewings with a white heart-shaped blotch. A mountain species, local in Scotland and mountains of Continental Europe. **Small Yellow Underwing** *Panemeria tenebrata* has duller forewings and a reduced area of yellow on the hindwings. Widespread and locally common.

Setaceous Hebrew Character
Xestia c-nigrum

Wingspan 35–45mm. A greyish-brown moth, with distinctive rectangular light-and-dark markings on the margin of each forewing, with a sinuous margin between the 2 shades.

Habitat Many different habitats; the larvae eat almost any herbaceous plant.

Status and distribution Widespread and common throughout, though less frequent in the north.

Season 5–10, most frequent in the second brood.

Similar species

Double Square-spot *X. triangulum* has 2 almost square dark marks in the equivalent position. Widespread and common.

Large Yellow Underwing

Small Yellow Underwing
Beautiful Yellow Underwing, larva

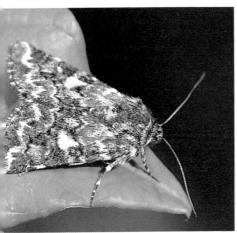

Beautiful Yellow Underwing

Setaceous Hebrew Character

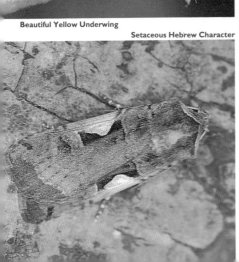

Dot Moth
Melanchra persicariae

A dark greyish-brown moth, with a wingspan of 40–50mm. The forewings have a bright dumb-bell-shaped dot in the centre of the front margin.

Habitat Many habitats, including gardens, waste ground, cultivated land. Larvae eat a wide range of herbs and shrubs.

Status and distribution Widespread and generally common, though absent from most of Scotland.

Season 6–9.

Similar species

Bright-line Brown-eye *Lacanobia oleracea* is very similar in size and shape, but more orange-brown in colour, with an orange dot in place of the white one. Very common throughout, frequently in gardens. (There is also a moth called the Brown-line Bright-eye *Mythimna conigera*, which is confusing in name if not in appearance!)

Cabbage Moth *Mamestra brassicae* is slightly larger, duller in colour than either, with a less distinct cream mark on the forewing. Common throughout; the larvae eat cabbages as well as many other herbaceous plants.

Broom Moth
Ceramica pisi

Most often seen as the caterpillar. The moth is brown, with a pale scalloped line towards the wing-tips. The larvae are boldly striped with yellow on a brown to green background.

Habitat Various habitats, including heaths, moors and open woodland. The larvae feed mainly on Broom, but also docks, Birch and Elm.

Status and distribution Widespread and common throughout.

Season Adult 5–7, larva 7–9.

Campion Moth
Hadena rivularis

An attractive moth, wingspan 30–35mm. Similar in general shape and pattern to the above few species, with a purplish-brown ground colour, and a triangle outlined in white on each forewing margin.

Habitat Various open habitats where species of campion occur.

Status and distribution Widespread and common throughout.

Season 5–9.

Chamomile Shark
Cucullia chamomillae

The adult moth is rather undistinguished, a typical Noctuid, with brown forewings and paler hindwings. The larvae, however, feed openly on the flowers of various mayweeds and related composites, and are often noticed. Variable in colour.

Habitat Wherever the food-plants occur – waste ground, cultivated ground and gardens.

Status and distribution Widespread in the UK from S Scotland southwards; widespread on the Continent.

Season 4–6 as adult, 5–7 as larva.

Mullein Moth
Cucullia verbasci

Like the above species, this is much more often seen as the caterpillar. The adults are pale brown, with darker margins to the wings; wingspan 45–50mm. The larvae are quite distinctive, hairless, grey-green brightly marked with yellow and black dots. They feed and rest openly by day.

Habitat Wherever the food-plants – various mulleins and figworts – occur, e.g. waste ground, riversides, fens, sunny banks.

Status and distribution Absent from N Britain, but widespread everywhere else, and moderately common.

Season 4–6 as adult, 6–7 as caterpillar.

Dot Moth

Bright-line Brown-eye

Broom Moth, larva

Mullein Moth, larva

Campion Moth

Chamomile Shark, larva

Merveille-du-jour
Dichonia aprilina

A beautiful moth, looking like a moth-shaped piece of green and black lichen! Very hard to spot when at rest on lichen-covered tree trunks. Wingspan 45–50mm.
Habitat Woodland and parkland, where oaks occur. Larvae feed on the buds and leaves of oak.
Status and distribution Widespread and moderately common, though absent from many areas.
Season 8–10.

Pink-barred Sallow
Xanthia togata

An attractive medium-small moth, with a wingspan of about 30mm. The forewings are mainly yellow, but with broad pinkish markings across them.
Habitat Open damp areas, such as fens, marshy commonland and neglected pasture. The main food-plant is Sallow.
Status and distribution Widespread and moderately common throughout.
Season 8–10.
Similar species
The Sallow *X. icteritia* is virtually identical in size and shape, but tends to have fewer pink markings and a yellower head. Similar habitats and distribution.
Dusky Sallow *Eremobia ochroleuca* is similar in size. Widespread in a variety of flowery habitats, but absent from Scotland.

Sycamore Moth
Acronicta aceris

The adult moth is relatively undistinguished, greyish mottled with brown and paler, with a wingspan of 40–45mm. The caterpillars are often noticed, and are unique, with their pattern of white dots edged with black, and long yellow and orange hairs.
Habitat Woods, parkland and gardens; the larvae feed on Sycamore, Field Maple and other trees.
Status and distribution Confined to S Britain, absent from Scotland; widespread

and frequent on the Continent.
Season Adults 5–7, larvae 8–9.
Similar species
Poplar Grey *A. megacephala*. The adults are very similar, though this species is darker with a conspicuous white spot in the middle of the forewing. The larvae are quite different, grey-green with pale hairs. Common throughout.

Alder Moth
Acronicta alni

Adult moths are attractively marbled deep brown, grey and pinkish-brown; wingspan about 40mm. The larvae are very striking – yellow with long black paddle-shaped hairs when older (but grey and white when younger, resembling a bird dropping).
Habitat Woods, commons and other areas with trees; the main food-plant is Alder, also other deciduous trees.
Status and distribution Local in England and Wales, absent further north; widespread but local on the Continent.
Season Adult 5–7, larvae 7–8.

Grey Dagger
Acronicta psi

Adults have a wingspan of 35–45mm. The forewings are pearly-grey, with a dark mark like an old-fashioned dagger. The caterpillars are very striking: grey, black and yellow, with red dots, and a narrow tuft of black hairs.
Habitat In a wide range of unspoilt habitats, such as woods, scrub, heaths; the larvae feed mainly on Hawthorn, Blackthorn and various trees.
Status and distribution Widespread and frequent throughout.
Season Adults 6–8, larvae 8–10.
Similar species
Dark Dagger *A. tridens*. Adults are slightly darker, but very similar. Larvae are similar, but with less yellow, and a less marked tuft of hairs. Similar habitats and distribution.
Knot-grass *A. rumicis* has a similar larva that is brown, white and red, with long brown hairs, feeding on docks and Knot-grass. Common throughout.

Merveille-du-jour

Dusky Sallow

Sycamore Moth, larva

Sycamore Moth

Alder Moth, larva

Grey Dagger

Grey Dagger, larva

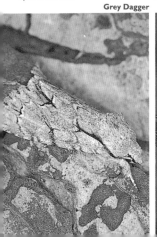

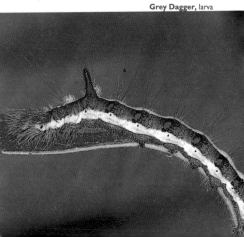

Copper Underwing
Amphipyra pyramidea

An attractive medium-large moth, with a wingspan of 47–54mm. Forewings deep brown, marbled paler and with a white spot; the underwings are orangey-brown and very noticeable.

Habitat Woodland and other habitats with trees.

Status and distribution Mainly southern in the UK, more widespread on the Continent.

Season 6–8.

Similar species

Svensson's Copper Underwing *A. berbera* is extremely similar, except on the underside of the hindwing which is paler and lacking a chequered margin. Similar habitats and distribution.

Old Lady
Mormo maura

A large moth; wingspan 70–75mm. The forewings are dark brown, with a marbled pattern over the top half that fancifully resembles a shawl over an old lady's shoulders!

Habitat Open woodland, commons, gardens; often seen in porches, occasionally in caves. Larvae feed on various herbs and shrubs.

Status and distribution Widespread and frequent in the UK, except in N Scotland; widespread on the Continent.

Season 6–8.

Angle Shades
Phlogophora meticulosa

A medium-sized moth; wingspan 48–53mm. The forewings are attractively marked, rather variable in ground colour, marbled pink, green and brown, with distinctive large triangles on each wing, their apices just meeting in the middle.

Habitat To be found almost anywhere, very mobile. Larvae feed on various herbs.

Status and distribution Widespread and common throughout.

Season Most common 5–9, but may be seen at almost any time.

Similar species

Small Angle Shades *Euplexia lucipara* resembles the above, but is smaller and less colourful. Widespread but less common.

Dark Arches
Apamaea monoglypha

A medium-sized moth; wingspan 45–55mm. A typical Noctuid, looking rather like many others. Brown forewings marbled light and dark, with zigzag markings towards the edge; very variable in colour (an example of industrial melanism, like Peppered Moth – see p.168). Hindwings usually very pale, edged darker, but may be all dark.

Habitat Almost everywhere. Larvae feed on various grasses.

Status and distribution Widespread and common throughout.

Season 6–10.

Similar species

The Exile *A. maillardii* is similar in size, shape and markings, but the markings are more clearly defined and brighter. A northern species, on moorland.

Dusky Sallow
Eremobia ochroleuca

A medium-sized moth; wingspan about 35mm. Forewings marbled brown on white, hindwings off-white with a broad brown edge.

Habitat Open, grassy, flowery places, such as dunes and downland. Larvae feed on various grasses.

Status and distribution Only in SE Britain; more widespread on the Continent.

Season 7–8.

Copper Underwing

Old Lady

Angle Shades

Dark Arches

Dusky Sallow

Bulrush Wainscot
Nonagria typhae
Wingspan 45–55mm. Forewings pale brown, streaked with white and dotted black; hindwings pale.
Habitat The larvae feed on Bulrush (Reedmace), which is found wherever they occur.
Status and distribution Widespread throughout, though rarer in the north.
Season 7–10.

Green Silver-lines
Pseudoips fagana
An attractive and distinctive moth; wingspan 35–40mm. Forewings bright green, with 3 diagonal silvery lines; hindwings off-white.
Habitat Woods and hedgerows with trees. Larvae feed on oak and Beech.
Status and distribution Common in southern UK, rarer further north. Widespread on the Continent.
Season 5–8.
Similar species
Scarce Silver-lines *Bena prasinana* is slightly larger, and has only 2 silvery diagonal lines. Widespread but local, absent from Scotland.
Cream-bordered Green Pea *Earias clorana* is a smaller version of these two, lacking the diagonal lines but with a white front margin to the forewing. Local, associated with willows in damp areas.

Burnished Brass
Diachrisia chrysitis
An attractive and distinctive moth, with a wingspan of 35–45mm. The forewings are brown, with 2 broad yellowish bands – the 'burnished brass' of its name. The head is orange.
Habitat In various open habitats, such as waste ground, gardens and commons, where Stinging Nettle grows.
Status and distribution Widespread and common throughout.
Season 6–9.

Similar species
Scarce Burnished Brass *D. chryson* has a single yellow patch, (not 2 stripes), and is otherwise brown. Occurs in damp places, feeding on Hemp Agrimony.
Slender Burnished Brass *D. orichalcea* is slightly smaller and has a single angled yellow stripe. Widespread in S Europe, a rare visitor to the north including Britain.

Golden Plusia
Polychrisia moneta
Wingspan 40–45mm. An attractive moth, with beautifully mottled and banded forewings, and a tuft of hairs on the thorax.
Habitat Particularly associated with gardens, as the larvae feed on Delphiniums, and the adults like *Buddleia* and other garden nectar sources.
Status and distribution Has spread within the UK this century, and now occurs throughout, though rare in the north; widespread on the Continent.
Season 6–9.

Silver Y
Autographa gamma
Wingspan 35–50mm. Variable in colour from grey to purplish-black, marbled with other colours, but nearly always with a white 'Y' in the centre of the forewing. Feeds at flowers, moving rapidly and continuing to beat its wings while feeding.
Habitat Anywhere with flowers. An extremely mobile species.
Status and distribution An immigrant from S Europe, appearing in variable numbers but often abundant. Fails to overwinter in UK and N Europe.
Season 5–11.
Similar species
Beautiful Golden Y *A. pulchrina* is more orange-brown in colour, with a less clear 'Y' mark next to a gold patch. Widespread and common throughout; resident.
Plain Golden Y *A. jota* is slightly duller, and has the 'Y' on a brownish rectangle. Common and widespread.

Burnished Brass

Golden Plusia

Green Silver-lines

Silver Y

Red Underwing
Catocala nupta

A large distinctive moth, with a wingspan of up to 90mm. Forewings attractively marbled brown, grey and pinkish-brown, but the underwings are bright orange-red with dark margins and a dark stripe. These are 'flashed' if they are disturbed, and – as with the yellow underwings (see p.184) – the moths 'disappear' when they settle after flying.

Habitat Woodlands, marshes, commons; the larvae feed on willows and poplars.

Status and distribution Widespread on the Continent, but only in the south of Britain.

Season 8–9.

Similar species

Rosy Underwing *C. electa* has paler forewings, and paler red on the hindwings. Rare and probably not resident in the UK; more frequent on the Continent.

Dark Crimson Underwing *C. sponsa* has more attractively marbled forewings and redder (less orange) underwings. Widespread but local in oakwoods; virtually confined to the New Forest in Britain.

Light Crimson Underwing *C. promissa* is slightly smaller, paler and greyer than the preceding species but has its redder underwings. Similar habitats and distribution.

Mother Shipton
Callistege mi

An attractive little day-flying, Skipper-like moth, with a wingspan of 30–35mm. The brown marbled forewings each have a mark like the face of an old witch, facing inwards – hence the name.

Habitat Flowery meadows, pastures and scrub. Food-plants include various legumes.

Status and distribution Widespread and locally common throughout, least common in the north.

Season 5–7.

Similar species

Burnet Companion *Euclidia glyphica* is similar in shape and habitats, but lacks the distinct 'face', and has reddish-orange hindwings, visible as it flies. Similar habitats and distribution, throughout.

The Herald
Scoliopteryx libatrix

Wingspan 45–50mm. A brownish moth, with orange patches on the forewings, a sinuous white transverse stripe, a white dot on each shoulder, and hook-tipped and wavy-edged wings.

Habitat Found in woodland, gardens, marshy places; overwinters as adult, and may be seen in outhouses, sheds and even caves.

Status and distribution Widespread throughout, though rare in Scotland.

Season Almost all year, but on the wing 7–10 and 3–6.

Snout
Hypena proboscidalis

A distinctively shaped small moth, with a wingspan of about 40mm. The palps which project forward from the head give the impression of a snout. Generally yellowish-brown, with transverse markings, and slightly hooked wing-tips.

Habitat Various open habitats, where Stinging Nettle occurs.

Status and distribution Widespread and common throughout.

Season 6–10.

Similar species

Beautiful Snout *H. crassalis* is slightly smaller, with attractively marked forewings. Local in UK, mainly western; feeds on Bilberry.

Red Underwing

Mother Shipton

The Herald　　　　　　　　　　**Snout**

Micro-moths

As described on p.152, this is a large and difficult group of moths. Only those which are distinctive at some stage are described here, including a number which are noticed readily in their larval stages, though rarely remarked on in the adult stage (e.g. the Serpentine mines on Bramble leaves). A large number of families are included within the heading 'micro moths'.

Green Longhorn Moth
Adela reaumurella (viridella)
A distinctive little moth, with a body about 10mm long, but antennae 2–3 times this length (longest in males). Wings metallic green. The moths fly by day and dance around bushes, such as Hawthorn, on sunny days.
Habitat Woodland edges, scrub and clearings.
Status and distribution Common virtually throughout.
Season 4–6.

Nemophora degeerella
Slightly larger than Green Longhorn, with even longer antennae and a conspicuous dark-edged yellow bar across the wing. Day-flying.
Habitat Damp woodlands, streamsides.
Status and distribution Widespread and generally frequent, though rare in Scotland.
Season 5–6.
Similar species
N. fasciella is smaller, with a darker band and shorter antennae. In scrub and rough places. Widespread but local.

PLUME MOTHS Micro-moths that have feather-like wings and long barbed legs.

Large White Plume
Pterophorus pentadactyla
A distinctive and familiar species, with a wingspan of about 20mm, pure white. Frequently seen in gardens, and often comes to windows. The larvae roll Greater Bindweed leaves. They should be welcome in gardens!
Habitat Gardens, hedges, scrub. Larvae feed on Bindweed especially the white-flowered Greater Bindweed.
Status and distribution Widespread and common throughout.
Season 5–8.

Triangle Plume
Platyptilia gonodactyla
Wingspan about 15mm. Wings pale brown or almost white, usually marbled darker, with a dark triangle on the front of each forewing.
Habitat In various rough habitats where the larval food-plant Colt's-foot grows.
Status and distribution Widespread and common throughout.
Season 5–9.
Other similar plume moths occur within the area. They are hard to separate without detailed examination.

Many-plumed Moth
Alucita hexadactyla
An attractive little moth, with a wingspan of 12–15mm. The brown wings are divided into many feathery plumes, forming a fan-like pattern.
Habitat Woodland edges, hedges and scrub. Food-plant Honeysuckle, the pink larvae feed amongst the buds and flowers.
Status and distribution Widespread and moderately common throughout, though easily overlooked.
Season Adults hibernate, most likely to be seen 8–10 and 4–6.

Green Longhorn Moth, male

Nemophora degeerella

Large White Plume

Triangle Plume

Many-plumed Moth

Brown China-mark Moth
Nymphula nympheata

An unusual moth, in having underwater larvae. Adults are marbled brown and white, with a wingspan of 20–25mm. The larvae leave even, roughly oval marks in the floating leaves of water-lilies, which can often be seen.

Habitat Around still and slow-moving waters, where water-lilies occur.

Status and distribution Widespread and common throughout.

Season 5–8.

Common Crimson-and-gold
Pyrausta purpuralis

Though small, with a wingspan of barely 20mm, this moth is surprisingly conspicuous. It has reddish wings with gold markings on the forewings, white on the hindwings, and flies by day (and at night), visiting flowers.

Habitat In various rough, open habitats, where the larvae feed on mints or thyme.

Status and distribution Widespread and common throughout.

Season 5–8.

Similar species

P. aurata is very similar, has darker forewings and yellower markings on the hindwings. The larvae feed on Catmint and other members of the mint family. Widespread but less common.

Gold Fringe *Hypsopygia costalis* has the same general colouring, in a different pattern – pinkish-red wings with a gold fringe. Local, absent from Scotland; widespread on the Continent.

Small Magpie
Eurrhypara hortulata

An attractive little moth, with a wingspan of 20–25mm. The wings are white, edged and dotted with black, and the insect has a yellow head.

Habitat Hedges, rough ground, gardens, on nettles and dead-nettles.

Status and distribution Widespread and common throughout.

Season 6–8.

Similar species

See Large Magpie and its close relatives (see p.164) which are unrelated but rather similar in general appearance.

Bramble Leaf-miner
Stigmella (Nepticula) aurella

These tiny moths are much better known in their larval stage; the larvae cause the attractive serpentine leaf mines in Bramble leaves, with the tunnel enlarging as it goes round. The adults are tiny, about 7–8mm wingspan, with a yellow stripe on each wing.

Habitat On Bramble, wherever it occurs.

Status and distribution Widespread and common throughout, except in the far north.

Season Adults 5–9, larval patterns visible through most of the summer and autumn until leaf-fall.

Similar species

Tischeria marginea makes a much less attractive blotch-mine in Bramble leaves. Similar habitats and distribution, but less common.

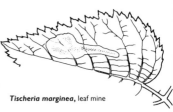

Tischeria marginea, leaf mine

Brown China-mark Moth

Pyrausta aurata, mating

Small Magpie **Bramble Leaf-miner,** mine in Bramble leaf

Green Oak Roller or **Oak Tortrix**
Tortrix viridana
A pretty little green moth, with a wingspan of about 20mm. Forewings green, with a thin pale margin; underwings greyish or white. The larvae are greenish, and lower themselves from trees by silken threads when ready to pupate. They can almost completely defoliate oaks, and are an important food source for birds with young.
Habitat Oakwoods and places where oaks grow.
Status and distribution Widespread and common.
Season 6–7.
Similar species
See Cream-bordered Green Pea, p.192.

Small Ermine
Yponomeuta padella
A small white moth, with a wingspan of about 20mm. Forewings white with black dots, hindwings grey. The larvae feed in dense silken tents on hedges and shrubs.
Habitat Hedgerows, woodland edges, scrub. Larval food-plants most commonly Hawthorn and Blackthorn.
Status and distribution Widespread and frequent.
Season Adults 6–8, larvae 7–9.
Similar species
There are several similar *Yponomeuta spp.* *Myelois cribrella* looks very similar, but hindwings have a clear white fringe. Occurs on thistles, and sometimes known as **Thistle Ermine**.

White-shouldered House-moth
Endrosis sarcitrella
One of several small moths sometimes known as 'clothes moths'. This species has a wingspan of about 15mm and marbled brown wings but with a distinct white 'shoulder'. Feeds on various fabrics.
Habitat Most frequent now in houses, though may also occur in old nests.
Status and distribution Widespread and common throughout.
Season Often all year in warm buildings.
Similar species
Brown House Moth *Hofmannophila pseudospretella* is similar in size and colour, but lacks the white shoulder. Similar habitats and distribution.
Common Clothes Moth *Tineola biselliella* is pale dull yellowish. The most frequent of the clothes moths, causing considerable damage at times. Widespread and common.

Coleophora caespitiella
The adults are tiny off-white moths that are rarely noticed. However, they have distinctive silken larval cases which are prominently attached to the flowers of various rushes, often in abundance.
Habitat Moorland and wet places, wherever rushes grow.
Status and distribution Widespread and locally common.
Season The cases are usually visible 7–9.

* *Oecophora bractella*
An attractive little moth, with a wingspan of 12–16mm. The wings are fringed, and coloured brownish-purple with a gold dot. Like other members of this family, there is a small tuft of hairs at the base of the antennae.
Habitat Damp ancient woodlands with old deciduous trees. The larvae feed on decaying oak and Beech.
Status and distribution Uncommon though widespread in Europe.
Season 5–6.

Green Oak Roller

Thistle Ermine

White-shouldered House-moth

Coleophora caespitiella, pupae

White-shouldered House-moth, pupae on felt

Oecophora bractella

CADDIS-FLIES
ORDER TRICHOPTERA

A medium-sized group of insects, with about 400 European species, and 350–400 in the area covered by the book. They resemble moths in some respects, and are distantly related. Virtually all caddis-fly larvae are aquatic, and those species that construct cases of débris around themselves are well known, though there are also naked larvae and net-making larvae, together with a very few terrestrial species.

caddis-fly, larva

The adults are generally brown, with long antennae, often much longer than the body. There are two pairs of wings, both hairy, especially the forewings. They are held roof-wise over the body when at rest. Compared with the Neuroptera, caddis-flies have relatively few cross-veins in the wings. Most adults are nocturnal, though a few are active in the day. They rarely feed, and have no proboscis like those of butter-flies and moths.

Caddis-flies are difficult to identify individually, with a few exceptions, and microscopic examination is often needed. The following are a small selection of commoner or more distinctive ones.

Great Red Sedge
Phryganea grandis
One of the largest species in the area, with a wingspan of 50–60mm. The wings are brown, mottled darker, though males lack the dark forewing stripe. The larvae live in cases constructed of plant fragments, arranged spirally.
Habitat Still and slow-moving water.

Status and distribution Widespread throughout and moderately common.
Season 5–7.
Similar species
P. striata is as large (and often included in the same English name), but the female has a narrower stripe broken up into dashes. Widespread and common.

Hydropsyche angustipennis
A small species, with a wingspan of 20–25mm. Grey and yellowish in colour, with antennae shorter than the body. Active both by day and by night.
Habitat Around still and flowing water.
Status and distribution Widespread and common.
Season 5–10.

Rhyacophila species
There are 4 species of this genus in the UK, reasonably distinctive as a group, but hard to separate individually. The wings are not very hairy; wingspan about 35mm. The larvae do not have cases, and are active predators.
Habitat Around faster-flowing and upland streams.
Status and distribution Generally common and widespread, mainly western in the UK.
Season 6–9.

Odontocerum albicorne
A largish distinctive species; wingspan 50–55mm. Wings brown, held close to the body; antennae almost twice as long as wings, but distinctly serrated, just visible with the naked eye, more easily seen under a lens (visible in the photo). Larval case covered with grains of sand.
Habitat Larvae live in faster-flowing streams with sandy bases.
Status and distribution Widespread and common where suitable habitat exists.
Season 6–10.

Hydropsyche angustipennis

Rhyacophila species

Odontocerum albicorne

TRUE FLIES
ORDER DIPTERA

An extremely large group of insects, comprising about 6,000 species in Britain alone (roughly a quarter of the total insect fauna, in terms of numbers of species). Overall, it is a reasonably distinctive group, with the primary linking feature being that the

fly halteres

insects have only 2 wings (hence the name *diptera*, meaning 2-winged). The hindwings are reduced to a pair of tiny club-shaped balancing organs known as halteres, visible in many of the pictures. A few parasitic species are wingless. The mouthparts are basically designed for sucking liquids of various sorts, with a variety of modifications for different feeding styles, including nectar-feeding, carrion-feeding and blood-sucking.

For identification purposes, the flies are a difficult group, and many species cannot readily be identified from casual observation. Nevertheless, a surprising number can be identified in the field, from relatively superficial observation of collected specimens, or from good photographs. There are a number of groups into which the flies can be classified, though these do not necessarily exactly follow family divisions, and many species do not fall within them. These are briefly introduced and described in the text, though many of the key differences between families are too microscopic for them to be useful field characters.

Crane-flies, Family Tipulidae

Also known as 'Daddy long-legs', which describes their long dangling legs and bumbling flight. Some species are quite colourful.

Giant Crane-fly
Tipula maxima
The largest and most distinctive of the crane-flies, with a wingspan of about 60mm. The wings are attractively marbled with brown, with triangular darker areas.
Habitat Damp acid areas, often shady.
Status and distribution Widespread throughout, but rather local.
Season 4–8.
Similar species
T. vittata is slightly smaller, and has the brown markings more restricted to the veins. Damp woods and boggy areas, throughout.

Tipula paludosa
The archetypal 'daddy long-legs', frequently coming into houses and gardens. Body greyish-brown, wings clear except for the leading edge.
Habitat Rough grassland and other open areas. The larvae ('leather-jackets') feed on roots, and may do considerable damage.
Status and distribution Widespread and common throughout.
Season 5–10, becoming most abundant in late summer/early autumn.
Similar species
T. oleracea is virtually identical, but has at least the first 3 antennae segments orange-red (only the first two in *T. paludosa*). The antennae are very small, and a lens is needed. Status and distribution as above.

Tipula rufina
A more delicate and smaller species than the above.
Habitat Damp areas, woodland and other less disturbed habitats.
Status and distribution Widespread but local.
Season 5–7.

Giant Crane-fly

Tipula vittata

Tipula paludosa, female

Tipula oleracea, female

Spotted Crane-fly
Nephrotoma appendiculata

An attractive species, with a wingspan of 40–50mm. Body yellow (particularly in females) with a black dot on each segment, and females have a sharp reddish tip to the abdomen. Wings clear.

Habitat Open woods, gardens, rough herb-rich areas.

Status and distribution Widespread and common throughout.

Season 5–9.

Similar species

N. crocata has a more boldly marked abdomen, black with 3 yellow rings. Widespread, locally common in damp woods and scrub.

N. quadrifaria resembles *appendiculata*, but the wings have a dark mark and streak. Local but widespread.

Ctenophora atrata

An attractive and distinctive species, with an orange, yellow or black abdomen, with a long pointed tip in females. Males have conspicuous feathery antennae. Wingspan 35–40mm.

Habitat Damp woods, unimproved farmland and wet commons.

Status and distribution Widespread but local, throughout.

Season 4–7.

Similar species

C. ornata tends to have a yellower abdomen with a more distinct 'waist', and remarkably large feathery antennae. Widespread, though local, in old woods where there is decaying timber.

Winter Gnat
Trichocera relegationis

These flies resemble crane-flies, but are smaller, and have different habits. They gather in dancing swarms in winter, even in quite cold weather. Individuals often settle on walls, windowsills and so on.

Habitat Woods, gardens, rough ground, almost everywhere.

Status and distribution Widespread and common throughout.

Season Virtually all year, though most conspicuous in winter.

Similar species

This is one example of a group of a dozen or so species, hard to separate in the field.

Mosquitoes and Midges, Family Culicidae and others

This group (see pp.206–8) is most familiar in the form of biting mosquitoes, though there are also many non-biting midges. Mosquitoes fall into two recognizable groups: culicines and anophelines. Culicines rest with the body slightly hunched and the abdomen parallel to the surface; anophelines hold their body sharply angled away

Culicine mosquito   Anopheline mosquito

from the surface. Female culicines have very short palps, anophelines have much longer ones. The only anophelines in this area are those in the genus *Anopheles*. There are 32 species of mosquito in Britain.

Culex pipiens

An undistinguished mosquito, brownish-grey, but with whitish bands on each abdominal segment. Females are said to bite man only rarely, though they feed on a wide variety of other animals.

Habitat Will breed in almost any still water-body, including puddles or even hoof-prints.

Status and distribution Widespread and common throughout.

Season Adults hibernate, and individuals may be seen all year. Most frequent 7–10.

Spotted Crane-fly, mating

Ctenophora atrata

Ctenophora ornata, male

Winter Gnat

Culex pipiens, male

Culex pipiens, female

Culiseta annulata

One of the more distinctive species of mosquito, with its large size (wingspan 17–20mm), banded black and white legs, and spotted wings. Frequently bites man, and most bites in winter are caused by this species.

Habitat Breeds in a very wide variety of still waters, including brackish water and very small tanks.

Status and distribution Widespread and common throughout.

Season May be seen in any month; adults hibernate, but may appear on the wing on warmer days.

Similar species

There are several other species of *Culiseta*, with varying patterns on wings, legs and bodies.

Chironomid Midge

Chironomus plumosus

One of a number of similar species. The individuals are frequently black, about 5–6mm long, with plumed antennae in males, and wings shorter than abdomen. They are non-biting. Males gather in clouds (see photo).

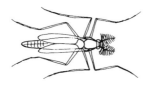

Chironomus plumosus

Habitat The larvae live in various types of still water, and the adults can be seen nearby.

Status and distribution Widespread and common throughout.

Season 5–9.

Similar species

There are several hundred related species, mostly smaller than *C. plumosus*. Specialist texts are required for identification.

Black-fly

Simulium equinum

One of many similar species of small fly, with a wingspan of 6–7mm, a black body, and a rather humped abdomen. Females bite various animals, including man. Not to be confused with the aphid 'blackfly'.

Habitat The larvae live in streams and rivers, and the adults occur around such habitats.

Status and distribution Widespread and common.

Season 3–11.

Similar species

There are numerous similar species.

Germander Speedwell gall

Jaapiella veronicae

See Galls (p.310).

Cerotelion lineatus

An undistinguished fly, with a brown body, and wings mottled with pale brown. The larvae are carnivorous, feeding on other insects associated with fungi.

Habitat Damp old woods.

Status and distribution Locally common in the south, rare further north.

Season 6–10.

Owl-midge or Moth-fly

Pericoma fuliginosa

Although very small (wingspan about 5mm), these little flies are surprisingly noticeable. As a group, they have hairy wings which they hold partly spread (some species fold them over the body, but they are less noticeable), resembling tiny moths.

Habitat Almost anywhere with rough vegetation, especially if slightly damp; the larvae feed on decaying vegetation.

Status and distribution Widespread and common throughout.

Season 3–11.

Similar species

One of hundreds of similar species. *Psychoda alternata* is particularly common around sewage farms.

Culiseta annulata

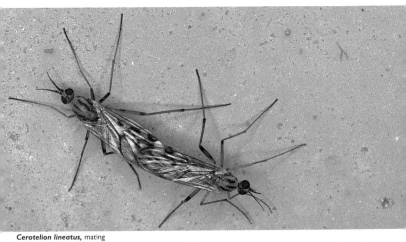

Cerotelion lineatus, mating

Chironomid Midge, swarm

Owl-midge

St Mark's Fly
Bibio marci

The largest and most distinctive and conspicuous of the bibionid flies. They have hairy black bodies, and clear wings with a brown front margin (wingspan about 20mm). The males fly slowly above vegetation in loose swarms, settling readily on flowers, leaves or posts.

Habitat Many rough unimproved habitats, especially scrub, hedgerows and woodland edges. Larvae mostly live in the soil.

Status and distribution Widespread and common throughout.

Season 4–5 (St Mark's Day is 25 April).

Similar species

B. hortulanus is less hairy, more slender, and reddish-brown. Widespread and common.

Soldier-fly
Stratiomys chameleon

The English name refers to the whole family (Stratiomyidae), but others are less conspicuous. This species is one of the largest (wingspan 20–23mm) with a broad abdomen boldly marked black and yellow. Soldier-flies resemble some hoverflies (see p.216), but have longer antennae and more flattened bodies, and hold their wings rather stiffly over the bodies, with wing-edges parallel.

Habitat Fens and marshes, especially with open water. Larvae are aquatic though some species emerge and travel some distance on land before pupating.

Status and distribution Local and southern in UK. More frequent and widespread on the Continent.

Season 5–9.

Similar species

S. potamida is similar in size, but has unbroken narrower yellow bands across the abdomen; similar habitats and distribution. *Odontomyia ornata* is slightly smaller, with the markings deeper yellow, and antennae not bent in the middle (as they are in *Stratiomys* species). Widespread but local in damp places.

Snipe-fly
Rhagio scolopacea

Distinctive fly, with a wingspan of 20–24mm. They have long narrow abdomens, marked with yellow and black, though this is not a very noticeable characteristic in the field. This species has wings with brownish marbling. They usually rest head-down on posts or other support, making quick darting flights.

Habitat Damp grassy and wooded places.

Status and distribution Widespread and moderately common throughout.

Season 5–8.

Similar species

There are several other slightly smaller species.

R. tringaria is similar but has clear unmarked wings. Widespread but local.

Horse-flies, Family Tabanidae

Robust flies, usually with large, brightly coloured iridescent eyes; females are blood-suckers, and have powerful blade-like mouthparts for piercing skin.

Horse-fly
Tabanus sudeticus

A large and fearsome-looking horse-fly, with a wingspan of 50–60mm. The body is broad, brown with dull yellow markings, including triangles down the centre line; wings clear except for the front margin.

Habitat Damp pastures, especially near woodland.

Status and distribution Widespread but local and mainly western in the UK; more generally distributed on the Continent.

Season 6–8.

Similar species

T. bovinus is smaller, paler brown in colour, with paler, narrower abdominal triangles. Similar habitats, especially frequent near rivers and ditches; mainly southern in the UK.

T. bromius is smaller again, dull greyish in colour, though variable. Frequent in damp pastures, mainly southern in the UK.

St Mark's Fly

Horse-fly, *Tabanus sudeticus*

Soldier-fly, *Stratiomys chameleon*

Snipe-fly

Cleg
Haematopota pluvialis

A familiar insect, which settles on the skin all too quietly (the larger horse-flies are clearly audible!). Wingspan about 20mm; body dull greyish-brown, with mottled wings. The females are very adept at finding people (or other animals) to bite.

Habitat Damp grassy places, woodland clearings, and even dry grassland.

Status and distribution Widespread and common throughout.

Season 5–9.

Similar species

H. crassicornis differs in having darker wings and wholly black antennae. More frequent in upland areas, in similar habitats.

Chrysops relictus

Members of this genus of horse-flies alight with their wings held out at an angle forming a triangle, and are often not recognized as horse-flies until they bite! Wingspan 20–24mm. Body dark with yellow patches; wings marbled with brown.

Habitat Open woodland, grassy clearings, usually near water.

Status and distribution Rather uncommon in the UK except in the New Forest; widespread but local on the Continent.

Season 5–9.

Similar species

C. caecutiens has an 'X'-shaped mark on the abdomen; males have almost black abdomens. Widespread and moderately common. There are several other very similar species of *Chrysops*, hard to separate in the field.

C. pictus is similar, but has a paler abdomen with dark markings and marbled wings. Uncommon, mainly southern.

Bee-fly
Bombylius major

A distinctive fly, resembling a small furry bumble bee, but with a long straight proboscis at the front. Wingspan about 20mm. Wings have dark markings towards the front edges. The females lay eggs close to the nests of mining bees, and the larvae enter and parasitize the bee larvae. Adults feed at flowers, hovering in front of them.

Habitat Flowery, warm, unspoilt places, such as woodland rides.

Status and distribution Common in S Britain, rarer to the north; widespread on the Continent.

Season 3–6.

Similar species

There are about 15 other *Bombylius* species in the area, mostly smaller and/or less common.

Thyridanthrax fenestratus

A medium-sized fly, with a wingspan of about 12–14mm. Distinctive by the conspicuous dark marbling which clouds the lower half of the wings. They are related to bee-flies, and behave similarly, but have a short retractable proboscis.

Habitat Dry flowery places, especially on sandy soils.

Status and distribution Local and southern in the UK; more widespread in Europe, though not common.

Season 6–8.

Similar species

* *Anthrax anthrax* is more bulky, darker-looking, and with about three-quarters of the wing area dark. Local in dry heathy places.

* *Villa hottentotus* is slightly larger than *Thyridanthrax*, but has wings clear except for the front margin. Like a less furry bee-fly with a short proboscis. Widespread and frequent on the Continent.

V. modesta is darker and less furry still. Local on dunes and heaths.

Chrysops relictus

Chrysops caecutiens

Chrysops pictus

Bee-fly

Thyridanthrax fenestratus

Robber-flies, Family Asilidae

Powerfully built predatory flies, usually very bristly, with dagger-like mouthparts. The Empid Flies (Empidae) are similar in habits, but less robust, and usually rest with the abdomen more raised.

Asilus crabroniformis

A very large and impressive fly, with a body length of up to 30mm, and powerfully built. Body black and yellow, face heavily bearded. Waits on a log or other perch, and attacks prey from there. It can deal with almost any size of insect, including wasps. Larvae feed in dung.
Habitat Open flowery places such as downs, heaths and warm woodland glades.
Status and distribution Very local and strongly southern in UK; more widespread on the Continent.
Season 7–10.

Laphria flava

Another large and robust robber-fly, with a body length of up to 25mm. The body is broad, hairy and yellowish-brown. The flies rest on logs in sunny clearings, attacking passing insects of all types.
Habitat Woodland clearings, especially in coniferous woods.
Status and distribution Very rare in UK, in Caledonian pinewoods only; widespread throughout the Continent, though local.
Season 6–9.
Similar species
L. gilva is slightly smaller and less furry. Local in deciduous woodland, rare in UK.
L. marginata is smaller and less robust than L. flava, with yellowish bristly hairs on the legs. Local in deciduous woodland.

Machimus atricapillus

A smaller robber-fly, though still with the fierce predatory appearance of the group.
Habitat Chalk and limestone grassland and scrub.
Status and distribution Local in southern UK, more widespread on the Continent.
Season 6–8.
Similar species
Epitriptus cingulatus is slightly smaller, with a body length of 11–12mm (compared to 12–15mm in Machimus), making it the smallest robber-fly in the area. It is paler, more yellowish, than Machimus, with pale hairs on the forehead (all black in the above species). Widespread and common in rough grassy and heathy places, throughout. On the wing through June and July.

Pamponerus germanicus

A medium-sized robber-fly with a body length of about 18mm. Wings with brown marbling, legs partly orange or yellow.
Habitat Most frequent in sand-dunes and other dry coastal habitats.
Status and distribution Local throughout southern UK; widespread but local on the Continent.
Season 6–8.

Dioctria rufipes

A relatively small robber-fly; body length about 10mm. Rests on vegetation, and preys on passing Ichneumons and other insects, especially Hymenopterans.
Habitat Rough flowery places of various sorts.
Status and distribution Widespread and common almost throughout.
Season 5–8.
Similar species
D. oelandica is larger, to 15mm, and differs in having darkened wings with a greenish-purple sheen. It is a local species of wood margins and scrub, confined to southern Britain; more widespread on the Continent.

Asilus crabroniformis

Laphria marginata, mating

Laphria flava

Machimus atricapillus

Pamponerus germanicus

Dioctria rufipes, with prey

Empis tesselata

The most frequent and noticeable of the empid flies, which resemble robber-flies but are more slightly built and have a downward-pointing proboscis. This species has a body length of about 12mm, brownish wings, and a rather hairy body. Like most empids, it is predatory on insects but also feeds on nectar.

Habitat A wide variety of flowery habitats such as wood borders, scrub, woodland rides.

Status and distribution Widespread and frequent throughout.

Season 5–8.

Similar species

E. stercorea is similar in size and habits, but has a yellowish body with a black stripe, and clearer wings. Widespread throughout. *Hilara maura* is dark-bodied, slightly smaller; the males have enlarged front tarsi, which are quite conspicuous. Frequent throughout, particularly near water.

Poecilobothrus nobilitatus

Though very small, with a wingspan of 12–14mm, this is an attractive and quite conspicuous little fly. Large numbers congregate on mud and around water; both sexes have mottled brown wings, but males have white tips, and they constantly court females or fight other males. Body metallic greenish.

Habitat Around still and slow-moving water-bodies.

Status and distribution Very common in S Britain, less common northwards; widespread and common on the Continent.

Season 5–9.

Similar species

There are many other flies in this group (the Long-headed Flies *Dolichopodidae*), though none are as easily identifiable as this species.

Hoverflies, Family Syrphidae

Although there are several hundred species in this important group, many are identifiable from superficial examination, thanks to their bright colours in reasonably stable patterns. They are attractive, harmless insects, sharing the habit of hovering readily then darting. All feed at flowers, on nectar or pollen particularly favouring the flowers of the Umbelliferae such as Hogweed or Angelica. Some mimic bees and wasps. The larvae vary considerably in form and life-style, many, such as *Episyrphus balteatus* are active carnivores, feeding especially on aphids. Other feeding habits include dung-feeding, wood-feeding and preying upon aquatic larvae. Hoverflies are covered more fully here than most other groups of flies because of their popularity with naturalists and relative ease of identification (pp.216–32).

Platycheirus podagratus

A smallish hoverfly, with a wingspan of about 12–15mm. One of a group of rather similar hoverflies with narrow bodies, black and yellow markings and a black stripe down the back.

Habitat Bogs, moorland and acid wet places.

Status and distribution Frequent in N Britain, widespread though local on the Continent, mainly in hilly areas.

Season 5–7.

Similar species

P. clypeatus is slightly more robust, with smaller yellow spots at the base of the abdomen; widespread and common, especially in the south.

Empis tesselata

Poecilobothrus nobilitatus

Platycheirus podagratus

Chrysotoxum bicinctum

An attractive and distinctive hoverfly, with a wingspan of about 25mm. The body is black, with 2 distinctive bands of yellow (hence the Latin name *bicinctum*) and 2 tiny yellow spots between them. The antennae are relatively long, and straight.

Habitat Grassland and scrub, especially on calcareous soils.

Status and distribution Widespread, locally common in the south, rarer in the north in UK; widespread and frequent on the Continent.

Season 5–9.

Chrysotoxum festivum

Slightly larger than *C. bicinctum*, but with similar antennae. Body black, with 3 interrupted yellow bands. Thorax black, with yellow edges.

Habitat Sheltered flowery places, such as woodland edges and scrub.

Status and distribution Widespread and moderately common northwards to S Scotland; throughout N Europe.

Season 6–10.

Similar species

C. vernale is very similar in size and markings, but the yellow bars are more evenly curved, not kinked. Rare in SW England only; more frequent, though southern, on the Continent.

Dasysyrphus tricinctus

A medium-sized hoverfly, with a wingspan of about 22mm. Thorax black, unmarked; abdomen black, rather diamond-shaped, with 3 yellow rings, the central one largest and usually uninterrupted, the other 2 thin and broken.

Habitat Woodland rides and margins.

Status and distribution Local and mainly southern in the UK. More widespread on the Continent.

Season 4–9.

Similar species

D. albostriatus has broader, curved yellow stripes, with the lowest one unbroken. Widespread through most of the UK and N Europe.

D. lunulatus has hooked yellow lunules rather than bars. Mainly northern in the UK, especially in woods. Widespread on the Continent.

Didea fasciata

A small to medium hoverfly, with a wingspan of about 20mm. Antennae shorter than in the above species. Abdomen black, with 1 interrupted yellow stripe and 2 complete ones.

Habitat Mainly in and around old woodland, but moving into flowery habitats (including gardens) to feed at flowers.

Status and distribution Widespread throughout, but very local in the UK, more frequent in wooded parts of the Continent.

Season 5–10.

Similar species

D. intermedia is very similar and hard to separate; it is slightly smaller, and has all-black halteres (part yellow in *D. fasciata*). Widespread but local, probably under-recorded.

Doros conopseus

A large distinctive species, with a wingspan of over 30mm. Body narrow, black with a 'waisted' appearance, a thin yellow band near the waist, and brown front margins to the wings.

Habitat Woodland edges and glades, or sheltered grassland.

Status and distribution Rare and local in Britain, confined to England; more widespread on the Continent.

Season 6–8.

Similar species

No other hoverfly resembles it, but it is similar to some solitary wasps, or conopid flies (see p.232).

Chrysotoxum bicinctum

Chrysotoxum festivum

Doros conopseus

Dasysyrphus tricinctus

Didea fasciata

Megasyrphus annulipes

A largish hoverfly, with a wingspan of about 25mm. Abdomen black with yellow stripes, like many similar species, but this one is larger and rather hairier than comparable species. The thorax is blackish-brown and shiny.

Habitat Found in woodland margins and rides.

Status and distribution Widespread but local in the UK, rather more frequent in Europe.

Season 5–10.

Similar species

No close relatives, but see *Syrphus ribesii* (see p.224)

Meliscaeva cinctella

A smallish hoverfly, wingspan about 20mm. Abdomen pattern rather resembles *Episyrphus balteatus* without the double black mark, though overall it is a slightly smaller and more slender species.

Habitat In scrub and rough flowery habitats; very mobile.

Status and distribution Widespread and frequent, probably migratory.

Season 5–10.

Similar species

Melangyna cincta is similar in size and general markings, but has more black, with the uppermost yellow markings reduced to 2 lateral triangles. Widespread, more frequent in the south.

Meliscaeva auricollis has the dark abdominal bands prolonged forwards into a pointed triangle. It is widespread in wooded places, common in the south, rarer further north.

Metasyrphus corollae

Wingspan about 16–18mm. Wings clear, thorax unmarked, abdomen black with 1 interrupted and 2 notched or interrupted stripes of yellow.

Habitat Almost any flowery habitat, including gardens.

Status and distribution Widespread and common throughout, with numbers probably boosted by migration in some years.

Season 5–10.

Similar species

M. latifasciatus has a rather broader abdomen, and areas of yellow more rounded. Widespread and moderately frequent in open flowery habitats, especially in damp places.

Metasyrphus luniger

Similar in size and general shape to the above 2 species but generally blacker in appearance, with 3 pairs of comma-shaped lunules of creamy yellow on the abdomen.

Habitat A wide variety of flowery habitats such as pastures, woodland rides, gardens.

Status and distribution Widespread and common, probably boosted by immigrants in some years.

Season 4–10.

Similar species

M. nielseni is very similar, but the lunules have blunter outer ends. Very local, mainly in Scotland in the UK, but occasional elsewhere; widespread but local in Europe. *M. nitens* often has the yellow bands joined, except the uppermost. Local, in old woodlands.

See also *Scaeva* species (p.222).

Megasyrphus annulipes

Meliscaeva cinctella

Metasyrphus corollae

Metasyrphus latifasciatus

Metasyrphus nitens

Epistrophe nitidicollis

A typical hoverfly, with yellow and black abdomen. Wingspan 22–24mm. The legs are entirely orange, and the thoracic pattern should be checked carefully against the photograph.

Habitat Woodland rides and glades.

Status and distribution Local in southern part of UK, more widespread on the Continent.

Season 5–8.

Similar species

E. diaphana has broader yellow bands on the thorax; local.

E. grossulariae has even broader bands, with the top one consisting of 2 almost square blocks. Widespread but local.

Episyrphus balteatus

Probably the most frequently noticed hoverfly. The orange body, with double black stripes across it (the lower one very narrow in each case) is distinctive.

Habitat May occur in almost any habitat where there are flowers; highly mobile, migrating widely.

Status and distribution Widespread and abundant throughout, though varying in numbers according to the number of immigrants.

Season Mainly 3–11, but could be seen in any month.

Leucozona lucorum

A distinctive medium-large hoverfly, with a wingspan of about 25mm and a broad body. Abdomen creamy-white above, black towards the tip; thorax black with brown hairs. The wings have a dark patch near the centre of the front margin.

Habitat Damp open woodland with rides and clearings.

Status and distribution Widespread, frequent in the south though rarer further north in the UK. Widespread on the Continent.

Season 5–8, most frequent 5–6.

Similar species

L. glaucia has less white on the abdomen, and a more slender body. Similar habitats, but more local.

Scaeva pyrastri

A largish conspicuous hoverfly, with a wingspan of about 25mm. The black abdomen, with 3 creamy-white pairs of lunules, is a distinctive combination (except for species below).

Habitat Most open sunny flowery habitats, including gardens; a very mobile species.

Status and distribution Widespread and generally common, with numbers boosted in some years by immigration.

Season 5–10.

Similar species

S. selenitica is superficially similar, but the white commas extend equally far up the abdomen at either end. Local but widespread.

Sphaerophoria scripta

One of a group of similar small species, with a wingspan of 12–15mm, and a yellow edge to the black thorax. Abdomen black and yellow; in this species, the long abdomen projects noticeably beyond the wings. Markings variable.

Habitat In most flowery habitats including gardens and waste ground.

Season 5–10.

Similar species

S. menthastri is slightly smaller, and has each yellow bar interrupted. Widespread and common throughout.

S. philanthus is smaller and darker, with 4 pairs of yellow dots. Mainly western in UK on heaths, moors, acid uplands.

Epistrophe nitidicollis

Episyrphus balteatus

Episyrphus balteatus, pupa

Leucozona lucorum

Scaeva pyrastri

Sphaerophoria scripta

Syrphus ribesii

A common and familiar 'typical' hoverfly. Wingspan 20–24mm. Thorax dark, unmarked. Abdomen broad, roughly oval, with 1 interrupted and 3 uninterrupted yellow bands; females have entirely yellow hind femora.

Habitat Most flowery habitats, such as rough grassland, hedgerows, gardens.

Status and distribution Widespread and common throughout.

Season 5–11.

Similar species

See *Megasyrphus annulipes* (p.220).

Syrphus vitripennis

This species resembles *S. ribesii* in general form and colouring. It is usually slightly smaller and more slender, and part of the hind femora of the females is always black (all yellow in the above species). Males are much more difficult to separate with certainty in the field.

Habitat Occurs in a wide variety of flowery habitats. They migrate widely and can appear almost anywhere.

Status and distribution Common and widespread throughout, varying in abundance according to immigrant numbers.

Season 3–11.

Xanthogramma pedissequum

An attractive medium-sized species, with a wingspan of about 22mm. Generally black, but with a yellow stripe on each side of the thorax, yellow triangles on each side of the abdomen, then 2 interrupted yellow stripes below that. Wings have dark patches towards the front margins.

Habitat Grassland, woodland rides and other flowery places, usually where there is some bare ground.

Status and distribution Widespread but local in UK; widespread on the Continent.

Season 5–9.

Similar species

X. citrofasciatum. Similar in size, shape and general appearance, but wings barely marked, and the first yellow markings on the abdomen are stripes rather than triangles. Widespread on the Continent, but local and southern in the UK.

Rhingia campestris

One of the most distinctive of hoverflies, once learnt. Wingspan 22–25mm. Abdomen brownish-orange, usually with a dark stripe down the centre (occasionally much reduced). The most distinctive feature is the extended snout, clearly visible from most angles.

Habitat Most closely associated with damp cattle pastures, but they are mobile and can turn up almost anywhere.

Status and distribution Widespread and common throughout.

Season 5–10, most frequent in early summer.

Similar species

R. rostrata is generally more orange, with virtually no dark stripe, and the snout is slightly smaller and paler – not always easy to separate from *R. campestris*. Local or rare, mainly in woodland.

Syrphus vitripennis

Xanthogramma pedissequum

Syrphus ribesii

Rhingia campestris

Drone-fly

Eristalis tenax

A common and familiar species, noted for its mimicry of male Honey Bee. Wingspan 24–28mm. Highly variable, basically deep brown with 2 narrow whitish rings, and greater or lesser amounts of orange on the edges of the abdomen. Rather hairy.

Habitat A very wide range of habitats, occurring almost anywhere that there are flowers.

Status and distribution Widespread and common throughout.

Season Can be seen in any month, and adults hibernate.

Similar species

E. horticola has a shorter, broader abdomen, a darkened area in the centre of the wing, and broad curved yellow marks on the abdomen. Widespread but local throughout.

Eristalis pertinax

Rather similar to Drone Fly, though slightly more slender with a strongly tapering abdomen, and with 1 pair of broad yellow markings on the abdomen; front legs wholly orange.

Habitat Found in a wide variety of habitats, wherever there are flowers. Larvae breed in wet, organically enriched situations.

Status and distribution Widespread and common throughout.

Season 3–10.

Eristalis intricarius

A furry bee mimic, similar in size to Drone-fly, though seeming more robust as it is much hairier. Body dark and light brown, legs black and yellow.

Habitat Various flowery places, especially if damp or semi-shaded.

Status and distribution Widespread throughout, but local.

Season 3–9.

Similar species

See Narcissus Fly (p.228), which is usually darker, and has all-black legs.

Eristalis nemorum

A smaller species than the above, with a wingspan of about 22mm, and a shorter body. Abdominal markings similar to *E. pertinax*, legs black and yellow, wing with just a small squarish dark mark.

Habitat A wide range of flowery habitats.

Status and distribution Widespread and common throughout.

Season 4–9.

Similar species

E. arbustorum can be almost identical in size and markings, though the face is usually pale without a dark stripe, and there is usually more yellow on the abdomen. Similar habitats and distribution.

Eristalinus sepulchralis

A small blackish fly, with a wingspan of less than 20mm. Thorax and abdomen black, with obscure greyish stripes on the abdomen. An active little fly, less approachable than many hoverflies.

Habitat Lowland marshes, damp grazing and similar damp flowery habitats.

Status and distribution Widespread but local throughout.

Season 4–9.

Similar species

E. aeneus is rather larger and longer-bodied, blacker in colour overall. A local species, occurring mainly in coastal habitats.

Drone-fly

Eristalis horticola

Eristalis pertinax

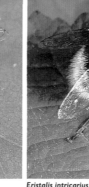

Eristalis nemorum

Eristalis intricarius

Eristalinus sepulchralis

Helophilus pendulus

A very attractive and distinctive hoverfly. Wingspan about 25mm. Thorax boldly striped with 3 black stripes on yellow; abdomen yellow and black; legs predominantly pale yellowish, with small patches of black.

Habitat Almost any rough flowery habitats, though especially common near water, where the larvae usually live.

Status and distribution Widespread and common throughout.

Season 4–10.

Similar species

H. hybridus is very like *H. pendulus*; males tend to have more continuous yellow markings down each side of the abdomen, and there is more black on the hind legs of both sexes. Local around well-vegetated ponds. Widespread.

Myathropa florea

Resembles the larger *Eristalis* species in size and markings, but is brighter in colour and more boldly marked, and the pattern is reasonably distinctive on close examination. Wings virtually clear.

Habitat Flowery rides and clearings in woodland, or on wooded commons.

Status and distribution Widespread but only locally common.

Season 5–10.

Narcissus-fly

Merodon equestris

A dark, hairy bumble bee mimic, with a wingspan of 22–24mm. Head and thorax basically all black, but widely variable in the colour of the hairs, mimicking various species of bumble bee, including the red-tailed ones; legs all black.

Habitat Woods and other sheltered flowery places. Unusually for hoverflies, the larvae live in monocotyledonous bulbs, mainly Wild Daffodils and Bluebells, but they can also be a horticultural pest on cultivated bulbs.

Status and distribution Widespread, though only rarely abundant.

Season 5–8; most frequently seen in May.

Sericomyia silentis

A most attractive largish hoverfly, with a wingspan of about 30mm. When seen in the field, the golden fringe of hairs is very noticeable. Legs yellow, wings clear except for a brownish main vein.

Habitat Damp well-vegetated acid areas, around peat-cuttings or bog pools. Frequently visits flowers of Devil's Bit Scabious in late summer.

Status and distribution A widespread species throughout and locally common in suitable habitats.

Season 5–10.

Similar species

See *Megasyrphus annulipes* (p. 220).

Sericomyia lappona

An attractive and distinctive species, resembling the above in general form, but smaller. The abdominal stripes are thinner and paler, more or less parallel-sided, and just meeting along the midline.

Habitat In damp places, especially associated with bogs or other peaty habitats.

Status and distribution A local species, though widespread both in Britain and on the Continent. Generally commoner northwards, where there is more suitable habitat.

Season 4–8.

Helophilus pendulus

Myathropa florea

Sericomyia lappona

Narcissus-fly

Sericomyia silentis

Volucella bombylans

A bumble bee mimic, largish by hoverfly standards, though small by bumble bee standards; wingspan 25–30mm. The thorax and abdomen are very hairy, variable in colour and mimicking different bumble bees, including red-tailed. The antennae, especially in some forms, are feathery, and the wing has a dark smudge halfway along.

Habitat Mainly in and around woodlands and clearings in woods, less frequently in scrub and rough grassland.

Status and distribution Widespread and moderately common.

Season 5–8.

Volucella pellucens

A large and very distinctive hoverfly, with a wingspan of about 35mm. The black and white abdomen and the black wing patch are diagnostic in conjunction with the large size. Legs dark.

Habitat Most frequent in woodland glades and rides, or scrub near woodland.

Status and distribution Widespread and moderately common in most areas.

Season 5–9.

Similar species

Unique once seen; *Leucozona lucorum* (see p.222) has a rather similar colour pattern, but is smaller, narrower, with more yellowish legs.

Volucella inflata

This species resembles *V. pellucens* in general form though is often slightly smaller. It differs in having brownish-orange in place of the white on the abdomen.

Habitat Usually associated with woodland areas, or other places with old trees.

Status and distribution Local in southern Britain, rare or absent further north. More widespread on the Continent, rarer northwards.

Season 5–8.

Volucella inanis

A large hoverfly, with the typical *Volucella* shape and a wingspan of over 30mm. The abdomen is bright yellow with 2 clear black bands and parts of a dorsal black line. Legs orange.

Habitat Woods, parks and gardens.

Status and distribution Very local and strongly southern in UK, more widespread in Europe.

Season 7–9.

Volucella zonaria

A large and impressive hoverfly, with a wingspan of up to 45mm, and a large body. Thorax brown, abdomen orange-yellow banded black – the whole effect is slightly reminiscent of a Hornet, though it behaves like a typical hoverfly, frequently sunbathing then darting off.

Habitat Most often seen in gardens and other flowery places; larvae probably live in wasps' nests.

Status and distribution Formerly very rare in Britain; now well established but local in the south, varying in numbers. Widespread and frequent on the Continent, becoming rarer northwards.

Season 5–10.

Brachypalpoides (Xylota) lenta

A distinctive and attractive hoverfly, similar in general pattern to *X. segnis*, but slightly larger, and with a broad red belt in place of the orange. Legs black.

Habitat Mainly old woodlands, especially where beech occurs.

Status and distribution Widespread in UK north to central Scotland, but very local. More frequent and widespread on the Continent.

Season 5–7.

Volucella bombylans

Volucella pellucens

Volucella bombylans

Volucella inanis

Volucella zonaria

Xylota segnis

A medium-sized hoverfly, with a wingspan of about 22–24mm, and a slender cylindrical body. The shape, and colour combination of yellow then black, is distinctive. Legs black and yellow; wings with a faint brown smudge in the middle. The wings obscure the abdomen when at rest.

Habitat Woods, rides, hedges and occasionally gardens; larvae live in rotting wood and other organic material.

Status and distribution Widespread and common.

Season 5–10.

Similar species

X. tarda is smaller and has a more bulbous abdomen, with a 'peak' of black extending down into the yellow patch. A local species, with scattered records, mainly in damp woodland.

Xylota sylvarum

Very similar in shape to the previous *Xylota* species, but abdomen black with golden hairs at near end, and marked with yellow towards the tip. Legs black and yellow.

Habitat Woodland and associated habitats.

Status and distribution Local in S Britain, rare further north. Probably widespread on the Continent.

Season 5–9.

Similar species

X. xanthocnema is extremely similar, and was not separated until relatively recently. Smaller (especially males), with hind tibiae entirely yellow (partly black in *X. sylvarum*). Apparently very local and southern, but probably overlooked.

Conops quadrifasciatus

One of the conopid flies, which have long probosces, and usually a 'waisted' abdomen. This species has a body length of about 10mm, and a banded black and yellow abdomen, rather like a wasp.

Habitat Rough flowery places; the larvae are internal parasites of bumble bees.

Status and distribution Widespread but local in the UK, more frequent on the Continent.

Season 6–10.

Myopa buccata

A rather deformed-looking fly, distinctly bent in the middle. Body length about 10mm, brown, wings veined with brown. Spends most of its time on flowers or sunbathing on leaves.

Habitat Rough, flowery places, often near water or wet places.

Status and distribution Widespread but local in the UK; widespread and more frequent on the Continent.

Season 5–8.

Xyphosia miliaria

One of the small but rather attractive 'picture-winged' flies. They are dark-bodied, with a wingspan of about 10mm. The wings are attractively marked with deep brown in a variety of patterns.

Habitat This species is always associated with thistles, especially Marsh Thistle.

Status and distribution Widespread and common throughout.

Season 5–7.

| *Urophora cardui* | *Xyphosia miliaria* | *Urophora solstitialis* |

'Picture-winged' fly wings

Similar species

There are a number of similar-looking close relatives.

Urophora cardui has wings with an attractive zigzag pattern (the galls formed by this species are shown on p.310).

U. solstitialis has transversely striped wings.

U. stylata has one stripe and a 'D' shaped mark at the tip.

Celery-fly *Euleia heraclei* looks similar, though has greenish eyes. The larvae mine the leaves of Celery and other Umbellifers.

Xylota segnis, male

Xylota sylvarum

Conops quadrifasciatus

Myopa buccata

Xyphosia miliaria

Sepsis fulgens

One of the little 'sepsid' flies, of which there are a number of species that cannot easily be separated in the field. They are small, with a wingspan of 7–8mm, but draw attention to themselves by waving their wings vigorously, and occasionally by occurring in large numbers.

Habitat Almost any tall vegetation; most common around farmland, especially in damper situations.

Status and distribution Widespread and common, often abundant in late summer.

Season They hibernate as adults, and can be seen at almost any time.

Fruit-fly or Vinegar-fly

Drosophila funebris

One of a number of similar species that fly around rotting fruit, opened wine bottles and other sources of sugary liquid. They are only 2–3mm long, but become noticeable by virtue of their presence in kitchens. Famous as the group whose chromosomes were investigated in detail.

Habitat Most often seen indoors around compost and opened foods.

Status and distribution Widespread and common throughout.

Season All year indoors; most frequent 6–10.

Tachinid Flies, Family Tachinidae

A large group of parasitic flies, all bristly-hairy in appearance.

Dexia rustica

One of the smallest of the tachinids, but frequently seen at flowers. Body length 10–12mm. Abdomen reddish-brown, with a dark dorsal stripe; females darker than males. Wings clear.

Habitat Rough flowery places; the larvae feed on beetle larvae in the soil.

Status and distribution Common in S UK, becoming rarer further north; widespread on the Continent.

Season 6–8.

Similar species

Gonia divisa has rather similar markings, but is a more robust swollen fly, with a projecting face. Moth parasite. Frequent at flowers, only in S Britain.

Tachina (Echinomyia) fera

A conspicuous fly, with a body length of 12–15mm, robust and swollen. Abdomen dark with orange-red at the edges (viewed from above), wings slightly coloured towards the base.

Habitat Rough flowery places, woodland clearings, riversides and so on. Larvae parasitize moth larvae.

Status and distribution Widespread and common.

Season 5–9.

Tachina (Echinomyia) grossa

A large fly, resembling a bumble bee in flight. Body length 20–25mm, large and swollen. Thorax and abdomen dark blackish-brown, wing bases yellowish-brown.

Habitat Most frequent around wooded heaths, also in older woodland. Larvae parasitize large moth larvae.

Status and distribution Widespread but local and never abundant.

Season 4–9.

Flesh-fly

Sarcophaga carnaria

A largish fly, with a body length of 13–19mm. Eyes red, feet large, body black, marbled paler, very hairy. Rather narrow-bodied compared to other similar flies.

Habitat Almost everywhere; especially common around habitations, though does not enter houses as readily as some of the House-fly relatives (muscids). Larvae feed in carrion (the females produce larvae rather than eggs).

Status and distribution Widespread and very common throughout.

Season 4–10.

Similar species

There are several very closely related species that are hard to separate in the field.

Sepsis fulgens

Dexia rustica

Tachina fera

Flesh-fly

Tachina grossa

Bluebottle
Calliphoria vomitoria

A very familiar fly (actually a small group of flies), frequent in and around houses. They have bluish bodies and red eyes.

Habitat Almost anywhere, but particularly frequent around houses and other buildings; the adults spend much of their time sunbathing. The larvae eat carrion.

Status and distribution Widespread and common throughout.

Season Can be seen at almost any time of year.

Cluster-fly
Pollenia rudis

Similar in size to Bluebottle, but more brownish-grey in colour, with a chequered abdomen. Thorax covered in golden-brown hairs.

Habitat May be seen almost anywhere. In autumn they gather on the walls of houses and congregate in attics for hibernation (hence the name Cluster-fly). The larvae parasitize earthworms and possibly other invertebrates.

Status and distribution Widespread and common.

Season All year, but most frequent 8–10 and 4–6.

Greenbottle
Lucilia caesar

A familiar fly, with a body length of 8–10mm. Thorax and abdomen metallic green, becoming duller and coppery with age. Eyes red, not hairy.

Habitat Almost anywhere, not strongly associated with houses. The larvae feed on carrion, the adults frequently visit flowers.

Status and distribution Widespread and common throughout.

Season 4–10.

Similar species

Although this is superficially one of the easiest flies to identify, there are actually a number of flies that look very similar. Within the genus *Lucilia* there are several other almost identical species.

L. sericata, whose larvae live in the wounds of animals.

Similar species from other genera include: *Dasyphora cyanella,* which is very similar, but has hairy eyes and a slightly narrower waist. Common throughout, frequently visiting flowers.

Gymnochaeta viridis is a tachinid fly (see p.234), and has the metallic green of Greenbottle, but is more hairy and has a longer body. Widespread and common.

Noon-fly
Mesembrina meridiana

A medium-sized fly, with a body length of about 10mm. Dark body and reddish eyes, but the most conspicuous feature is that the lower third of the wing is stained yellowish-brown. They spend much time on tree-trunks and walls sunbathing, and this feature is then clearly visible.

Habitat Flowery places, most often seen feeding at flowers or sunbathing. Larvae feed in dung.

Status and distribution Widespread and common throughout.

Season 3–10, particularly visible in late summer.

Similar species

* *M. mystacea* is larger and hairier, but has similar wings. Widespread in Europe.

Phaonia viarum

A rather undistinguished medium-sized fly, with a body length of 8–10mm. The thorax is obscurely striped, and the abdomen is rather chequered.

Habitat A wide variety of flowery habitats, where it basks in the sun and visits flowers. The larvae breed in rotting vegetation.

Status and distribution Widespread and common throughout.

Season 4–11.

Bluebottle

Cluster-fly

Greenbottle

Noon-fly

Phaonia viarum

Sweat-fly
Hydrotaea irritans
A smallish fly, body length 5–7mm. They are familiar as the flies that swarm around the heads of walkers in hill country; they are only attracted by the sweat and do not bite. Males are dark, females are pale greyish.
Habitat Most frequent in woods, especially where bracken is present.
Status and distribution Widespread and common, especially in hilly areas.
Season 6–9.

Graphomyia maculata
A surprisingly attractive little fly (body length 6–8mm), with a conspicuously black and grey chequered abdomen (yellowish in males) and striped thorax. Males have pale yellowish wings, females' wings only yellowish at the base.
Habitat Most flowery habitats, especially close to water. Larvae live in damp or wet places.
Status and distribution Widespread and common throughout.
Season 5–10.
Similar species
Stable-fly *Stomoxys calcitrans* resembles the female in size and markings, though behaves differently; these are biting insects, attacking animals and man. Frequent wherever animals are kept, especially barns and stables.

Face-fly
Musca autumnalis
One of the 'house-flies'. Body length 7–8mm. Thorax blackish, abdomen orange and black, though not clearly visible through the wings. They swarm around cattle and other animals, or sunbathe on walls.
Habitat Associated with domestic animals and habitations.

Status and distribution Widespread and common throughout.
Season 2–10; in autumn they gather on walls to enter buildings for hibernation.
Similar species
House-fly *M. domestica* is slightly smaller and more slender, and there is more of a gap between the eyes. They are in greater evidence in the height of summer, and are much more likely to be in houses at this time of year.
Lesser House-fly *Fannia canicularis* is smaller, duller and more slender, though it has the same habits. Common throughout.

Yellow Dung-fly
Scathophaga stercoraria
A conspicuous slender-bodied fly, with a body length of 8–10mm. Males are brownish with golden-yellow hairs; females are duller, less hairy and less frequent.
Habitat Almost everywhere, but most frequent where there is a plentiful supply of dung.
Status and distribution Widespread and very common.
Season 4–10.
Similar species
There are several closely related species.

Bot-fly
Gasterophilus intestinalis
These are dark brown, largish flies, with a body length of about 15mm. The abdomen tapers gradually to a blunt point. The females lay eggs on the fur of horses or related animals, constantly flicking eggs onto the coat as they fly and hover close by.
Habitat Wherever horses, donkeys and similar animals occur.
Status and distribution Widespread and moderately common.
Season 6–9.

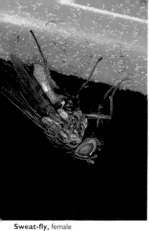

Sweat-fly, female

Graphomyia maculata, female

Face-fly

Yellow Dung-fly, mating

Yellow Dung-fly, eggs on dung

Bot-fly

Bot-fly, eggs

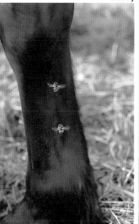

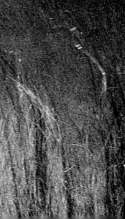

ANTS, BEES, WASPS, SAWFLIES AND THEIR RELATIVES
ORDER HYMENOPTERA

A very large order of insects, with thousands of representatives in N Europe alone. They are very varied in form, but essentially are insects with 2 pairs of membranous wings, the front pair larger than the hind pair. The wings are joined together to act as a single unit on each side by a row of hooks. The wing venation is reasonably distinctive, with relatively few veins enclosing a small number of large, often rectangular, cells.

Normally, these insects have slender necks, and very mobile heads, on which there are 3 quite visible ocelli (simple eyes, see p.9) in addition to the 2 compound eyes. The mouthparts are variable through the group, but are usually adapted for biting. The antennae vary from short to long, and are generally longer in males than females.

There is a single major division within the order, and a number of other recognizable sub-groups such as bees, ants, ichneumons and so on. The primary division is into Symphyta, sawflies, and Apocrita, the remainder.

Most of the gall-forming insects belong to the Hymenoptera. They are described in more detail on pp.302–11. Those galls that have conspicuous adult insect phases are also described in this section.

Sawflies
Suborder Symphyta

The sawflies are distinguishable by their lack of any 'waist' on the abdomen (a key feature of the rest of the Hymenoptera). The females have ovipositors with saw-teeth (hence the name of the group), though these are not necessarily visible in the field. The antennae vary, though generally they are quite long, occasionally clubbed. Sawfly larvae are all plant-eaters, often causing considerable damage. They resemble moth caterpillars, but have 6 or more pairs of prolegs, whereas Lepidopteran larvae never have more than 5, usually 3. The adults have a wide range of feeding habits.

Horntail
Urocerus gigas

A conspicuous and distinctive insect, though often confused with hornets by the general public. Female body length is over 40mm (including the spike-like ovipositor), boldly banded with black and yellow. Males are smaller, more orange than yellow. The ovipositor is used to drill into coniferous wood and lay eggs.
Habitat Coniferous woodland, though adults may turn up anywhere as they emerge from transported wood.
Status and distribution Widespread throughout, but local and rarely abundant.
Season 6–10.

Rose Sawfly
Arge ochropus

A small to medium sawfly; body length about 10mm. Mainly yellow, with the front edge of the wings brown. The females lay eggs on rose shoots in a double row, and the larvae later feed in a group.
Habitat On wild and cultivated roses, wherever they occur; occasionally becomes a pest in gardens.
Status and distribution Widespread and locally common.
Season 6–8.
Similar species
A. *cyanocrocea* has yellowish wings with a dark patch running across the middle; hind legs black-tipped (all yellow in A. *ochropus*). Larvae feed on Bramble; mainly southern in UK.
A. *ustulata* is similar in size and shape, but metallic blue-green in colour. The larvae feed communally on Sallow and Birch. Widespread and common.

Horntail

Rose Sawfly, laying eggs

Arge ustulata, larva

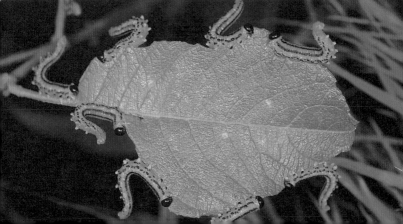

Birch Sawfly
Cimbex femoratus

One of the largest sawflies, with a body length of about 25mm. Abdomen dark, with yellow and brown bands; wings with a dark band around the tips and across the middle; antennae clubbed.

Habitat Always associated with Birch; the larvae feed singly on Birch leaves.

Status and distribution Widespread though rather local.

Season 5–8.

Similar species

Hawthorn Sawfly *Trichiosoma tibiale* is slightly smaller, generally darker, and the larvae feed on Hawthorn. Mainly southern in UK, widespread elsewhere.

Rhogogaster viridis

A largish attractive sawfly, with a body length of 12–14mm. Whole body green, marked variably with black down the central line; wings veined with green. Most often seen on flowers; adults predatory on other insects.

Habitat Flowery places, especially near woods and scrub; larvae feed on various herbaceous plants.

Status and distribution Widespread and locally common throughout.

Season 5–8.

Tenthredo arcuata

Body length about 10mm. Abdomen and thorax black banded with yellow above, bright yellow underneath (in males); antennae gradually expanding towards the tip.

Habitat Rough flowery grassland; the larvae feed on Red Clover.

Status and distribution Widespread and moderately common throughout.

Season 4–8.

Similar species

There are large numbers of *Tenthredo* species in N Europe, many of them very similar. Males of *T. atra* are fairly distinctive, with a broad red band on the abdomen. Widespread and frequent.

Pine Sawfly
Diprion pini

Females have a body length of about 10mm; males are smaller. Females are robust and swollen. Abdomen dull greyish-black, though female may be banded with dull yellow markings.

Habitat Pinewoods, where the larvae feed on pine needles, sometimes becoming a serious forestry pest.

Status and distribution Widespread and locally common throughout.

Season 5–8.

Gooseberry Sawfly
Nematus ribesii

Adults are much less familiar than the larvae and the damage they cause. Adults 7–9mm long, yellowish. The larvae strip the leaves of gooseberries and currants, leaving the bushes almost defoliated.

Habitat Wherever gooseberry and currant bushes occur, including gardens.

Status and distribution Widespread and common throughout.

Season 5–9.

Similar species

Several species of *Pontania* are rather similar in size and shape, though they are usually darker in colour. They form characteristic galls on willows, described in more detail on p.308.

Solomon's Seal Sawfly
Phymatocera aterrima

The adults of this species are black, small, and rather smoky-winged. The greyish larvae and their effects are much more familiar: they strip the leaves of Solomon's Seal *Polygonatum* plants thoroughly.

Habitat Wherever the host plant occurs; frequent in gardens.

Status and distribution Widespread and common, having extended its range considerably in recent years.

Season 6–7.

Birch Sawfly

Rhogogaster viridis

Gooseberry Sawfly, larva

Tenthredo arcuata

Suborder Apocrita

The *Apocrita* are more typical of the general idea of hymenopterans, with strongly 'waisted' abdomens. They comprise a very varied group, including a number of readily recognizable families. Most entomologists make a primary division into the *Parasitica* and the *Aculeata*.

Section Parasitica, Parasitic Hymenoptera

The *Parasitica* are (as the name suggests) generally parasites, with a few exceptions. The group includes the ichneumons, the chalcid wasps, the braconid wasps and others.

Torymus nitens

A small parasitic species, greenish-black in colour, with a body length of 4–5mm, excluding the female's ovipositor. The ovipositor is used to pierce galls such as oak apples (see p.306) to insert eggs into the gall-former's larvae.
Habitat Woodlands and other places where oak trees occur.
Status and distribution Widespread and common throughout.
Season 4–7.

Pteromalus puparum

A small dark greenish insect, no more than 3–4mm long, which parasitizes the pupae of common white butterflies, laying eggs through the skin before it finally hardens. Numerous wasps emerge the following spring from parasitized pupae.
Habitat Wherever the hosts occur – almost anywhere; common in gardens.
Status and distribution Widespread and common throughout.
Season 4–9.

Apanteles glomeratus

One of the braconid wasps. The adults are very small, about 3mm long, and blackish. The females lay eggs into the larvae of Large and Small white butterflies; the larvae become slower-moving, and remain much less well concealed than their healthy counterparts. The wasp larvae emerge just before the caterpillar reaches pupation stage, and spin themselves little yellow silken cocoons, visible in large numbers around the shrivelled remains of the caterpillar.
Habitat Wherever abundant Whites occur.
Status and distribution Widespread and common throughout.
Season 4–7.

Ichneumons, Family Ichneumonidae

Relatively large insects, often with long ovipositors; a few species are virtually wingless.

It should be noted that there are a very large number of ichneumon species (for example, over 500 species have been recorded from one garden), so it is hard to make certain identifications from a general guide such as this. Only the most conspicuous and identifiable species have been selected.

Rhyssa persuasoria

One of the largest of the ichneumons, with a body length of 30mm or more, and an ovipositor at least as long again. Body black with yellowish dots, and legs red. The long ovipositor is used to drill into wood, into the larvae of Horntail (see p.240), which they pinpoint precisely.
Habitat Coniferous woods, where Horntails occur.
Status and distribution Widespread but local.
Season 6–9.

Torymus nitens, female

Rhyssa persuasoria, female

Pteromalus puparum, female

Apanteles glomeratus, pupa

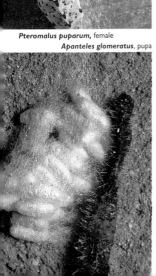

Lissonota (Lampronata) setosa

Another large ichneumon, about 20mm long excluding the long ovipositor. Body predominantly black, with orange-red legs and pale brown wings.

Habitat Parasitizes the larvae of Goat Moth (see p.152) which live in dead and dying willow and poplar wood.

Habitat Wherever the hosts might occur.

Status and distribution Widespread but local and declining.

Season 5–7.

Similar species

L. fundator is smaller, and parasitizes the larvae of clearwing moths (see p.156) in willows and other tree stems.

Yellow Ophion
Ophion luteus

One of the most familiar ichneumons, as it often comes into houses on summer and autumn evenings. Body dull yellowish-red, 15–20mm long; there is no long ovipositor. Wings virtually clear. Mainly nocturnal (see also picture on p.4).

Habitat Various rough flowery habitats such as woods, unimproved grassland, sand-dunes. Parasitizes various moth larvae.

Status and distribution Widespread and common throughout.

Season 7–10.

Similar species

Netelia testaceus is similar in size and shape, perhaps slightly smaller, but has its body tipped with black. It is parasitic on moths. Widespread and moderately common.

Amblyteles armatorius

A large, conspicuous and identifiable ichneumon, with a body length of about 15mm, without a long ovipositor. The body is banded black and yellow, and the antennae are long and dark. The insects move rapidly over vegetation, waving their antennae, searching for caterpillars of noctuid moths (see p.182).

Habitat In rough flowery places, including gardens.

Status and distribution Widespread and common throughout.

Season Most of the summer; adults hibernate.

Similar species

A. elongatus is similar in size, though rather more slender, and dark in colour except for a small yellow patch on the back; legs reddish. Similar habitats and distribution.

Ichneumon suspiciosus

Similar in size and shape to Amblyteles. Body black except for a broad red band on the abdomen; legs banded red and black. Frequently seen on flowers, and could be mistaken for a sawfly or some other hymenopteran at first glance.

Habitat Various rough flowery places, including gardens. Larvae parasitize moth caterpillars.

Status and distribution Common throughout.

Season 4–10, and adults hibernate.

Similar species

There are a number of closely related species in the same genus. Protichneumon pisorius is larger, and has a wholly red-orange abdomen. Similar habitats and distribution, less common.

Lissonota setosa

Yellow Ophion

Amblyteles armatorius

Section Aculeata, Aculeate Hymenoptera

The aculeate hymenoptera are divided into bees, wasps, ants and several other groups.

Ants, Family Formicidae

Social insects, showing specialization within the group into wingless workers and winged sexual phases. The antennae are elbowed.

Red Ant
Myrmica rubra
Smallish ants, about 4mm long, familiar to most people because they are common and they sting. Males are dark brown, workers and queens are paler red-brown. They are social species (like all ants) occurring in small underground nests.
Habitat Short turf and other grassy places, including gardens.
Status and distribution Widespread and common.
Season Can be found all summer; mating flights usually 7–9.
Similar species
This is but one of several very similar species, sharing the same common name. They cannot be identified in the field without considerable experience or detailed knowledge. The group includes *M. scabrinodis* and *M. ruginodis*.

Black Ant
Lasius niger
One of the commonest and best-known of ants, often entering houses. Similar in size to red ants, they are black or dark brown in colour. They eat almost everything, and are often seen 'milking' aphids for honeydew.
Habitat Gardens, other grasslands, and almost anywhere.
Status and distribution Widespread and common throughout.
Season Present all summer; the familiar mating swarms (with masses of flying ants – winged males and queens) take place on warm days from July on, in highly synchronized fashion.

Shining Jet Black Ant
Lasius fuliginosus
A distinctive ant, which lives up to its name. Larger than common Black Ant; workers can be up to 7mm long.
Habitat Gardens, woods and parkland. Most commonly in rotten tree-stumps where they make nests of a paper-like substance, though they also nest under stones.
Status and distribution Widespread, but more local than Black Ant.
Season 4–10.
Similar species
Formica fusca and *F. lemani* are similar in size, and black in colour, but they are dull not shiny. *F. lemani* is hairier than *F. fusca*. Both are widespread, with *F. lemani* commoner in the north.

Yellow Meadow Ant
Lasius flavus
More familiar for its homes than its individuals. The workers are small, dull yellowish. They make perennial nests of soil in undisturbed conditions; therefore, the larger the nests are, the older they are. Some ancient pastures have hundreds of anthills in a small area, each up to 50cm high.
Habitat Various grazed grasslands. They cannot stand being overshaded for long.
Status and distribution Widespread and common; the large nests only occur in undisturbed pasture.
Season Visible all year; adults active through the summer.

Wood Ant
Formica rufa
One of our largest ants; workers are about 10mm long, queens and males slightly larger. The workers are red and black. The nests are huge piles of leaves, needles, and twigs, swarming with workers. The ants spread out over a large area, along trails.
Habitat Usually in coniferous woodland, occasionally in other shady places.
Status and distribution Widespread and locally common throughout.
Season Visible 3–10; mating flights 5–6.

Red Ant, workers and pupae at nest

Red Ant, winged

Black Ant, winged, with workers

Shining Jet Black Ant, workers with white wood louse

Wood Ant, worker pulling leaf

Yellow Meadow Ant, anthills in chalk downland

Wood Ant, nest

Ruby-tailed Wasp
Chrysis ignita

An attractive little insect, about 10mm long, metallic in colour. Head and thorax greenish-blue, abdomen red. Most frequently seen resting in the sun, or flying around the nest holes of solitary bees and wasps.

Habitat Various habitats, most commonly dry, warm, sandy places, where the larval hosts – mason bees in particular – are common. Heathlands are its most favoured habitat.

Status and distribution Widespread but local in the UK, widespread and common over most of the Continent.

Season 5–9.

Similar species

There are a number of ruby-tailed wasps varying in the degree and pattern of red and green markings, and some are much smaller.

C. fulgida has the first third of the abdomen green, the bottom two-thirds red.

Velvet Ant
Mutilla europaea

An unusual species that is really neither a wasp nor an ant, but the wingless females resemble ants. Body length 13–15mm, dark, with paler stripes on the abdomen, and silvery hairs; female has a red thorax and no wings.

Habitat Most likely to be seen in heathy places; they parasitize bumble bees in their nests.

Status and distribution Widespread but very local throughout.

Season 3–5 and 7–9; adults hibernate.

Digger Wasps, Family Sphecidae

A very large family of solitary wasps, many of which dig nests in the ground.

Slender-bodied Digger Wasp
Crabro cribrarius

As the name suggests, this species has a noticeably slender abdomen, and a body length of 12–14 mm. It is black and yellow, like many digger wasps, but the greatly enlarged front tibia of the males are reasonably distinctive (though there are close relatives).

Habitat Sandy heaths.

Status and distribution Widespread, though local, throughout.

Season 5–9.

Field Digger Wasp
Mellinus arvensis

A typical digger wasp, 12–14mm long, strongly waisted with a distinct petiole (a visible very narrow stem), with black and yellow on the abdomen. There is a single yellow spot on the scutellum, just below the thorax, and thin black stripes on yellow on the abdomen. Unlike some similar species, the front of the head has no silvery hairs.

Habitat Sandy places; the larval nests are stocked with flies.

Status and distribution Widespread and common throughout; one of the most frequently encountered digger wasps.

Season 5–9.

Similar species

Most other black and yellow diggers do not have so much yellow or such a distinct petiole.

Ectemnius cephalotes is rather similar in colouring, with a broader head. Local, mainly southern.

Ruby-tailed Wasp

Velvet Ant

Field Digger Wasp

Argogorytes mystaceus

Body length about 12mm. A rather dark species, predominantly black with few yellow rings, and no petiole. Males have long antennae; legs pale yellowish-brown, black at the base.

Habitat Dry flowery places; the larval nests are stocked with froghoppers. The males are the main pollinators in the UK of the Fly Orchid, by a process known as pseudocopulation – they think the flower is a female wasp.

Status and distribution Widespread throughout, but local.

Season 5–8.

Similar species
Nysson spinosus is a 'cuckoo wasp' which lays its eggs in those of *Argogorytes*, and looks very like it, except for having redder legs, and 2 little spines just above the waist. Widespread but local.

Sand Wasp
Ammophila sabulosa

A very distinctive large species, with a body length of 20–24mm. The narrow waist expands gradually along the abdomen, which is red except for the last few black segments. The females catch caterpillars, and drag them to pre-dug nests, stocking each nest with a single large caterpillar and laying an egg on it, before covering it.

Habitat Sandy places, especially heathland.

Status and distribution Widespread; mainly southern in the UK, throughout on the Continent.

Season 5–9.

Similar species
A. pubescens is the only other UK species in this genus. It is slightly smaller, and the rear part of the abdomen has no metallic blue sheen (noticeable in *A. sabulosa*). This sand wasp is unusual in continuing to look after its developing larvae, checking the nests and reprovisioning them as required. Less common.

Podalonia hirsuta

Another sand wasp. Similar in size and colouring to *Ammophila* but differing in having a strongly marked petiole that expands abruptly to the swollen part of the abdomen. Behaviour is also different – this sand wasp catches a caterpillar and then excavates a nest.

Habitat Sandy heaths, dunes and similar dry places.

Status and distribution Only in the south of Britain, local. More widespread on the Continent.

Season 4–8.

Similar species
P. affinis differs merely in minor details, and is slightly smaller. Only in England and Wales; more widespread on the Continent.

★ *Bembix rostrata*

An impressive insect, very like a social wasp, but with different habits, and holds its wings flat when at rest. Builds nests in sandy ground, which the females provision with flies for the larvae, continuing to bring prey of suitable size as the larvae grow.

Habitat Sandy heaths.

Status and distribution A southern species, extending up to N France.

Season 5–8.

Sand Wasp, *Ammophila sabulosa*

Podalonia hirsuta, dragging moth larva to burrow

Bembix rostrata

Astata pinguis
A small digger wasp, with a body length of 6–8mm. Body black and red, with a marked waist. The male has a large white spot on the face.

Habitat Heaths, dunes and other sandy places.

Status and distribution Only in southern UK; more widespread on the Continent.

Season 5–8.

Similar species
A. boops is slightly larger, and males lack the white spot on the face. Similar habitats and distribution though it is more widespread within Britain.

Spider-hunting Wasps, Family Pompilidae

Similar to digger wasps, though all pompilids catch spiders. Generally long-legged and very active. They mainly run, rarely flying far.

Priocnemis perturbator
One of the larger spider-hunting wasps, with a body length of about 20mm. Colour red and black (like many other pompilids).

Habitat Dry places, such as heaths and downs.

Status and distribution Mainly southern in the UK. More widespread on the Continent.

Season 4–9.

Anoplius viaticus
Similar in size to *Priocnemis*. Red and black, but with the tip of the female's abdomen covered with stiff black hairs. The males have broader, flattened abdomens.

Habitat Dry flowery places, such as woodland edges, heaths. Preys on wolf spiders. Males frequently visit flowers such as Hogweed in early summer.

Status and distribution Confined to S Britain; more widespread on the Continent from Germany southwards.

Season 5–9.

Similar species
There are several closely related species that are hard to separate in the field.

Potter Wasp
Eumenes coarctatus
Body length 12–14mm. Thorax black, abdomen yellow and black, with a long waist. The nest is a 'pot' made from mud, with a small hole, attached to plants such as heather. The pots are stocked with caterpillars as food for the single wasp larva inside.

Habitat Heaths and moors.

Status and distribution Confined to the far south of Britain; Widespread but local on the Continent.

Season 6–9.

Similar species
Odynerus spinipes has a less marked waist. It builds nests in sandy ground. Widespread but local, especially on heaths.

Potter Wasp, nest

Astata pinguis, male

Anoplius viaticus

Potter Wasp

Social Wasps, Family Vespidae

Familiar winged insects, some species of which become a nuisance in late summer. They live in tight-knit colonies in nests made of paper, which they manufacture from chewed wood. The colonies consist of large numbers of female workers, and larger queens. Males appear from late summer onwards. The colonies break down at the end of summer, and only the mated queens survive.

Common Wasp
Vespula vulgaris

The typical familiar wasp, about 20–25mm long, boldly marked with black and yellow. Queens are largest, with a slightly more swollen body; males have longer antennae than the female workers.

Habitat Almost anywhere; the nests are usually in holes in the ground, but may be in buildings.

Status and distribution Widespread and common throughout.

Season 6–10.

Similar species

Cuckoo Wasp *V. austriaca* is usually slightly more yellow, has antennae yellow at base, and only 2 (not 4) yellow spots on the thorax. They make no nest, acting as 'cuckoos' in the nests of Red Wasp (see below). A widespread but uncommon species. German Wasp (see below) is very similar – see under that species for differences.

German Wasp
Vespula germanica

Very similar to Common Wasp in size and markings, and usually combined under the same common name. Differs mainly in having 3 black dots on the face rather than a dark anchor-like mark; more extensive black markings on the back of the abdomen which are more like diamonds than triangles; and the vertical yellow stripes on the thorax tend to be parallel-sided in Common, rather convex in German. These distinctions apply most accurately to worker females.

Habitat As Common Wasp.

Status and distribution Widespread and common throughout.

Season 6–10.

Similar species

Red Wasp *V. rufa* is similar to all the above, but generally has a reddish first segment to the abdomen. Widespread and frequent, but less common than the Common and German.

Dolichovespula media

Recently dubbed as the 'killer wasp', this species has spread northwards in recent years. It is larger than the above species, up to 30mm long, with variable amounts of black, but often much blacker overall, and sometimes tinged reddish on the thorax. The nest is hung from bushes or small trees.

Habitat Almost anywhere; particularly associated with gardens, scrub and open woodland.

Status and distribution Widespread on the Continent, currently still spreading northwards and westwards in the UK.

Season 6–10.

Similar species

Tree Wasp *D. sylvestris* has a rather similar nest in bushes and small trees, but the insects are distinctly smaller, and the thorax has 2 (not 4) yellow spots. Widespread and moderately common, though easily overlooked.

Norwegian Wasp *D. norvegica* looks very like Tree Wasp, except that there is often red on the thorax, and the face has a vertical black bar (cf. a single spot in Tree). Widespread and moderately common throughout.

Common Wasp, male

German Wasp, nest

German Wasp, on rotten apple

Red Wasp

Dolichovespula media, female collecting wood for paper

Dolichovespula media, nest in laburnum

Hornet

Vespa crabro

An impressive insect, unlikely to be con-fused with anything else (though the hov-erfly Volucella zonaria occasionally is – see p.230). Very large, body length 30–40mm, with a much more reddish appearance than the smaller wasps. Not as aggressive as popularly supposed, though they can become dangerous if 'pushed' and have a powerful sting.

Habitat Various habitats, but most often associated with woodland and parkland; individuals travel widely from their base. The nests are usually in old trees, or some-times buildings.

Status and distribution Widespread in the UK but not common, though varying markedly from year to year. Widespread and frequent on the Continent.

Season 6–10.

Polistes gallicus

These attractive little wasps are most often noticed for their nests, rather than as adults. The nest is a flattish plate, without any covering, attached to a plant or other surface by a stalk, and is rarely more than a few centimetres across. Generally similar in markings to other wasps, but with a longer 'waist'; usually seen on the nest.

Habitat Rough unspoilt habitats such as downland and heathland.

Status and distribution Widespread and frequent further south in Europe, becoming rarer northwards; occasional in Britain.

Season 5–10.

Similar species

There are a number of similar Polistes species further south in Europe. They are difficult to identify without some specialist knowledge.

Bees, Family Apidae and others

A large and variable group, hard to charac-terize, but all feeding on nectar or pollen; not predatory. Bees often have pollen 'bas-kets' on their back legs,. and are nearly always hairy. The great majority are solitary or live in loose colonies but a few (such as the Honey Bee) are social.

Colletes davisiana

One of a group of very similar species in the same genus, characterized by the very hairy head and thorax, and narrow parallel bands of white hairs on the abdomen. Body length 9–12mm.

Habitat Nest in loose colonies in hard sandy ground or occasionally in soft mor-tar.

Status and distribution Widespread and moderately common.

Season 7–9.

Similar species

About a dozen other Colletes species, very hard to separate.

Halictus xanthopus

One of a large group of similar species, which mostly have a hairless central ridge towards the tip of the abdomen. Body length 10–12mm. This species has white bands across the abdomen, and golden-yellow legs.

Habitat Dry sandy places, especially where there are banks; occasionally nests in mortar.

Status and distribution Widespread and moderately common.

Season 4–10.

Similar species

There are 40 or so other species in the genus. H. tumulorum is greenish and smaller. Widespread.

Hornet, nest interior

Hornet

Polistes gallicus

Colletes davisiana

Andrena haemorrhoa

One of the mining bees, which all have rather flattened abdomens. Body length 11–14mm. Thorax hairy golden-brown (redder in female), abdomen dark tipped with gold (redder in female).

Habitat Associated with dry flowery places, where they make burrows in the soil. Appears early in the year and feeds on Sallow, Blackthorn and other spring flowers.

Status and distribution Widespread and common.

Season 3–8.

Similar species

A. hattorfiana is the largest UK species, similar in shape to the above but larger, with a darker thorax. Appears later, from midsummer onwards.

Tawny Mining Bee
Andrena fulva

Best known for its little volcano-like nest mounds in dry places such as heaths, dry lawns and so on. Sometimes also known as the Lawn Bee. The adult females are tawny orange, very hairy, and relatively distinctive. Body length 12–14mm. Males are darker and smaller. Often seen at currant flowers.

Habitat Dry, flowery places; quite frequent in gardens.

Status and distribution Widespread and common.

Season 4–9.

Wool Carder Bee
Anthidium manicatum

An attractive and distinctive bee. Males are larger than females, with a body length of 10–13mm. They are black, with yellow edging to the abdomen. They collect hairs from plants and carry them in a ball to their nests.

Habitat The nests are in pre-existing holes in wood or masonry. Frequent in gardens, where they particularly like 'Lamb's Ear' (*Stachys lanata*) plants. They can be encouraged by providing holes for them.

Status and distribution Widespread but local in the UK; widespread and frequent on the Continent.

Season 6–8.

Similar species

★ *A. variegatum* has much more yellow on the abdomen. Similar habits and habitats.

Osmia rufa

A small reddish bee, body length about 10mm, females slightly larger. The females are more distinctive, with 2 little dark horns on the head, and a densely hairy abdomen. Males have white hairs on their faces.

Habitat A wide variety of flowery habitats; they make mud nests in buildings, holes and other situations. Frequent in gardens.

Status and distribution Common in S Britain; widespread on the Continent.

Season 4–7.

Similar species

There are many other *Osmia* species in Britain and N Europe.

O. bicolor is obscurely banded with yellow and brown on the abdomen, and it nests in old snail-shells in dry, flowery places such as downland. Local, mainly southern.

Leaf-cutter Bee
Megachile centuncularis

An undistinguished-looking bee, usually noticed for its effects. Adults about 10mm long, dark brown with orange pollen brush below in females. The females cut semicircular to almost circular patches from leaves with their sharp mandibles (fascinating to watch, and completed remarkably quickly), and carry them to their nests to make cells for the larvae. This species particularly likes the leaves of roses, so it is often noticed in the garden.

Habitat Gardens, scrub, woodland rides. Nests in holes in wood, or in plant stems.

Status and distribution Widespread and common throughout.

Season 5–8.

Similar species

There are several related leaf-cutter species. *M. maritima* is slightly larger, and females have a bicoloured pollen brush, white at the front, dark orange to brown behind. Local, mainly coastal and southern.

Andrena haemorrhoa, male

Wool Carder Bee

Leaf-cutter Bee, nest

Leaf-cutter Bee

Leaf cut by Leaf-cutter Bee

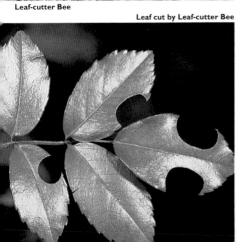

Nomada lineola

One of a group of similar species known as 'cuckoo bees' because they build no nest of their own. They stealthily enter the nests of other species, usually *Andrena* spp. where they feed initially on the food brought in by the host species, and later on its larvae as well. They are small, 8–10mm long, black and yellow, and hard to distinguish from some solitary wasps, especially as they are almost hairless.

Habitat Various rough, flowery habitats, where the host bees occur.

Status and distribution Widespread but local.

Season 4–7.

Similar species

There are many similar bees in this genus, hard to separate in the field.

N. ruficornis has more red on the abdomen and the thorax. Local, and uncommon, mainly southern.

Eucera longicornis

Females of this species are medium-sized, about 10mm long, undistinguished brown with a paler tip to the abdomen. Males are more distinctive, with very long antennae for a bee – almost as long as the body.

Eucera longicornis

Habitat The nests are made in dry sandy ground; most frequent on heaths and other suitable dry places.

Status and distribution Local and mainly southern in the UK; more widespread on the Continent.

Season 4–7.

Flower Bee
Anthophora plumipes

One of a group of similar species with the same English name. They are largish, robust bees, body length 12–14mm, reminiscent of small bumble bees. Females black, hairy, with orange pollen brushes; males browner especially on the thorax.

Habitat Flowery places, where there are walls or banks in which to nest. Regular visitors to garden flowers such as Lungwort and Aubrieta.

Status and distribution Common in S Britain, widespread on the Continent.

Season 3–6.

Similar species

A. acervorum has greyish pollen brushes on the middle pair of legs. *A. retusa* males have a hairless patch on the abdomen. Both species are local, mainly southern.

Honey Bee
Apis mellifera

One of the most familiar insects in the world. Adults rather undistinguished, basically brown but variable in colour; there are a number of different races with varying amounts of orange or darker brown. Most bees seen are probably from domestic hives, though there are also many wild colonies. Thought not to be a native of Europe, coming originally from S Asia.

Habitat Almost anywhere flowery; hives are moved by their keepers to follow the flowers and produce particular types of honey; wild colonies are most frequent in woods and parkland.

Status and distribution Widespread and common throughout.

Season 3–10.

Similar species

Several hoverflies, such as the Drone Fly (*Eristalis tenax*), mimic bees. They have 2 (not 4) wings, and differ in various details (see p.226).

Nomada lineola

Flower Bee

Swarm of bees, on apple tree

Honey Bee

Melecta luctuosa

One of a small group of similar greyish cuckoo bees, nesting in the burrows of flower bees. Body length 12–14mm, greyish-black with white edging; eyes reddish.
Habitat Similar habitats to flower bees.
Status and distribution Local, confined to S Britain; more widespread on the Continent.
Season 4–6.
Similar species
M. albifrons. The thorax is browner and the abdomen darker, with fewer pale spots. Similar habits and distribution.

★ Violet Carpenter Bee
Xylocopa violacea

A conspicuous large bee, easily recognized in the field (though there are a few very closely related species). Body length 20–25mm, robustly built, dark violet, with lovely purplish-blue wings. Flies rapidly and noisily from flower to flower.
Habitat A variety of rough, flowery habitats; nests in dead wood, excavating its own holes (hence 'carpenter').
Status and distribution Absent from the UK except as a rare vagrant; a southern species, becoming rarer northwards.
Season 3–9.

BUMBLE BEES These are familiar large, furry, 'bumbling' bees from the genus *Bombus*. Members of another genus *Psithyrus* look very similar, and are parasitic on bumble bees; they tend to have thinner fur coats, such that the shiny abdomen can be seen, and the females have no pollen baskets.

They are a difficult group to identify, not only because there are many species, but also because the size of workers varies considerably according to time of year, and there are many regional or local colour variations within species.

Bombus hortorum

A largish bee, 19–24mm long. It is a white-tailed species, with yellow behind the head, and alternating yellow and deep brown. It has a particularly long tongue, and tends to visit tubular flowers such as Red Clover, Honeysuckle and balsams.
Habitat Nests in the soil or close to the soil surface, and may occur in any rough habitat where there are suitable flowers, including gardens.
Status and distribution Widespread throughout, though never abundant. Colonies are usually rather small and widely spaced.
Season 4–9. Workers do not usually appear until May.
Similar species
B. jonellus is slightly smaller and has a shorter face and tongue. Pollen baskets reddish, not black. Widespread but local, mainly on heaths.

Bombus lucorum

Rather similar in size and markings to *B. hortorum*. This species may be distinguished by the lack of a yellowish band around the 'waist', though the smaller males may have a yellowish area here.
Habitat A wide variety of flowery places. The nests are below ground.
Status and distribution Very common and widespread.
Season 4–9.
Similar species
B. pratorum has rather similar markings, but it is smaller, and has a short reddish tip to the tail (not white). Common throughout.

Violet Carpenter Bee

Bombus pratorum

Bombus hortorum, male

Bombus lucorum, female

Bombus pascuorum

This is the only common bumble bee to have a uniformly reddish thorax. The abdomen is variable, dark brown to grey, but usually with a reddish tinge. One of the so-called carder bumble bees, because they collect material by combing to line the nests with.

Habitat Rough flowery places such as old pasture or woodland rides; also in gardens. The nests are built in vegetation, or just below the soil.

Status and distribution Widespread and common throughout.

Season 5–10.

Similar species

B. muscorum is slightly larger, on average, and has no black hairs on the upper side of the abdomen; coat very long. A local species, apparently declining; most frequent in fens and marshes.

B. humilis is extremely similar, but generally has a more triangular abdomen, and occurs in drier places, such as chalk downland and other rough pastures.

Bombus lapidarius

One of the attractive 'red-tailed' bumble bees. A largish species, up to 25mm long. Most of the body is deep brown to black, but the lower half of the abdomen is red. The smaller males also have a thin yellowish collar behind the head.

Habitat Many rough, flowery places, including gardens. Nests in the ground or under stones.

Status and distribution Widespread and generally common throughout the lowlands.

Season 5–9.

Similar species

B. ruderarius is very similar in size and general markings, but the pollen basket is edged with red (not black) hairs. A local species, mainly southern and lowland in the UK, more widespread on the Continent.

B. monticola is smaller and has a longer red tip to the abdomen. Mainly northern and upland areas.

Cuckoo Bee Psithyrus rupestris looks extremely like B. lapidarius, which it parasitizes, differing in the general characteristics described in the introduction to the genus.

Psithyrus barbutellus

One of the cuckoo bumble bees, in this case a parasite on Bombus hortorum. Body length about 20mm (males smaller, as with bumble bees). Has a tawny collar, a dark centre to the thorax, with a shiny appearance where the hair covering is thin; and a white tail – very like its host species.

Habitat Various rough flowery habitats, wherever the host species occurs.

Status and distribution Widespread throughout, though less common than its host.

Season 5–8.

Similar species

P. vestalis is slightly larger, and usually has a gold band just above the white on the tail. Parasitizes Bombus terrestris. Widespread.

Bombus pascuorum, female

Bombus pascuorum, female

Bombus lapidarius

Psithyrus barbutellus

BEETLES
ORDER COLEOPTERA

A huge order of insects, with hundreds of thousands of species known in the world, about 20,000 in Europe, and over 4,000 in Britain alone.

Despite the large numbers, and their wide variation in size, habits and colouring, beetles are still quite easily recognizable as such. Their most obvious characteristic is the forewings, known as elytra: they are toughened and hard, and cover the whole abdomen, meeting neatly along the midline of the abdomen. The hindwings are folded away underneath them. (Shield bugs, which can look rather beetle-like, do not have the forewings meeting along the midline.) The rove beetles (see p.272) share the general characteristics, but have wings that are very short, leaving the segments of most of the abdomen clearly exposed.

The mouthparts are of the biting type, sometimes particularly adapted for an aggressive predatory way of life, such as those of the tiger beetles. Most beetles are plant-feeders, exploiting a wide range of foods, from stored man-made products such as flour; to leaves, stems, seeds and flowers; or pollen and nectar. Some of the leaf-feeders are well-known pests such as the Colorado Beetle or the Turnip Flea Beetle. Many species feed on dead wood, normally in dead and dying trees although some, such as Death Watch Beetle or Furniture Beetle (woodworm), have adapted to processed timbers. Carnivorous species include some of the ladybirds, the water-beetles and the ground beetles.

Green Tiger Beetle
Cicindela campestris
A distinctive beetle, about 18–20mm long, bright green in colour with yellow spots on the elytra, though they can be surprisingly

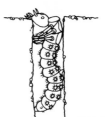

Green Tiger Beetle, larva

inconspicuous in the field. Voracious predators, with well-developed jaws. The larvae live in the soil in vertical tunnels with their jaws at the surface, waiting for prey.
Habitat In sandy soil, where tunnels can be constructed; most frequent on heaths and dunes.
Status and distribution Widespread and locally common throughout.
Season 5–7.
Similar species
C. germanica is similar in colour, sometimes darker, but smaller with just a few yellow dots on the margins of the elytra. Rare and local in the UK, confined to S coast; more widespread on the Continent in dry places.

Wood Tiger Beetle
Cicindela sylvatica
Slightly larger than Green Tiger Beetle, though very similar in shape and life-style. Colour dark grey, with cream stripes and dots on the elytra.
Habitat Heathy woods and wooded heaths.
Status and distribution More local than Green Tiger Beetle and confined to the south of Britain.
Season 5–8.
Similar species
C. hybrida is slightly smaller, more greenish with a red tinge. Elytra have 3 yellow stripes on each side. Local on heaths and other sandy places in early summer after hibernation, then again in late summer.

Green Tiger Beetle

Wood Tiger Beetle

Ground Beetles, Family Carabidae

Fast-moving, ground-dwelling predatory species, often metallic. The front tarsi are enlarged. The larvae are also predatory.

Violet Ground Beetle
Carabus violaceus

One of the more distinctive of the Ground Beetles; body length 25–30mm, noticeably violet-black in colour, particularly towards the edges. Nocturnal and highly active.
Habitat Various habitats, wherever there is plenty of cover and other insects for food.
Status and distribution Widespread and common throughout.
Season Adults active virtually all year, except in the coldest months.
Similar species
C. nemoralis is slightly smaller, and more bronze-green, sometimes violet towards the edges. The elytra are marked with ridges and pits. Common and widespread in similar habitats, with similar habits.

Carabus granulatus

An attractive and moderately distinctive ground beetle. Body length about 20mm. Overall coppery-brown to greenish-black in colour, with strongly marked ridges and bumps in 3 rows on each elytra. An active nocturnal predator.
Habitat Damp grassland and riversides.
Status and distribution Locally common almost throughout.
Season All year, hibernating in cold winter weather.

Harpalus affinis

A smallish ground beetle; body length 12–15mm. Body variable in colour, from bright metallic green to blackish-bronze; males are brighter than females. Legs and antennae orange-red. Mainly nocturnal, though occasionally active in sunshine.
Habitat Almost any habitat where there is cover and ample invertebrate prey.
Status and distribution Widespread and common throughout.
Season Adults all year, but most often seen 4–7.

Pterostichus madidus

A shiny black beetle, with brownish-red legs. Body length 12–15mm. The pronotum covering the thorax is roughly square, with blunt corners. A flightless nocturnal predator, though it also eats fruit on the ground.
Habitat Gardens, fields and other vegetated places with a mixture of cover and open areas.
Status and distribution Widespread and common throughout.
Season Adult all year, hibernating in cold weather.

Pterostichus madidus   Pterostichus nigrita

Similar species
P. nigrita has black legs, and the hind corners of the pronotum are sharply angled. This species is able to fly. Widespread and common in suitable habitats.

Bombardier Beetle
Brachinus crepitans

A distinctive little beetle, about 10mm long. Head and thorax orange-brown, elytra metallic greenish. It has a curious habit: when disturbed, it fires a burning liquid from its rear end accompanied by a puff of smoke and a soft popping, like a tiny cannon going off – hence the name.
Habitat Chalk downland and other dry habitats.
Status and distribution Widespread but local and easily overlooked, as it usually hides under stones. Most frequent in the south of Britain.
Season 7–9.

Violet Ground Beetle

Carabus nemoralis

Harpalus affinis

Pterostichus madidus

Burying Beetles, Family Silphidae

Distinctive beetles with clubbed antennae, and often with shortened elytra. They live on carrion which they bury by digging below it, even moving the body to a better site if necessary.

Nicrophorus (Necrophorus) investigator

One of a group of very distinctive beetles. Body length 20–24mm long, black with 2 broad orange-red stripes across the elytra. The antennae are clubbed, as in all this family. They are attracted to corpses which they bury by excavating a hollow underneath, usually working in pairs. The eggs are laid on the corpse and the developing larvae feed on it.

Habitat Wherever there are suitable corpses, which may include mammals, birds and reptiles.

Status and distribution Widespread, though not very common.

Season 4–7.

Similar species

N. vespillo has strongly curved hind legs. Similar habitats and distribution.

N. interruptus has both the broad reddish stripes noticeably interrupted with black in the middle. Local, mainly southern.

N. vespilloides has the posterior red band reduced to 2 large spots, and it has all-black antennae (they are all orange-tipped in the above species). Widespread.

Nicrophorus humator

Resembles the above species in general shape, but it is slightly longer, and all black in colour, lacking the red bands. Close examination shows that it has red-tipped antennae.

Habitat Similar to the above species.

Status and distribution Widespread, but local.

Season 4–7.

Rove Beetles, Family Staphylinidae

A huge and varied group, which share the characteristic of very short elytra, leaving most of the abdomen exposed. Two species are described here.

Devil's Coach-horse

Staphylinus (Ocypus) olens

A familiar and distinctive beetle, with a body length of about 25mm. Black all over, and clothed with black hairs. The beetle raises its abdomen in the air when threatened, whilst opening its jaws. Mainly nocturnal, but occasionally seen in the day.

Habitat Woods, gardens, heaths and other habitats.

Status and distribution Widespread and common.

Season 4–10.

Similar species

Creophilus maxillosus. This is very similar in form, though slightly smaller and clothed with grey and black hairs on the abdomen. Occurs mainly around carrion, where it preys on visiting insects.

There are numerous other rove beetles, many of them very small.

Oxyporus rufus

A rather slender beetle, with a body length of about 10mm. Head and jaws black; red and black patches on the body, ending in a black tip. Somewhat arched when viewed from the side.

Habitat Associated with fungi in woodlands.

Status and distribution Widespread and moderately common.

Season 6–10.

Similar species

Paederus littoralis is even more slender, and has a rather similar colour scheme, though the elytra are all green or bluish. A flightless species, widespread in damp places.

Nicrophorus (Necrophorus) investigator

Nicrophorus vespilloides

Devil's Coach-horse

Oxyporus rufus

Stag Beetle
Lucanus cervus

One of the most impressive and distinctive of insects in this area – males are impossible to confuse with anything else. Body length of males, excluding 'antlers', is 35–40mm, females slightly smaller, though both sexes are surprisingly variable in size. The male has greatly enlarged jaws, which are used for fighting with other males.
Habitat Mainly in old woodland, but also in parks and gardens in some areas; the larvae develop in old wood, taking several years.
Status and distribution Local and strongly southern in the UK, though quite frequent in the New Forest and south of London; widespread on the Continent.
Season 5–7.

Lesser Stag Beetle
Dorcus parallelipipedus

This species resembles female Stag Beetle but is distinctly smaller (body length 26–32mm), and lacks the brown tinge that Stag Beetle elytra usually have. The males do not have enlarged antlers.
Habitat Woodlands, parks and gardens. The larvae live in rotting wood.
Status and distribution Not infrequent in southern Britain; more widespread on the Continent.
Season 5–10.

Rhinoceros Beetle
Sinodendron cylindricum

A distinctly cylindrical, parallel-sided beetle, with a body length of 17–20mm. Wholly black, with a coarsely sculptured surface. Male has a projection like a rhinoceros horn on the head.
Habitat In woodlands. The larvae feed in rotting tree stumps, especially beech, and the adults feed on sap.
Status and distribution Widespread throughout, but local and never abundant.
Season 6–8.

Dor Beetle
Geotrupes stercorarius

A large, bulky black beetle, with a body length of about 20–25mm. Each elytron has 7 fine ridges. The beetles are all black viewed from above, but usually metallic blue or green below. There are no horns or other projections. They are often heavily infested with mites (as are many other beetles) giving rise to the alternative name of 'Lousy Watchman'.
Habitat Found in and around pastures, especially those in which cattle are present. They dig holes below the dung and bury it, as larval food.
Status and distribution Widespread virtually throughout, though not common and probably declining.
Season 4–10.
Similar species
G. spiniger is very similar and hard to separate in the field.
G. stercorosus is smaller, with wing-cases less deeply grooved. Local in woodland.
G. vernalis is dark bluish-black, with smooth, shiny wing-cases that have fine rows of tiny dots. Widespread but local, often active in the day.

Minotaur Beetle
Typhaeus typhoeus

A distinctive beetle, about the same size as Dor Beetle, but with 3 distinct horns on the thorax of the male; females resemble Dor Beetles but are not metallic, and have more strongly ribbed elytra.
Habitat Dry grassland and heathland; they bury rabbit droppings, less often cow dung, as larval food. Their holes are often visible in suitable habitats.
Status and distribution Mainly southern in Britain, though locally common in suitable places; widespread on the Continent.
Season All summer, most often 3–5 and 8–10.

Stag Beetle, male

Stag Beetle, larvae

Lesser Stag Beetle

Rhinoceros Beetle

Dor Beetle

Minotaur Beetle, male on rabbit dung

Geotrupes vernalis, with sheep dung

Scarabs and Chafers, Family Scarabaeidae

Often large beetles, with clubbed fan-like antennae. Scarabs are dung-feeders, chafers feed on plants and are often hairy.

English Scarab
Copris lunaris
Body length 20–23mm. A black beetle, with a single long 'rhinoceros' horn on the male (shorter in female). Elytra heavily striped. The beetles bury balls of horse and cattle dung in underground chambers as food for their developing larvae.
Habitat Sandy heaths and similar places.
Status and distribution Extremely rare in the UK, only in the far south.
Season 4–6 and 8–10 mainly.

Aphodius fimetarius
A small dung-eating beetle, about 10mm long. Head and thorax blackish, elytra red. Feeds on and around the droppings of various grazing animals, though does not bury the dung. Nocturnal.
Habitat Pastures and grazed woodland.
Status and distribution Widespread and common.
Season 5–10.
Similar species
A. rufipes is distinctly larger, and all black. Similar habitats and distribution. There are many other species in the genus.
A. inquinatus is representative of a group of smaller beetles, 4–6mm long, with dark thorax and pale brown elytra marked with darker patches. Common and widespread around dung.

Cockchafer or Maybug
Melolontha melolontha
A familiar and distinctive large chafer; body length 25–30mm. Predominantly brown, with a blackish thorax, and beautifully feath-ered antennae. Like other chafers, this one is very hairy. Flies in the evening and at night, often coming to lighted windows.
Habitat The larvae feed on the roots of plants, especially in unimproved permanent pastureland. The adults travel a consider-able distance.
Status and distribution Formerly abun-dant, often in pest proportions, but now much reduced; widespread but local.
Season 5–6.

Summer Chafer
Amphimallon solstitialis
This beetle resembles the Cockchafer, but is smaller, rarely exceeding 20mm, and the thorax is paler and much hairier. Noctur-nal.
Habitat The larvae live underground in permanent pasture, and are most frequent in old-fashioned pastoral farmland with plenty of hedges and trees.
Status and distribution Widespread but local and probably declining, through-out the area.
Season 6–7.
Similar species
A. ochraceus is slightly paler and day-flying. Uncommon.

Garden Chafer
Phyllopertha horticola
A small but distinctive chafer; body length 12–15mm. Head and thorax green to almost black; elytra reddish-brown, though variable, often with a greenish sheen. Diur-nal, often gathering in large numbers in sun-shine.
Habitat Permanent pastures such as chalk downland; larvae feed on plant roots, adults feed on trees.
Status and distribution Widespread and moderately common, but generally declining.
Season 5–7.

Aphodius inquinatus

Cockchafer

Cockchafer, larva

Summer Chafer

Garden Chafer

★ *Hoplia caerulea*

A striking beetle, unlikely to be confused with anything else. Body length 11–14mm. The whole body, viewed from above, is a bright metallic blue, visible from some distance away. Females are similar in shape, but duller, greyish.

Habitat Rough, flowery places, especially along rivers.

Status and distribution A southern species, reaching northwards to N France.

Season 6–8.

Bee Chafer
Trichius fasciatus

An attractive and distinctive chafer; body length 12–14mm. The whole body, with the exception of the elytra, is covered with golden-brown hair, giving some resemblance to a bumble bee. Elytra are reddish marked with black, though variable from yellow to brown.

Habitat Rough, flowery places near woodlands; the larvae live in rotting stumps, especially Birch, and the adults feed at flowers.

Status and distribution Very local in the UK, only in the north and west; widespread and locally common on the Continent, especially in hilly areas.

Season 5–7.

★ *Oxythyrea funesta*

A small chafer, about 10mm long. Predominantly black, with a bronzey iridescence when young, marked with creamy-white stripes and dots.

Habitat Rough, flowery places, where it is frequently seen on flowers.

Status and distribution Widespread in S Europe, extending northwards to N France and Switzerland.

Season 5–7.

Rose Chafer
Cetonia aurata

A beautiful beetle, with a body length of about 20mm. Bright, metallic, jewel-like green, with whitish marks · and stripes across the elytra.

Habitat Sunny flowery places, including gardens. The larvae live in old tree-stumps, and the adults visit various flowers including roses.

Status and distribution Widespread and moderately common, though declining, in the UK; still widespread and common on the Continent.

Season 6–9.

Similar species

C. cuprea, sometimes known as the Northern Rose Chafer, is duller green, and the elytra taper slightly towards the rear end. Despite their similarity, this and the Rose Chafer have different life-histories – the larvae of this species live in ants' nests, especially those of wood-ants. Widespread but uncommon.

★ *C. aeruginosa* is larger, and not marked with white. In and around woodland, from Germany southwards.

Gnorimus nobilis, see below.

★ *Gnorimus nobilis*

Similar to Rose Chafer in general appearance and size, metallic green in colour. It differs in having a slightly more tapered, almost pear-shaped body, and in the wrinkled wing-cases.

Habitat Most frequent in wooded areas with flowers. The larvae live in rotting wood, especially old stumps, and the adults visit flowers, especially Umbellifers like Hogweed. They are active during the day.

Status and distribution Local and mainly southern in the UK, widespread over most of N Europe.

Season 6–8.

Hoplia caerulea

Bee Chafer

Oxythyrea funesta, on privet

Rose Chafer

Click Beetles, Family Elateridae

Slender, flattened beetles, which share the ability to click their bodies suddenly to leap into the air, either to escape a potential predator, or to right themselves if they have landed upside-down.

mechanism of a click beetle's 'click'

Ampedus cinnabarinus
Body length 12–14mm long. A typical elongated, slender click beetle, with black head and thorax, and red elytra, clothed with pale brown hairs.
Habitat Woodland, especially where old trees are present; the larvae eat other larvae.
Status and distribution Widespread but local throughout.
Season 5–7.

Ctenicera cuprea
Body length 14–16mm long, in typical click beetle shape. Head and thorax blackish-violet, wings metallic brown variably suffused with violet. Antennae long and toothed along one side, especially noticeable in males.
Habitat Grassy places, sand-dunes and other open habitats.
Status and distribution Local and mainly northern and western in Britain. More widespread on the Continent with a northern bias.
Season 5–7.
Similar species
C. pectinicornis is slightly larger and more conspicuous, greenish or bronze metallic all over. Antennae similar. Similar habitats and distribution.

Elater sanguinolentus
Body length 10–12mm. A striking red and black species, differing from comparable relatives by the oval black patch in the centre of the midline of the elytra.
Habitat Flowery clearings in woodland, especially in damp places.
Status and distribution Local, in the southern half of Britain only; on the Continent, widespread almost throughout, though local.
Season 7–10.

Athous haemorrhoidalis
Body length 12–14mm. Head and thorax dark, elytra reddish-brown, strongly grooved. A rather hairy beetle.
Habitat Woodlands, hedges and unimproved pastures; has a particular liking for acid soils with bracken.
Status and distribution Widespread and common throughout.
Season 5–8.
Similar species
Agriotes lineatus is a smaller version, only 8–10mm long, with dull yellowish-brown elytra. The larvae (together with those of several other species) are known as 'wireworms' and can cause considerable damage to crops planted in ploughed permanent pasture. Widespread and common.

Byrrhus pilula
An inconspicuous little beetle, 8–10mm long, oval in outline and strongly domed. The greyish or brown elytra are obscurely marked with yellow. When disturbed, the beetle retracts its legs and antennae, feigning dead and looking more like a seed than a beetle.
Habitat Short turf in sandy places such as dunes or machair.
Status and distribution Widespread and moderately common throughout.
Season Adult all year, most often seen 5–8.

Ampedus cinnabarinus, posing dead

Ctenicera cuprea

Athous haemorrhoidalis

Elater sanguinolentus

Soldier Beetle
Cantharis rustica
Body length 13–16mm. A slender beetle, with a red thorax that has a dark spot in the middle; and dark bluish-black elytra; legs partly red.
Habitat Rough flowery places, especially near woodland and along hedges.
Status and distribution Widespread and common.
Season 5–8.
Similar species
C. fusca has a black spot towards the front of the thorax, and all-black legs. Similar habitats and distribution.

C. cryptica has paler reddish-brown wing-cases, with raised hairs; common throughout.

C. livida is similar in colouring, but larger. Common and widespread.

Black-tipped Soldier Beetle
Rhagonycha fulva
A small slender beetle, about 10mm long, orange-red with a distinct black tip to the elytra. Sometimes called the 'Bloodsucker' because of its colour, and various less polite names because they are almost always seen as mating pairs!
Habitat Many types of flowery habitat, especially woodland edges, hedgerows and downland.
Status and distribution Very common throughout.
Season 5–8.

Yellow-tipped Malthine
Malthinus flaveolus
A slender beetle, about 10mm long. Thorax orange, elytra brownish, but made distinctive by being short and tipped with bold yellow spots.

Habitat Woodland margins, hedges and rough flowery places. The larvae live in rotting wood.
Status and distribution Widespread and common.
Season 5–9.

Glow-worm
Lampyris noctiluca
Male glow-worms look like undistinguished brownish soldier beetles, about 10mm long. They fly at night in search of wingless females, which look like larvae. The females emit a greenish glow from the last few segments of the abdomen. Both adults and larvae feed on snails, injecting digestive juices into them, then ingesting the resulting soup. The empty, unbroken snail shells lying on grassland are a useful guide to where to look for glow-worms at night.
Habitat Warm grassy, flowery places, especially on limestone.
Status and distribution Local and probably declining in the UK; commonest towards the south. More widespread on the Continent in suitable habitats.
Season 6–7.

Ant Beetle
Thanasinus formicarius
A small rather ant-like beetle, about 10mm long. They are downy, and boldly marked with red, black and white with a distinctive double 'W' on the elytra.
Habitat Woodland, where they occur under the bark of trees or in other damp, hidden places.
Status and distribution Widespread and moderately common.
Season 4–6.

Soldier Beetle

Black-tipped Soldier Beetles, mating

Glow-worm, female

Yellow-tipped Malthine

Ant Beetle

★ *Trichodes alvearius*
A beautiful, boldly marked beetle. Body length 14–18mm, downy all over. Some specimens are a dramatic combination of royal blue and red; others have the blue replaced by black.
Habitat Rough flowery places, often seen visiting flowers. Larvae live on the larvae of some solitary bees.
Status and distribution Widespread and moderately common on the Continent, especially towards the south.
Season 5–7.

Cardinal Beetle
Pyrochroa coccinea
An attractive and distinctive beetle, about 20mm long, with a dark head and the rest of the body bright orange-red. Antennae strongly toothed.
Habitat Around woods and hedges; the larvae live under bark on fallen or dying trees, adults visit flowers.
Status and distribution Widespread throughout, but rarely common.
Season 5–7.
Similar species
P. serraticornis, also known as Cardinal Beetle, is slightly smaller, and has a red head; otherwise very similar. Similar habitats, mainly southern in the UK.
Dictyoptera aurora looks like a headless Cardinal Beetle; antennae less toothed. Associated with old coniferous woods; local and northern in the UK.

Red-tipped Flower Beetle
Malachius bipustulatus
Although less than 10mm long, this is quite a conspicuous little beetle. It has a slender body, expanding slightly towards the abdomen tip, bright metallic green except for 2 large red dots at the ends of the elytra.

Habitat Rough, flowery places, especially around woods.
Status and distribution Widespread, but only common in the south in Britain. Widespread and common on the Continent.
Season 5–8.
Similar species
M. aeneus is a very similar shape, but has a broad red 'V' around the abdomen. Local and mainly southern.

Endomychus coccineus
A brightly coloured little beetle, about 4–5mm long, resembling a scarlet ladybird with 4 spots, but flatter in profile, and with longer antennae.
Habitat Woodland and parkland. Feeds on fungi under the bark of various deciduous trees.
Status and distribution Common and widespread.
Season 4–7.
Similar species
The ladybird *Coccidula scutellata* is rather similar, but does not have the same clearly defined 4 dots, and the antennae are shorter.

Anthocomus rufus
An attractive little beetle, about 8mm long, with a slender body and bright red wing-cases. The last few segments of the black abdomen project beyond the elytra.
Habitat Fens and wet grassy places.
Status and distribution Local and mainly southern in the UK; more widespread on the Continent.
Season 6–8.
Similar species
A. fasciatus is similar in shape and size, but has darker greenish-black elytra with 4 red dots. Local and mainly southern.

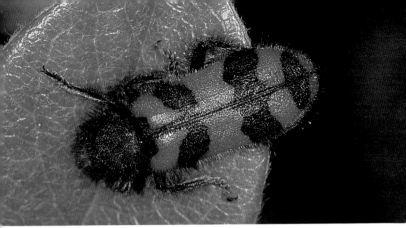

Trichodes alvearius, blacker form

Pyrochroa serraticornis

Red-tipped Flower Beetle

Endomychus coccineus, feeding

Anthocomus rufus

Ladybirds, Family Coccinellidae

Almost hemispherical beetles, with very short heads. Legs short. Mostly carnivorous, but some species are vegetarian.

24-spot Ladybird
Subcoccinella 24-punctata
A small ladybird, only 4–5mm long, reddish-orange, with 24 black spots of varying size.
Habitat A wide range of rough grassy habitats.
Status and distribution Widespread and common throughout.
Season 5–10.

7-spot Ladybird
Coccinella 7-punctata
Easily the most familiar ladybird. Oval, 7–9mm long, with a black head and red elytra; each elytra has 3 black spots, and there is one shared central one – 7 in all. Adults and larvae are predatory, mainly on aphids.
Habitat Almost anywhere. A highly mobile species, and resident populations are often reinforced by immigrants (see p.28).
Status and distribution Widespread and common throughout.
Season 3–10.

Eyed Ladybird
Anatis ocellata
The largest British ladybird, just over 10mm long. Apart from its size, it has distinctive spots that are black edged with yellow. The thorax is black and yellow.
Habitat In woods, almost always associated with pines and other conifers.
Status and distribution Widespread but local throughout.
Season 6–8.

22-spot Ladybird
Thea 22-punctata
A small but conspicuous ladybird, about 5mm long. Bright yellow, heavily dotted with 22 black spots. Feeds on fungi, especially mildews, on leaf surfaces.
Habitat Almost anywhere.
Status and distribution Widespread and common throughout.
Season 4–8.

2-spot Ladybird
Adalia bipunctata
A common and distinctive small ladybird, about 5–6mm long. Most commonly they have red elytra with 2 black spots; other forms are black with 2 red spots, and there are a number of forms which have additional markings. They may occasionally be yellow with black markings. Legs black.
Habitat Almost everywhere.
Status and distribution Widespread and common.
Season 3–10.

10-spot Ladybird
Adalia 10-punctata
Similar in size to 2-spot, and almost as variable, such that the two overlap in appearance. Usually orange with black dots, but it may be almost black, with varying numbers of dots. The legs are always yellowish.
Habitat Almost anywhere, though more associated with trees than the 2-spot.
Status and distribution Widespread and common.
Season 3–10.

Propylea 14-punctata
This species is 5–6mm long, yellow, with a pattern of black dots and marks, with a line down the centre; amount of black variable.
Habitat On trees and shrubs anywhere.
Status and distribution Widespread and common throughout.
Season 4–9.

Halyzia 16-guttata
A distinctive, boldly-marked species, slightly larger than *Propylea*
Habitat Deciduous woodland, especially associated with Sycamore.
Status and distribution Thought to be rare, but now found widely in southern Britain; widespread on the continent.
Season 6–8. Adults overwinter.

7-spot Ladybirds **7-spot Ladybird**, pupa **7-spot Ladybird**

Ladybird, larva **Eyed Ladybird**
22-spot Ladybird, grazing *Propylea 14-punctata* *Halyzia 16-guttata*

Larder Beetle
Dermestes lardarius

A small beetle, 6–8mm long, narrowly oval. Blackish-grey, with a paler patch across half of the elytra. Legs black.

Habitat On carrion, or a pest of stored dried meats.

Status and distribution Widespread and common throughout.

Season 4–10, or all year indoors.

Similar species

Hide Beetle *D. maculatus* lacks the pale patch, though it is pale underneath. Feeds on carrion, fur and leather; these beetles have been used by museums to clean skulls and skeletons!

Flour Beetle
Tribolium confusum

Very small beetles, 3–5mm long, brown with a darker thorax. They may occur in abundance in flour and other processed cereal products.

Habitat Mills, granaries, stores and domestic situations.

Status and distribution Widespread and common throughout.

Season All year indoors.

Similar species

Gnatocerus cornutus. A slightly larger beetle. Males have 'horns' on either side of the head. Similar habitats and distribution, though more frequent in the wild.

Furniture Beetle or Woodworm
Anobium punctatum

This species is most familiar as the small round larval exit holes, 1.5–2mm across, in

timber, denoting woodworm infestation. The adults are brown, cylindrical, 5–6mm long. **Habitat** Wood, including stored timber, worked wood,

Furniture Beetle, adult

and standing old trees. The larvae reduce timber to powder if unchecked.

Status and distribution Widespread and common throughout.

Season Adults: 5–7. Larvae and holes visible most of the year.

Similar species

Death Watch Beetle *Xestobium rufovillosum* has both adults and larvae larger than Furniture Beetle. The larvae cause considerable damage to building timbers. Adults make tapping noises (the 'death watch') in spring to attract mates. The larval exit holes are 3–4mm across. Widespread but more local.

Pollen Beetle
Meligethes aeneus

A small blackish beetle, only about 2mm long, with paler brown legs. These beetles become conspicuous because they occur in large numbers in flowers (see picture of a group in a wild rose flower) and around the tops of plants. May become a pest on Oilseed Rape.

Habitat Anywhere flowery, including suitable cultivated crops.

Status and distribution Widespread and common throughout; it is often abundant.

Season 5–8.

Lagria hirta

A smallish, slow-moving, soft-bodied beetle, about 10mm long. The head and thorax are dark blackish-brown, and the elytra are reddish-brown – a common enough combination, but this species is distinctive because it is covered throughout with fine golden down.

Habitat Various rough habitats, especially along woodland edges.

Status and distribution Widespread and moderately common throughout.

Season 5–7.

Larder Beetle, on carcass of deer

Death Watch Beetle, exit holes in old timber

Pollen Beetles, on wild rose

Lagria hirta

Mealworm Beetle
Tenebrio molitor

The larvae are familiar as the 'mealworms' sold as pet food and fish-bait. The adults are brownish-black, about 12–14mm long, with parallel-sided elytra.

Habitat Under the bark of trees, or in various stored cereal products.

Status and distribution Widespread and common throughout.

Season 6–8 outdoors, maybe all year indoors.

Cteniopus sulphureus

A smallish beetle, 8–9mm long. Usually pale yellow all over, though occasionally the head and thorax are darker. Day-flying, and frequently seen visiting flowers.

Habitat Sand-dunes and other dry flowery places; the larvae live in the soil, eating roots.

Status and distribution Local, mainly southern and coastal in Britain; more widespread on the Continent.

Season 5–8.

Oedemera nobilis

A slender beetle; body length about 10mm. Both sexes are bright metallic green, with gaping elytra. The males have markedly swollen hind femora. The beetles visit flowers, where they feed on pollen.

Habitat Rough flowery places – downland, hedgerows, woodland rides and so on.

Status and distribution Widespread, commoner in the south.

Season 5–8.

Oil Beetle
Meloe proscarabeus

Large distinctive beetles, with a curious life-history. Female 30–35mm long, with a very swollen abdomen; male shorter and less swollen. Both have overlapping elytra. The females lay thousands of eggs in holes and crevices, and these hatch into active little larvae which swarm over vegetation. To survive, they have to find a bee to attach themselves to, and be taken to the bee's nest, where they commence feeding on the larvae. They change into more typical beetle larvae and grow rapidly, feeding mainly on honey. The adults emerge in the spring. They can emit an unpleasant-smelling oil.

Habitat Rough grassy places.

Status and distribution Widespread but local, most common near the coast in Britain.

Season 4–7.

Similar species

M. violaceus is similar but has a stronger bluish tinge, and finer dots on the thorax and elytra. Local, mainly southern.

M. variegatus has coloured stripes on the abdomen. Rare in UK in grassy places; more widespread and frequent in Europe.

Longhorn Beetles, Family Cerambycidae

Beetles with very long antennae. The larvae all feed in wood, and the adults usually feed on pollen or other parts of plants, though a few adults do not feed.

Musk Beetle
Aromia moschata

A large longhorn beetle, though very variable in length, up to 35mm. Normally metallic green, but may be darker or more coppery. Male has antennae longer than the female's, and longer than his own body. Smells strongly of musk.

Habitat Associated with willows and poplars; the larvae live in the timber. Adults fly by day and visit flowers.

Status and distribution Formerly widespread in the UK, now very local; still widespread and locally common on the Continent.

Season 6–8.

Mealworm Beetle

Cteniopus sulphureus, on sea holly

Oedemera nobilis, female on Black Mullein

Oedemera nobilis, male

Oil Beetle

Musk Beetle

Poplar Longhorn

Saperda carcharias

A medium-large longhorn, 25–30mm long. Antennae about as long as body, banded dark and pale. Elytra variable in colour, but usually brown finely speckled with black.

Habitat Associated with poplars, on which the larvae feed, sometimes causing considerable damage.

Status and distribution Local in Britain; widespread and common on the Continent.

Season 6–9.

Wasp Beetle

Clytus arietis

A small but distinctive longhorn, about 20mm long. As the name suggests, it is black marked with yellow, though unlikely to be confused with a wasp. Flies in sunshine, settling on wood, flowers or other surfaces.

Habitat Flowery places near woodland or old trees; the larvae live in dead timber.

Status and distribution Widespread but local, and probably declining.

Season 5–7.

Similar species

Plagionotus arcuatus is larger, with 3 distinct yellow bands, together with dots, on the black elytra. Similar habitats, though more local; rare in the UK.

Strangalia maculata

One of the most familiar and distinctive of longhorns. Head and thorax black, elytra yellowish marked with black stripes and almost continuous black towards the tip. Antennae yellow at base.

Habitat Flowery places close to woodland; the adults feed on pollen, the larvae live in rotten stumps.

Status and distribution Widespread and moderately common.

Season 6–8.

Similar species

S. quadrifasciata is slightly larger, and has 4 more distinct areas of black on the elytra. Similar habitats, but less common.

Agapanthea villosoviridescens

Rather similar in size and shape to Poplar Longhorn, though the antennae are slightly longer. Greyish-brown to almost black, marked with gold hairs. Antennae banded light and dark.

Habitat Rough, flowery habitats; the larvae feed in the stems of various thistles.

Status and distribution Widespread but local throughout; uncommon in the UK.

Season 5–7.

Rhagium mordax

A medium-sized brownish longhorn, about 20mm long, with relatively short antennae. The elytra are marked with 2 red stripes separated by a black band.

Habitat Woodland, both coniferous and deciduous, where the larvae live on old timber.

Status and distribution Widespread and moderately common throughout.

Season 5–9.

Similar species

★ *R. sycophanta* is larger and more boldly marked. *R. inquisitor* is duller, variable yellowish or brown with black markings on the elytra. Similar habitats and distribution to *R. mordax*.

R. bifasciatum is more slender, with 2 rather obscure yellowish 'commas' on each elytra. Widespread.

Pogonochoerus hispidulus

A curious truncated-looking longhorn, with a body length of about 15mm. Basically brown, but with a large greyish patch on the elytra. There are 2 teeth at the tip of each elytron.

Habitat Woods, hedgerows and old farmland.

Status and distribution Widespread but local and easily overlooked.

Season 4–10.

Wasp Beetle

Strangalia maculata

Strangalia maculata

Strangalia quadrifasciata

Agapanthea villosoviridescens

Rhagium mordax

Rhagium bifasciatum

Pogonochoerus hispidulus

Leptura rubra
A brownish-red beetle, with a marked variation in size between the sexes. Female is 22–24mm long, male shorter. Male has black head and thorax, female has thorax red. Antennae relatively short for a longhorn.
Habitat It is associated with coniferous woodlands, where the larvae feed in rotting timber; adults visit flowers.
Status and distribution Widespread but uncommon in Britain; more frequent on the Continent.
Season 5–7.
Similar species
L. 6-guttata is black, boldly marked with 6 red spots. Around deciduous woods. Very local in UK, more widespread in Europe. *L. sanguinolenta* is more distinctly red, sometimes with blackish markings on the elytra. Local in England, widespread in Europe; associated with conifers.

Variable Longhorn Beetle
Stenocorus meridianus
A variable species, as the name suggests; normally it has a black head and thorax and ochre-coloured elytra, but these may be almost all black at times. Even the antennae and legs vary in colour. They also vary greatly in size; females are much larger than males. Day-flying, frequently visiting flowers.
Habitat In and around deciduous woods, and old hedges.
Status and distribution Widespread and moderately common in the south, rarer in north Britain; widespread on the Continent.
Season 5–7.

★ *Dorcadion scopoli*
A distinctive longhorn; body length 10–14mm. Greyish-black, strongly banded longitudinally with greyish-white. More skulking than most longhorns. Flightless.
Habitat Dry, open places, such as downland and steppe.
Status and distribution A southern and eastern species.
Season 4–6.

The Leaf Beetles, Family Chrysomelidae

A large and varied family of herbivorous beetles, usually oval, and domed when viewed from the side. Heads short.

Reed Beetle
Donacia vulgaris
A member of a small group of beetles, reminiscent of small longhorns. This species is about 10mm long, greenish or coppery, with a broken reddish stripe down its back.
Habitat Associated with bur-reeds *Sparganium* spp, close to water.
Status and distribution Widespread and common.
Season 5–8.
Similar species
D. aquatica has reddish elytra with a green stripe; they are gold (cf. silvery in *D. vulgaris*) underneath. Associated with Floating Reed-grass. Local.

Variable Reed Beetle
Plateumaris sericea
Similar in size and shape to the above 2 species. Green or bronze in colour, with shorter hind legs than *Donacia* species. Frequently visits flowers.
Habitat Around still and slow-moving water-bodies, usually on emergent plants.
Status and distribution Widespread and common.
Season 5–7.

Asparagus Beetle
Crioceris asparagi
An attractive and distinctive little beetle, 6–8mm long, and boldly marked with red, black and white. Often occurs in abundance on the tips of growing Asparagus.
Habitat Gardens and rough, flowery places where wild forms of Asparagus grow. Larvae and adults eat Asparagus.
Status and distribution Moderately common in S Britain; more widespread on the Continent, absent from the north.
Season 5–8.

Leptura rubra

Variable Longhorn Beetle

Dorcadion scopoli

Reed Beetle
Variable Reed Beetle

Asparagus Beetles, on asparagus

Cryptocephalus hypochaeridis

An attractive metallic green beetle, only 4–6 mm long, but often conspicuous as 2 or 3 of them sit openly on flowers. They particularly favour yellow Composites, such as hawkweeds and Cat's-ear. The generic name means 'hidden-head', which is very appropriate.

Habitat Rough, flowery places.

Status and distribution Widespread and common.

Season 5–8.

Similar species

★ C. sericeus is slightly larger and more coppery. Similar habits and habitats, though more frequent on umbellifers.

Bloody-nosed Beetle
Timarcha tenebricosa

One of the largest and most distinctive of the leaf beetles, up to 20mm long, shiny deep bluish-black, strongly domed, and flightless, with large feet. The common name comes from the habit of exuding a drop of red liquid when alarmed, said to deter predators.

Habitat Rough grassy places, where bedstraws occur.

Status and distribution Widespread and locally common in the UK, especially in the south. Absent from the far north of Europe.

Season 4–8.

Mint Leaf Beetle
Chrysolina menthastri

A beautiful and distinctive beetle, about 10mm long, bright metallic green in colour. Readily visible in daylight on its food-plant.

Habitat Particularly associated with mints, also other Labiates. Common in gardens.

Status and distribution Locally frequent in S Britain, rare or absent further north. Widespread on the Continent except further north.

Season 5–9.

Similar species

C. polita is similar in size and shape, but has a greenish thorax and red elytra. Widespread and common, also occurs on mints.

★ Colorado Beetle
Leptinotarsa decemlineata

A well-known and very distinctive beetle, about 10mm long, domed, and boldly marked with yellow and black. The beetles feed on various members of the Nightshade family Solanaceae, and become a pest when they turn to potatoes.

Habitat Various rough grassy places, and potato fields.

Status and distribution Widespread and common on the Continent, mainly southern; originally introduced from N America. Occasional in the UK, where considerable attempts are made to keep it out.

Season 4–9.

Poplar Leaf Beetle
Chrysomela populi

An attractive and relatively large leaf beetle, about 10mm long. Predominantly red, with a dark greenish thorax. Often visible in the daytime on its food-plant.

Habitat Feeds on poplars and various willows, including Creeping Willow.

Status and distribution Widespread and common throughout.

Season 4–9.

Similar species

C. tremulae lives mainly on Aspen.

Galerucella lineola

A rather dull beetle, about 8mm long, yellowish-brown and hairy, with variable darker markings. Antennae about half as long as the body.

Habitat On willows and alders, near water.

Status and distribution Widespread and common throughout.

Season 4–9.

Similar species

Pyrrhalta viburni is very similar, slightly darker and more bulky. It feeds on Wayfaring Tree, stripping the leaves to the veins. Widespread and common.

Cryptocephalus hypochaeridis

Bloody-nosed Beetle

Bloody-nosed Beetle, larva

Colorado Beetle, eggs

Mint Leaf Beetle

Colorado Beetle

Chrysolina polita

Poplar Leaf Beetle

Green Tortoise Beetle
Cassida rubiginosa

One of two species referred to as Tortoise Beetle both because of their shape and because the elytra extend well beyond the body, like a shell. Body length about 8–9mm, wholly green from above.

Habitat Grassy places, especially along rivers. Often seen on thistles.

Status and distribution Widespread and moderately common throughout.

Season 6–9.

Similar species

C. viridis looks very similar, but has the angles of the pronotum (covering the thorax) more rounded, less sharply angled. Similar habitats.

* *C. sanguinolenta* has a reddish tinge to the elytra.

C. nobilis is more slender, and has a blue stripe along each elytra. Local.

Weevils, Various Families

Most weevils have a predominant snout (the rostrum), with jaws at the end of it, and elbowed antennae attached halfway along. They are vegetarian.

Hazel Weevil
Apoderus coryli

An attractive and distinctive weevil, about 6–7mm long. The head is black, and strongly narrowed towards the thorax; the remainder of the body is bright red.

Habitat Woodland and scrub, feeding mainly on Hazel, sometimes other deciduous shrubs; the larvae feed in rolled leaves.

Status and distribution Widespread and common throughout.

Season 5–7.

Similar species

Red Oak Roller *Attabelus nitens* has a more parallel-sided head. Feeds mainly on oaks. Widespread.

Rhynchites aequatus has a similar colour-scheme, but its snout is much longer. Associated with Hawthorn, and the adults visit the flowers. Widespread.

Clay-coloured Weevil
Otiorhynchus singularis

A medium-large weevil, up to 10mm long, greyish-brown in colour, streaked paler.

Habitat On a variety of trees and shrubs, especially Hazel.

Status and distribution Widespread and frequent.

Season 5–9.

Phyllobius pomaceus

About 10mm long, with a narrow body and short snout. Covered with greenish or bluish scales, which gradually rub off to reveal black below.

Habitat Strongly associated with nettles, wherever they occur.

Status and distribution Widespread and common.

Season 4–9.

Similar species

P. argentatus is smaller, up to 6mm long, and more shiny. Associated with Hazel and other shrubs. Common.

P. calcaratus is up to 10mm long, with green scales and often small bare patches; legs finely white-downy. Local on deciduous trees.

Lixus paraplecticus

A distinctive long, narrow weevil, up to 20mm long. Elytra dark green, but covered with yellowish scales. Snout long.

Habitat Riversides and marshy places; feeds on umbellifers such as Angelica.

Status and distribution Rare and local in the UK, mainly southern on the Continent; most frequent in France.

Season 4–6 and 8–10.

Green Tortoise Beetle   *Cassida viridis*   Hazel Weevil

Red Oak Roller

Rhynchites aequatus   Clay-coloured Weevil

Phyllobius pomaceus, on nettle   *Lixus paraplecticus*

Pine Weevil
Hylobius abietis
A largish weevil, 10–12mm long, rather variable in colour. Essentially black, with varying amounts of gold or brown markings; legs black, occasionally reddish-black.
Habitat Coniferous woodland, particularly associated with pines and spruces; adults eat foliage, larvae live in old stumps.
Status and distribution Widespread and common throughout; sometimes abundant in plantations.
Season Adult all year, though well hidden in cold weather.
Similar species
★ *H. piceus* is slightly larger, with smaller pale markings; occurs on spruces and Larch.

Sandy Clover Weevil
Hypera punctata
Body length about 8mm, dull brown in colour, obscurely striped with dark.
Habitat The larvae live on clovers and other legumes, pupating in open netting cocoons; adults are active by day sometimes, in rough grassy places.
Status and distribution Widespread throughout and moderately common.
Season 5–8.

Elm Bark Beetle
Scolytus scolytus
Familiar in name as the carrier of the Dutch Elm disease that devastated elms throughout Britain. The adults are small, 3–6mm long, shiny brown and black; the larval chambers under the bark are distinctive; in this group, there is a central 'egg gallery' excavated by the female, and secondary galleries excavated by the growing larvae.
Habitat Wherever elms occur.
Status and distribution Widespread and common.
Season 5–9.
Similar species
Ash Bark Beetle *Leperisinus varius* produces rather similar galleries in Ash. The beetles are dull greyish-brown. Widespread and common.

Water Beetles,
Family Dytiscidae and others

Beetles that are structurally modified for life in water. The hind legs are enlarged for swimming, and the outline is streamlined. The diving beetles are strongly carnivorous.

Great Diving Beetle
Dytiscus marginalis
A large and impressive aquatic beetle, 30–38mm long. Deep reddish-brown, with a yellowish border all round the elytra and thorax (pronotum). Females have more finely ridged elytra than males.
Habitat Well-vegetated pools, lakes and ditches.
Status and distribution Widespread and locally common throughout. Both adults and larvae are fierce predators.
Season Adult all year, quiescent during very cold weather.
Similar species
★ *Cybister laterimarginalis* has no yellow border across the join between the thorax and the abdomen; otherwise very similar. Widespread in N Europe in similar habitats.

Whirligig Beetle
Gyrinus natator
One of a small group of similar species, with very distinctive habits. They gather in groups on the water surface, where they whirl round and round in seemingly random fashion. Body length about 10mm, black with brown legs. Their eyes are in 2 parts, one part for seeing underwater, the other in air. Both adults and larvae are predatory.
Habitat Still and slow-moving water-bodies.
Status and distribution Widespread and common throughout.
Similar species
Hairy Whirligig *Orectochilus villosus* is hairier and slightly larger. Found mainly in running water, and active only at night. Widespread.

Pine Weevil

Sandy Clover Weevil

Elm Bark Beetle, galleries on dead Wych Elm

Great Diving Beetle, female

Whirligig Beetles

Acilius sulcatus

A medium-sized water beetle, about 20mm long. Both sexes are orange-brown; females (shown here) have ribbed elytra, striped with paler hairy grooves; males have smooth elytra.
Habitat Well-oxygenated ponds, canals and other slow-moving waters.
Status and distribution Widespread and common.
Season Adult all year, inactive in cold weather.

Great Silver Beetle
Hydrophilus piceus

A very large beetle, up to 45mm long. They resemble diving beetles, but are vegetarian. Shiny blackish-green above, silvery below when submerged. The eggs are laid in cases which have a special air funnel up to the surface.
Habitat Weedy and muddy ponds and ditches.
Status and distribution Uncommon and mainly southern in Britain, declining. Widespread but local on the Continent.
Season Adult all year, but inactive in cold weather.

Great Silver Beetle, larva

STYLOPIDS
ORDER STREPSIPTERA

A little-known group of insects, once classified with the beetles but now separated into their own order. They are all very small, and are hardly ever noticed. The early stages are spent as parasites of other insects, such as *Stylops melittae*, which parasitizes solitary bees. The females remain larva-like and legless; the males are winged, with antler-like antennae, but are only about 2mm long. They are widespread and common.

Stylopid

PLANT GALLS

Plant galls are a familiar feature of the countryside, often meriting familiar names: Robin's Pincushion, Oak Apple, Marble Gall, Currant Gall and so on. There is even an 'Oak Apple Day' celebrated in some parts of Britain. As described on p.22, galls are produced as the result of an attack on the plant tissue by some form of gall-causing organism, to which the gall is the plant's response. Fortunately, these responses are generally quite consistent, and it is a relatively easy matter to identify the gall, and therefore its causative agent, in most examples.

Insects are the main causers of conspicuous galls in Britain and N Europe. There are other gall-causers, particularly mites and fungi. Since this book is concerned with insects, we have concentrated on the insect galls, with just a few examples of non-insect galls to show what they are like.

In the following section, the galls are classified by host plant, beginning with those that bear the greatest number of galls. In most of the examples, the host plants are familiar species such as Oaks, Rose, Willows, so this is a relatively simple way of subdividing the galls and speeding up the process of identification.

Galls on Oaks, Quercus spp.

Oaks support a large number of galls, on their flowers, acorns, leaves and even roots. In fact, the same species of insect may cause different, but consistent, galls at different stages of its life-cycle.

Common Spangle Gall
Neuroterus quercusbaccarum

This is caused by a gall wasp (*Hymenoptera*). These galls are flat 'Mexican-hat'-shaped structures, up to about 6mm across, and may occur abundantly on the underside of a leaf. They are usually orange-pink, speckled darker. The leaves and galls fall to the ground, and the gall wasps emerge in early

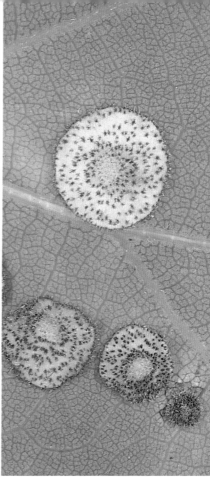

Currant Galls, on male oak flowers

Common Spangle Galls, on oak Leaf

spring; the females lay eggs into oak buds and the next generation causes **Currant Galls** on developing male oak catkins.

Habitat Wherever oak trees occur.

Status and distribution Widespread and common throughout.

Season 5–6 for Currant Gall, 8–11 for Spangle Gall.

Similar species

Smooth Spangle *N. albipes* is similar in size and position, but the galls are saucer-

Neuroterus quercusbaccarum

N. albipes

N. tricolor

shaped, curling away from the leaf surface, and hairless. Common throughout.

Cupped Spangle *N. tricolor* is also saucer-shaped, but very hairy, especially around the rim. Locally common. The sexual generations of these 2 species are not especially conspicuous.

Silk Button Spangle Gall
Neuroterus numismalis

Attractive little galls on the undersides of the leaves, roughly similar in size to Spangle Gall, but more like a thicker disc, with a central depression, pressed tightly against the leaf surface. They are covered with golden silky hairs. The life-cycle is similar to Spangle Gall, but the sexual stage is not conspicuous.
Habitat On oaks, wherever they occur.
Status and distribution Widespread and common; there may be very large numbers on a single leaf.
Season 8–11.
Similar species
Trigonaspis megaptera produces kidney-shaped yellow to brown swellings, about 2mm long, on the undersides of leaves close to veins. Local and mainly northern; 9–10.

Marble Gall or Oak Nut
Andricus kollari

These familiar and highly distinctive galls are often wrongly referred to as 'oak apples' (see below). These are very hard, spherical galls, green at first, becoming brown, up to about 25mm across, singly or in groups. Parasitized examples fail to develop evenly and are smaller. The gall wasps leave in late summer by a conspicuous hole, but the galls remain on the tree through the winter.
Habitat On oaks, especially young ones.
Status and distribution Widespread and common throughout. Originally introduced from the Middle East.
Season Mature and visible 7–4.
Similar species
A. lignicola, sometimes referred to as the Cola-nut Gall, resembles a small misshapen Marble Gall, but is ovoid rather than spherical, and rough rather than smooth. Now widespread through England, having spread northwards. Widespread in Europe.

Artichoke Gall
Andricus fecundator

Swollen buds which vaguely resemble small globe artichokes, about 10–15 mm long. A hard gall forms inside these, and falls out when the bud scales open. Occasionally called Hop Gall.
Habitat Wherever oaks occur, especially on younger trees.
Status and distribution Widespread and common throughout, except N Britain.
Season 6–10.
Similar species
A. curvator galls are much smaller, and have a conical tip free of scales. They are widespread.

Andricus inflator

Two distinct types of gall are formed by this species. Some are spherical, up to 8mm across, soft, greenish, with net-veining on the surface, formed on twigs, often on the trunk of mature trees. The other galls are ovoid-spherical, up to about 10mm across, mainly enclosed by scales when on the tree. The second type is more common.
Habitat Oaks, especially mature trees.
Status and distribution Widespread, but rather local.
Season All year.

Knopper Gall
Andricus quercuscalicis

A distinctive gall on acorns, causing the acorn to become enlarged, green and heavily ridged; eventually it turns brown.
Habitat On oaks, almost anywhere.
Status and distribution Now widespread in England and Wales, though only recently introduced. Widespread in Europe.
Season 8–11.

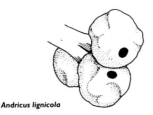

Andricus lignicola

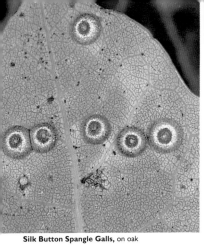

Silk Button Spangle Galls, on oak

Marble Gall, on oak

Andricus quercuscalicis

Artichoke Gall

Knopper Gall, on oak

Cotton Gall
Andricus quercusramuli

A distinctive gall, in the form of a mass of cotton wool, up to 20mm (rarely 30mm) across, formed on a male catkin.

Habitat On Common Oak.

Status and distribution Widespread but very local.

Season 5–6.

Cherry Gall
Cynips quercusfolii

Large cherry-like galls, up to 20mm across, attached to the undersurface of leaves. They are green at first, becoming red as they mature. There may be several on one leaf.

Habitat On oaks.

Status and distribution Widespread and common throughout.

Season 7–10, but remaining visible on the fallen leaves through some of the winter.

Similar species

C. divisa forms the galls which are smaller (less than 7mm across), hard and woody. There may be many on a single leaf. Widespread and common.

C. longiventris produces galls up to 10mm across, but distinctively covered with bumps in stripes, with an overall appearance of yellow striped with red. 6–10. Locally common.

Oak Apple
Biorrhiza pallida

A familiar and distinctive gall, the subject of much folklore. Oak Apple Day (29 May) is still celebrated in some areas in commemoration of the restoration of the British monarchy. The galls themselves are irregular spongy spheres, up to 40mm across, greenish-yellow at first, becoming redder. They contain numerous larvae of the gall wasp, which emerge as adults June–July.

Habitat On oaks, including young trees.

Status and distribution Widespread and common.

Season Visible from 5 onwards, persisting through the winter but gradually shrivelling and blackening.

Galls on Roses, Rosa spp.

Bedeguar Gall or Robin's Pincushion
Diplolepis rosae

A very familiar and distinctive gall, consisting of a ball of long, branched, tangled hairs, up to 10cm across in large specimens, usually much less. Greenish at first, gradually becoming redder.

Habitat On rose bushes of various species.

Status and distribution Widespread and common.

Season 7–10, then remaining visible over winter but gradually blackening and losing hairs.

Similar species

D. mayri consists of smaller galls with unbranched spines (though often coalescing into a larger structure), on Sweet Briar *Rosa rubiginosa*. Rare and local.

Spiked Pea Gall
Diplolepis nervosus

Attractive and distinctive galls on the underside of rose leaves, consisting of spherical structures with up to 6 pointed projections. They are up to 5–8mm across, green gradually reddening. They resemble tiny naval mines.

Habitat Wherever roses grow, including gardens.

Status and distribution Widespread and common.

Season 7–10.

Smooth Pea Gall
Diplolepis eglanteriae

Generally similar to Spiked Pea Gall, but simply spherical, lacking the projections. Several galls can occur on one leaflet. They are green initially, gradually reddening.

Habitat On rose bushes.

Status and distribution Widespread but less common than Spiked Pea Gall.

Season 7–10.

Cherry Gall, on fallen oak leaves

Oak Apple

Robin's Pincushion, on rose

Spiked Pea Gall, on rose

Smooth Pea Galls, on rose

Galls on Willows and Poplars, Salix and Populus spp.

Bean Gall
Pontania proxima

Red or brown swollen galls on the leaves of White and Crack Willow (*Salix alba* and *S. fragilis*), roughly bean-shaped, up to 12mm long. The gall-causer is a sawfly. For the identification of this and the following *Pontania* galls, it is very helpful to know the species of willow.

Habitat Wherever the willows occur.
Status and distribution Widespread and common.
Season 6–10.
Similar species
P. viminalis is roughly spherical, up to 10mm across, warty and slightly hairy; reddish. Occurs on *Salix viminalis*, *S. fragilis*, *S. purpurea* and others. Widespread.
P. collactanea is similar, only on Creeping Willow *Salix repens*; mainly northern.
P. vesicator projects more from the undersurface of the leaf, and is thinner-walled. Mainly northern, on *S. purpurea*.

Pontania pedunculi

A spherical gall on the undersides of willow leaves, up to 8mm across, but with long whitish hairs making it more conspicuous. Occurs mainly on Sallow and Eared Willow *S. cinerea*, *S. caprea* and *S. aurita*.

Habitat Where these species of willow occur.
Status and distribution Widespread and moderately common.
Season 6–10.

Rhabdophaga salicis

This gall midge produces swellings on young stems of Sallow and Eared Willow. Greenish, ovoid, and about 20mm long, though sometimes several merge together.
Habitat On the above willows, mainly in damp places.
Status and distribution Widespread but local.
Season 8–10.

Harmandia globuli

These galls are reddish globular or cylindrical, up to approximately 3mm across (but often several together), on the upper surface of the leaves of Aspen *Populus tremulus*. The gall-former is a gall midge (Dipteran).
Habitat Wherever Aspens occur.
Status and distribution Widespread but local.
Season 6–10.
Similar species
H. cavernosa produces similar, slightly larger, galls on the undersides of Aspen leaves. Local.

Galls on other Broadleaved Trees

Maple Nail Gall
Eriophyes macrorhynchus

This and the following species are mite nail galls. They are caused by mites, which are not insects but form conspicuous galls that could be mistaken for insect galls. This one is a common and familiar nail gall on Field Maple. Each gall is a tiny red projection from the upper surface of the leaf, but the galls frequently occur in very large numbers, becoming highly conspicuous.
Habitat Found wherever Field Maples occurs.
Status and distribution Widespread and common in S Britain; widespread on the Continent.
Season 6–10.

Lime Nail Gall
Eriophyes tiliae

A variable species, causing tall conical hairy projections, up to almost 10mm long, on the upper surfaces of Lime leaves. They can be present in great abundance.
Habitat On limes, especially Common Lime.
Status and distribution Widespread and common.
Season 6–10.

Bean Galls, on Crack Willow leaf

Gall on Sallow, caused by *Pontania viminalis*

Harmandia globuli

Maple Nail Galls, on Sycamore

Lime Nail Gall, on Lime leaf

Holly Leaf-mine
Phytomyza ilicis
Conspicuous blotches on the leaves of Holly, caused by a small fly. On some trees, almost every leaf is affected.
Habitat Wherever Holly occurs.
Status and distribution Widespread and common throughout.
Season All year.

Beech Gall-midge
Oligotrophus fagineus
Ovoid projections from the veins on the upper surface of Beech leaves, up to 10mm high; green becoming reddish.
Habitat On Beech trees.
Status and distribution Mainly southern in UK; widespread on the Continent.
Season 6–9.
Similar species
Mikiola fagi galls, also on Beech, are narrower and more cylindrical, up to 6mm high.

Galls on Coniferous Trees

Yew Artichoke Gall
Taxomyia taxi
A distinctive species, forming conical, slightly artichoke-like swollen galls on the growing tips of Yew shoots. They are 10–20mm long. The gall-causer is a gall midge.
Habitat Wherever Yew occurs.
Status and distribution Widespread and common throughout.
Season The galls develop from spring onwards, and remain on the tree; they can be seen in any month.

Galls on Herbaceous Plants

Germander Speedwell Gall
Jaapiella veronicae
Hairy, swollen galls formed at the tips of Germander Speedwell by a gall midge. The galls are about 7–9mm across, and are partly enclosed by the stunted leaves.
Habitat Grassy and flowery places, wherever Germander Speedwell occurs.
Status and distribution Widespread

and common throughout.
Season May be seen in almost any month in mild areas; mainly 4–9.

Thistle Stem-gall
Urophora cardui
Conspicuous swollen stems, usually towards the top of Creeping Thistle, up to 10cm long, oval in shape, green then brown. They are caused by a picture-winged fly (see p.232).
Habitat Arable land, or waste ground.
Status and distribution Widespread and common throughout.
Season 7–10.
Similar species
Phanacis hypochaeridis is a gall wasp that causes a similar swelling on the stems of Common Cat's Ear *Hypochoeris radicata*.

Diastrophus rubi
A distinctive stem gall on blackberries, occasionally raspberries. The galled part of the stem becomes swollen, distorted and curled, and generally lacks prickles. Old galls persist, perforated with exit holes.
Habitat Wherever Bramble occurs.
Status and distribution Widespread and common.
Season Galls develop from 6–11 and persist through the winter. Most conspicuous when fully developed in late autumn.

Ground Ivy: Lighthouse Gall
Dasyneura glechomae
Erect cylindrical swellings, up to 4mm high, with a swollen top, on the upper surface of Ground Ivy leaves. The galls begin green then turn pink, and are hairy.
Habitat Almost anywhere, wherever Ground Ivy grows.
Status and distribution Widespread and common.
Season 5–9.
Similar species
Liposthenus latreillei are galls on the same plant caused by a gall wasp. They are irregular globular swellings on the leaves or stems. Widespread but local.

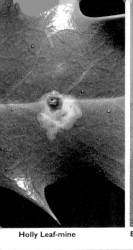

Holly Leaf-mine

Beech Gall-midge, gall on beech leaf

Yew Artichoke Gall

Germander Speedwell Gall
Diastrophus rubi

Thistle Stem-gall
Liposthenus latreillei

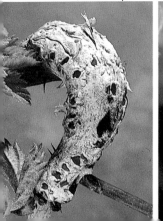

Bibliography

Askew, RR, *The Dragonflies of Europe* (Harley, 1988). Large and expensive, but very comprehensive.

Bellmann, H, *A Field Guide to the Grasshoppers and Crickets of Britain and Northern Europe* (Harper Collins, 1988). A good photographic field guide.

Carter, DJ and Hargreaves, B, *A Field Guide to the Caterpillars of Butterflies and Moths in Britain and Europe* (Harper Collins, 1986). Not perfect, but very useful, and there is nothing better.

Chinery, M, *Collins Guide to the Insects of Britain and Western Europe* (Harper Collins, 1986). An excellent field guide.

Chinery, M, *New Generation Guide to the Butterflies and Day-flying Moths of Britain and Europe* (Harper Collins, 1989). Good field guide, covering the whole of Europe.

Chinery, M, *Collins Field Guide to the Insects of Britain and Northern Europe*, 3rd Edition (Harper Collins, 1993). Actually less useful as a field guide than the above, but full of information.

Gibbons, R, *Hamlyn Guide to Dragonflies and Damselflies of Britain and Northern Europe* (Hamlyn, 1994). Good pocketable field guide.

Gibbons, R and Gibbons, E, *Creating a Wildlife Garden* (Hamlyn, 1988). A good practical guide to attracting wildlife, including insects, into the garden.

Hammond, CO and Merritt, R, *The Dragonflies of Great Britain and Ireland* (Harley, 1983). Well-illustrated detailed book, but not a field guide.

Marshall, JA and Haes, ECM, *Grasshoppers and Allied Insects of Great Britain and Ireland* (Harley, 1988). An excellent book, and a tape of calls is available with it.

Prys-Jones, O and Corbett, S, *Bumblebees* (Richmond, 1987). One of the excellent Richmond natural history books, which cover a number of insect groups.

Skinner, B, *Colour Identification Guide to Moths of the British Isles* (Viking, 1984). Comprehensive guide to the macro-moths.

Stubbs, A and Falk, S, *British Hoverflies* (BENHS, 1994). The standard work on British hoverflies, with excellent illustrations.

Thomas, J, *Hamlyn Colour Guide to the Butterflies of the British Isles* (Hamlyn, 1993). Excellent field guide to British butterflies.

Whalley, P, *Mitchell Beazley Pocket Guide to Butterflies* (Mitchell Beazley, 1981). A remarkably compact guide, covering the whole of Europe.

Useful Addresses

British Dragonfly Society, 68 Outwoods Road, Loughborough, Leicestershire LE11 3LY.

BENHS – The British Entomological and Natural History Society, c/o Institute of Biology, 20 Queensberry Place, London SW7 2DZ.

The Royal Entomological Society, 41 Queen's Gate, South Kensington, London.

Royal Society for Nature Conservation, The Green, Witham Park, Waterside South, Lincoln LN5 7JR. The 'umbrella' organization for the county wildlife trusts, with nature reserves all over the country. They can provide the address for your local Trust.

Index